THE ILLEGAL ALIEN

FORWARD

You don't have to agree with everything in Raoul's book, not to recognize the enormous contribution that immigrants have made and continue to make our nation.

Among the millions of ethnic Americans, Mexican Americans in particular, are among the most productive and patriotic, which is why my old friend Raoul Contreras has taken "his pen in hand" to the irrational left as well as the xenophobic right. *Viva la libertad*!

The Honorable Jack Kemp,

Former United States Secretary of Housing and Urban Development; former Congressman; 1996 candidate for

Vice-President of the United States; Number 15, Quarterback of the original San Diego Chargers of the NFL...

Contents

Part 1

Chapter 1—Professor Samuel P. Huntington of Harvard

Chapter 2—Anglo-Protestants, The Two Faces Of

Chapter 3—Lingua Franca, Savvy?

Chapter 4—The Nativist and Roman Catholics

Chapter 5—The Mexicans Are Coming! The Mexicans Are Coming!

Chapter 6—Two Peoples, Two Languages?

Chapter 7—Professor Huntington Gets Something Right

Chapter 8—The Professor's Little Big Lies

Chapter 9—The Professor Fails, Mexicans Pass

Chapter 10—Mexicans Steamroll Blacks

Chapter 11—I Only Speak Anglo Saxon

Chapter 12—Mexican or American, Choose

Chapter 13—The Professor's Black Helicopters

Chapter 14—Dream On, Professor

Part 2

Professor Victor Davis Hanson's *Mexifornia*

Chapter 15—The Professor Speaks from His Tractor

Chapter 16—Mexican Americans Fail In School

Chapter 17—The Angry Mexican

Chapter 18—Anglo-Protestant Bounties for Indian Scalps

Chapter 19—Hanson Doesn't Know Assimilation When He Sees It

Chapter 20—Where Is The Little Red Schoolhouse?

Chapter 21—Are Mexicans Armenians, Italians or Space Aliens?

Chapter 22—Hanson Vents

Chapter 23—Living Off The Public Trough

Chapter 24—The Welfare Myth

Chapter 25—Where's Hanson's Numbers?

Chapter 26—Americans by Choice, Not Accident

Chapter 27—Americans per the Constitution

Chapter 28—Hanson v. Huntington

Chapter 29—Race, Tribe and Religion

Part 3

Congressman Tom Tancredo and His Racist Associates

Chapter 30—Who Is Tom Tancredo?

Chapter 31—Fanatic Anti-Immigrant Tom Tancredo

Chapter 32—Congressman Tancredo Speaks

Chapter 33—American Yuppie Swallows Propaganda

Part 4

Jon E, Dougherty Writes a Book

Illegals: the Imminent Threat Posed by Our Unsecured U.S.-Mexico Border, Wnd Books, 2004

Chapter 34—An Amateur Is Published

Chapter 35—Dougherty says...

Chapter 36—Dougherty's Coming Revolution

Chapter 37—Dougherty Speaks For F.A.I.R

Chapter 38—There must be A Pony in Here

Part 5

Race, Illegals and Problems

Chapter 39—Xenophobia

Chapter 40—Illegal Immigrants, Serious Problems

Chapter 41—Serious Problems, Illegals Notwithstanding

Chapter 42—Amnesty

Chapter 43—1994, Watershed for Paranoia

Chapter 44—The Border Militias

Chapter 45—Just How Many Illegals make it to the USA?

Part 6

Fantasies of Fanatics

Chapter 46—Fantasies on the Internet

Part 7

The Good, the Bad, the Law, the Lawbreakers

Chapter 47—Laws and Lawbreakers

Chapter 48—Immigrants Fight for America, Others Run and Hide

Chapter 49—Positive Contributions of Illegals

Chapter 50—Taxes, Social Security and Illegals

Part 8

The End of the Beginning

Chapter 51—Standing on the Corner...

Chapter 52—A Happy-Face Police State

Part 9

The Beginning of the End, January 7, 2004

Chapter 53—President George W. Bush speaks and the Nation Awakens

Part 10

Democrats try to catch up—Tuesday, May 4, 2004

Part 11

About The Author

ACKNOWLEDGMENTS

Many people had input into this book. The initial impetus for it came from a suggestion by University of California Regent Ward Connerly that he and I write a joint Op-Ed piece on how to solve the illegal alien problem. My first draft of the Op-Ed piece was 3,000 words long and quickly grew to 20,000 words, then 40,000, then on to the finish.

Then entered Republican Congressional candidate Mike Giorgino who, while researching his opponent anti-war Democrat Bob Filner discovered that Congressman Filner and Republican Tom Tancredo had signed advertisements in support of a viciously anti-American terrorist group from Iran. Giorgino directed me to Professor Paul Sheldon Foote of Cal-State Fullerton who sent me the information on Tancredo's support of Iranian terrorists.

I offer my everlasting thanks and appreciation to two university professors, one in California and one at Harvard.

First, Cal-State-Fresno Professor Victor Davis Hanson, whose book *Mexifornia*, was published by Encounter books while I was drafting the first few thousand words of this book, for he gave me a target rich environment to refer to and quote.

Finally, there is the world famous Harvard Political Science and Department Chairman, Dr. Samuel P. Huntington. He is the highest-ranking racial jingoist in the modern United States of America. In publishing his article (*The Hispanic Challenge*) in the *Foreign Policy Magazine* which was derived from his new book Who Are We? He provided this former Marine a marksman's dream — a larger-than-life target. He did this writer the greatest favor of all, he outlined how he considers Mexicans to be the greatest threat ever to this country and its *Anglo-Protestant* culture.

Racists throughout the country exulted in Huntington's words because they finally have some "intellectual" validation for their racist hate against Mexicans.

I exulted also. Huntington was too good a target, what with his juvenile observations, lack of proof, and documentation. More importantly, was his total disregard for the history of this country since the first Roman Catholic landed in Maryland and Mexicans died fighting in the American Revolution.

Those "threatening" Mexicans have died fighting for America since 1779 up to and including the present war in Iraq.

I dedicate this book to Jesús Suárez de Solar and José Angel Garibay, both Mexican citizens, and José Antonio Gutiérrez, a citizen of Guatemala, who were all United States Marines when they died in the first few days of the Iraq invasion.

These men were buried as American citizens. They died as Americans, fighting for America. These immigrant men's lives and deaths overshadow Professors Hanson and Huntington and all those who revel in their widely held shallow unsubstantiated views.

The Illegal Alien: A Dagger into the Heart of America???

"I believe with all my heart that massive illegal immigration into our country is a dagger pointed at our heart...It will determine whether we are to be a country – or not."

Representative Tom Tancredo, ®-Colorado), October 23, 2003, *San Diego Union Tribune*

"Unlike past immigrant groups, Mexicans and other Latinos have not assimilated into mainstream U.S. culture, forming instead their own political and linguistic enclaves—from Los Angeles to Miami—rejecting the *Anglo-Protestant* values that built the American dream. The United States ignores this challenge at its peril." (*The Hispanic Challenge, Foreign Policy*)

Professor Samuel P. Huntington, Chairman, Harvard Academy for International Area Studies

"Massive illegal immigration from Mexico into California, coupled with a loss of confidence in the old melting pot model of transforming newcomers into Americans, is changing the very nature of the state." (*Mexifornia: A State of Becoming*, Encounter Books)

Professor Victor Davis Hanson, California State University, Fresno

"Almost one-quarter of California's inmates are from Mexico, and almost a third of recent drug-trafficking arrests involved illegal aliens." (*Mexifornia: A State of Becoming*, Encounter Books)

Professor Victor Davis Hanson, California State University, Fresno

"The only effective way to close the Mexican-American border (or any other) is to punish those who get caught and that is not politically practical. Jailing illegals would cause a major row with Mexico. Perhaps even more important, it would almost certainly be unpopular with American voters as well. Americans see work as a moral virtue. They are unlikely to favor jailing people whose only sin is that they want a job." (*New York Review of Books*)

Professor Christopher Jencks, Social Policy Professor, Harvard University

"…Some US and Mexican politicians are plotting to merge both nations' (U.S. and Mexico) social security systems, even as the economic impact of immigration—legal and otherwise—is dooming budgets in a number of states. Add to this mix a high (and climbing) unemployment rate in the U.S., including the loss of thousands of jobs that are being filled by illegal aliens, and in many ways American taxpayers are finding they are supporting not one country but two." (*Illegals: The Imminent Threat Posed By Our Unsecured U.S.-Mexico Border*, WND Books)

Jon E. Dougherty

"Not every opponent of immigration is racist, but every racist opposes immigration."

Raoul Lowery Contreras

"At this late hour, only an affirmation that we are White and that we must do whatever is necessary to ensure that our race survives can save us. White people have an absolute nonnegotiable right to exist, to organize and govern ourselves, to have our own exclusive territories for our nations and peoples, and to keep the products of our labor for ourselves and our posterity. Only by taking that uncompromising stand and backing it up with all the wealth and will and power we can muster, do we have a chance to provide for future generations of our people.

"We are Americans, White people of Western civilization. Our values, and the great culture and science and wealth we have created, are ours and ours alone. Our survival depends on us keeping them for ourselves, and on keeping the land that sustains us, as our property and no one else's. Furthermore, the very existence of that culture and that science depends on our continued existence, and we cannot risk losing what we are by mixing with other and incompatible races."

American Dissident Voices Broadcast of March 20, 2004

"They (illegals) do not pay taxes. Illegals in this country are un-American. It (illegal residency) flies in the face of the Constitution."

Maryland State Representative Patrick L. McDonough ®,February 19, 2004, *Baltimore Sun*

"President Bush's plan to grant amnesty to millions of undocumented workers and allow millions more to enter the country is a fundamental disconnect with reality and should be rejected out-of-hand."

Mark Krikorian, Center for Immigration Studies

"America is, essentially, an elegant idea, engraved in a social contract of shared rights and obligations. The President would rip up that contract."

Mike McGarry, Colorado Alliance for Immigration Reform, *Denver Post*, February 22, 2204

"The President's proposal is unrealistic, lacks basic credibility and is insulting to the intelligence of anyone who has studied this problem for any length of time."

Dan Stein, Federation for American Immigration Reform (FAIR)

"…What the President is proposing is that we have a kind of one-way merger with Mexico."

Glenn Spencer, American Border Patrol

"The Huntingtons arrived in Boston in 1633. Almost all Huntingtons in the U.S. are descended from Simon and Margaret Huntington, who were part of a group of settlers from Norwich, England, who founded Norwich, Conn."

This statement was made in the New York Times Magazine, May 2, 2004. Here Harvard's Dr. Samuel P. Huntington explains why he is an immigration snob and dislikes Hispanics;

particularly Mexicans with this reference to his people immigrated here first.

***

ILLEGAL IMMIGRATION MUST BE STOPPED

"Illegal immigration, particularly as it pertains to narco republic Mexico, is out of control. It has an immense social, political, economic and demographic cost on American citizens.

Through his relentless pro-illegal immigration columns on these pages, who knows how many Mexicans, including felons, writer Raul (sic) Contreras encouraged and emboldened to break our immigration laws.

More and more we're hearing heartbreaking stories of heinous crimes committed against Americans by Mexican illegals. Recently two police officers were killed by Mexican illegals. Crimes of person and property are dramatically on the rise by this group of lawless desperadoes.

Thanks to Gov. Gray Davis, who with his cronies has ruined California, and the Bush administration, nothing is being done about this grave and costly problem. Be prepared to protect yourself and your family.

This unchecked illegal Mexican assault on our country, our borders, language and culture, is costing us dearly in blood and treasure. Watch as this most serious problem explodes and shakes the foundations of your world. "

Gary Walker, Escondido, San Diego's *North County Times,* June 28, 2003

"The Emigration Party of Nevada indorses (sic) a shoot on sight policy for illegal border crossers."

Emigration Party Update 688, Wednesday, February 11, 2004, www.sendemback.org

" The Emigration Party of Nevada endorses a shoot to kill on sight policy for all illegal border crossers. No warning should be given. While the vast majority of illegal aliens border crossers are Mexicans, this should be done without regard to age, gender, sexual orientation, citizenship, national origin, or race. We want to shoot Heidi from Switzerland just as quickly as poor pregnant Maria from Chiapas. They take jobs away from Americans, depress our standard of living, use our welfare, ruin our schools, raise our taxes, and overload our infrastructure. Within days of a shoot on sight policy being instituted, illegal border crossing will stop. Shooting illegal alien border crossers on sight is no different than shooting a burlar (sic) in the act of breaking into your home. It will take only a handfull (sic) to get the word out in Mexico. All illegal border crossing traffic will stop overnight. We could even sell illegal alien bag permits, somewhat like a deer tags (sic). To be elgible (sic) for one you would have to show that you are a good marksman and are familiar with the border. This is a better way that (sic) wasting expensive ammunition on the border and cleaning up rotting carcasses."

Emigration Party of Nevada, Update 725 Friday, 19 March, 2004, www.sendemback.org

"From the rural Mexican cultures of the 1920s to modern urban America today is a very long journey in human terms. Most Mexican Americans have come a long way on that journey."

Dr. Thomas Sowell, *Ethnic America*, Basic Books, 1981

A Credo to Live By, by Critics of *Illegal Aliens*

"...The factual accuracy of Contreras's argument is not important..."

Peter Brimelow, *Alien Nation* Random House, 1995

INTRODUCTION

PARANOIA AND XENOPHOBIA

(XENOPHOBIA=FEAR OF FOREIGNERS)

There are people like Tom Tancredo, Gary Walker, uneducated amateurs like *author* Jon Dougherty and the Emigration Party of Nevada who attack the relatively serious problem of illegal aliens with false charges, profound emotionalism and huge doses of pure hatred of Mexicans. As isolated extremists, they are easy to handle intellectually and we shall do so easily. Unfortunately, they obviously have some appeal to some in our country.

Recent statements by the "Emigration Party of Nevada" of shooting illegal aliens on sight are not accidental, nor made in a vacuum. The statements result from inflamed and infectious excitement among Mexican-haters caused by the demagoguery of Tancredo, Walker, Dougherty and those who absorb their views and pass them on with a high energetic level of bigoted gusto.

Less easy to confront are the newer forces emerging against illegal aliens from Mexico. These people grace the faculty at Harvard, Cal-State Fresno (one professor), the University of California, Santa Barbara (one professor) and San Diego State University (one professor). They gleefully toss profound intellectual statements around like *Anglo-Protestant*, or drool over Cal-State Fresno's Professor Victor Davis Hanson's 150-page book, *Mexifornia: a State of Becoming.*

Nonetheless, facts and the reality of 2004 and ten-or-so-million illegal aliens in the country, plus Aristotelian reason will publicly expose these "doctors of philosophy" immigration critics for what they are, ethnic jingoists. The only difference between these professors and people like ill-educated Gary Walker, Jon Dougherty and the Emigration Party of Nevada, are clearly university pedigrees and tenured positions as professors.

Regardless of doctorates, or lack of them, these people cut the ground out from under reasoned discussion over the illegal alien problem in America. Their intellectual obtrusiveness obstructs intelligent proposals to define and solve the problem. Their definitions of the problem, like Walker's, are clouded by emotion, blatant lies, bone-deep racism and a deep-seated fear that some people in this country don't want to act like Anglo-Protestants, especially if they aren't Anglo or Protestant.

Thus, if their definitions and data aren't accurate, dispassionate or objective, obviously any of their proposed solutions will lack intellectual integrity, or veracity, that is—if they offer any solutions at all.

These critics, academics and otherwise, believe that the country is collapsing under the weight of illegal aliens. They believe that the American culture, the American civilization, if you will, cannot continue or flourish as long as the "invasion" from Mexico continues.

They believe "criminals," criminals with dark skins who speak Spanish, who are Roman Catholic, and refuse to learn English and the American Way, are overwhelming the country. They believe there is a massive conspiracy of American-hating Mexicans to recapture California and the Southwest by infiltration (*reconquista*), political theft and destruction of

American institutions. They really, truly believe this conspiracy exists. Some live and breathe this imagined conspiracy 24-hours-a-day. That now includes a well-placed, world famous Harvard intellectual, Dr. Samuel P. Huntington.

For the record, Professor Huntington is not only a traditional Anglo Protestant, he is a Democrat and once served on President Jimmy Carter's National Security Council, the same security people on whose watch the Iranians kidnaped 54 Americans and held them hostage for over 400 days.

In a coincidence of history, Professor Huntington has now joined forces with Congressman Tom Tancredo of Colorado in implementing hate words against Mexicans. Huntington watched helplessly from the White House while terrorist Iranian Mujahedin kidnaped Americans and murdered others. Tancredo now supports those very terrorist Mujahedin in an attempt to legitimize their place in the world—What a coincidence.

Some of these people (especially Harvard professors) refused to believe that the Soviet Union truly posed a threat to the West, or that Soviet Communist agents were burrowed deeply into our government and institutions like Hollywood filmmaking and the academy.

Unlike the Cold War days, today, they are totally convinced that Mexican peasant Indians and the Mexican White elite are plotting in Rural Mexico to demographically reconquer the American Southwest. Specifically, they think, the principal target is the "nation-state" of California, the fifth largest economy in the world. Any objective word analysis of Tancredo's and Walker's statements, for example, clearly demonstrates that these two people are irresponsible emotionally-whacked out paranoids who are truly dangerous in a civil constitutional democratic society. Their manner and base lies reflect a fascist society, not the United States of America, as we know it. As to the academics, they will be examined individually, statement by statement, word by word and proven wrong, with their own words and, more importantly, with irrefutable scientific evidence. For example, what intellectual and personality defects does Tancredo appeal to with his use of such inflammatory words as "dagger" and the image of a "dagger pointed at our hearts?"

He implies the worst crime of all, murder. In other words, illegal aliens are murdering us as a people, not as a culture as asserted by the academics, but as a people. His use of the word "massive" implies a huge invasion of illegals. Factually, his implication leaves much to be desired. One in 29 people living in the United States is in the country illegally. "Massive...One in 29?

Moreover, despite lawsuits by former California Governor Pete Wilson who alleged the United States was not protecting California as required in the Constitution (Article IV, Section 4) when an "invasion" occurs, the courts have dismissed the law suits. Why? Because they ruled, there was no "invasion."

The courts have defined "invasions" as by armed military forces, organized and directed by a command and control structure. Unarmed Mexican peasant farmers and young unemployed urban men, women and some child Mexicans sneaking across the border looking for work cannot be legally, Constitutionally characterized as an "invasion" force.

As for Mr. Walker, "...narco republic Mexico..." is the first example of prejudice in his screed. According to law enforcement, more marijuana is grown and sold in Northern California by middle-aged pony-tailed American "hippies" than is smuggled in from Mexico. Absolutely no cocaine is grown or processed in Mexico, yet it is the narcotic of choice on the streets of suburban White America, as is it's derivative, "crack" is among America's Blacks. About 60 percent of all cocaine transits Mexico. The remaining 40 percent transit myriad routes, but not through Mexico.

The United States Coast Guard intercepted three boatloads of cocaine on the high seas in March 2004, that amounted to almost a third of a billion dollars value on the street, enough, according to the drug enforcers of the DEA, to supply American cocaine habits for almost a year. The boats were from South America, not Mexico.

Only 5 percent of all heroin used in the United States comes from or through Mexico, according to the U.S. Drug Enforcement Agency (DEA). 95 percent of heroin comes from mostly Moslem South/Central Asia (Afghanistan, Pakistan, Iran, Turkey, Lebanon) and Southeast Asia countries like Mynamar-Burma, Thailand, Laos and South China—Golden Triangle).

So, Mr. Walker, what does "narco republic" mean? As the primary market in the world for illicit narcotics, isn't the United States a "narco republic?" If not, please explain how tons of cocaine manage to find their way across thousands of miles of American streets and highways into the neighborhoods of drug users who have never even heard of Mexico. Mexico is not the center of the illicit drug world Mr. Walker, Colombia and Asia are the production centers of the illicit drug world. Northern California, Hawaii and Canada are the centers of the illicit marijuana trade. Mexico is only one of a number of marijuana producing countries that supply the United States. There are people that think marijuana shouldn't be illegal. There are laws on the California books that permit marijuana users to smoke the weed if they can get a letter from fellow marijuana smokers with medical degrees.

His words "immense" cost in "social, political, economic and demographic" areas of America are not documented or quantified, nor are there quotes from bona fide studies, just Mr. Walker's flat declaration. The Rand Corporation, in several studies, concludes that the country makes money off of illegal aliens. Some studies show a positive impact on the national Gross Domestic Product while others shows a slight cost, but no legitimate study concludes there is an "immense" cost to the 285-million people in the country who are not illegal aliens.

Moreover, despite emotional claims to the contrary by Walker and others, illegal aliens are not a zero-sum economic cost vis a vis tax revenue. Some costs, yes; however, they also produce revenue, they pay taxes, substantial taxes. They pay the most regressive of taxes, sales and property taxes. Plus, they produce value, produce Gross Domestic Product. Then, he uses the words "relentless pro-illegal immigration columns" by me in an American newspaper seldom read by people in Mexico. He uses "encouraged" (I encouraged Mexicans) as my motivation for writing such pieces and that they "emboldened" people to "break" immigration laws. His proof, he doesn't say, and he offers none. Perhaps he is living by Peter Brimelow's credo that my "facts" are irrelevant.

Has any apprehended illegal alien ever responded to a Border Patrol agent's demand to know why the illegal came to America—I came because Raoul Lowery Contreras encouraged me to in his Saturday political newspaper column? Then, he writes "More and more we're hearing heartbreaking stories of heinous crimes committed against Americans by Mexican illegals." He cites two cases. Then, "Crimes of person and property are dramatically on the rise by lawless desperadoes." His facts...his statistics? None! Ten million or so illegals in the country and he offers no evidentiary statistics from any official source of any sort.

Actually, the state of California—the state Attorney General himself—reports that crimes of all sorts, violent and nonviolent, have fallen over the past decade to 1967 levels (though some crimes have gone up slightly since 2000, all violent crime levels are down to levels not seen since 1967). What is interesting is that the number of illegals from Mexico has, perhaps, doubled or tripled in the exact same time period that crime levels have plunged. "Lawless desperadoes?" I think not.

Critics can't explain why crime has plunged so deeply while illegal border crossing numbers have spiked upward by millions and, as noted, doubled or tripled in California. Nonetheless, when this writer even points out that incongruity, the Anglo-Protestants decry the question and the theory it posits because scientific evidence generated by "experts" isn't presented with the question.

My answer, the evidence is in plain view for all to see. Experts are not needed to explain the connection between the drop in crime while the numbers of illegals climb. The connection is obvious. Violent crime is not on the minds of many illegals, jobs are. Of the illegal alien prisoners in state prisons, according to prison officials and all their paperwork from the courts, the majority is there for crimes of property, not violence.

In the Federal prison system, well over 80 percent are in custody for immigration or smuggling charges, not violent crimes.

"…nothing," Walker writes, "is being done about this grave and costly problem. Be prepared to protect yourself and your family." Walker smugly proclaims nothing is being done because, perhaps, Mexicans are not being machine gunned on the streets and on the border (as advocated by some talk show hosts and the Emigration Party of Nevada). While he states "nothing" is being done, myriad congressmen of both parties and the Bush Administration itself are negotiating programs in the halls of Congress to craft realistic solutions to parts, if not all, of the illegal alien problem. Some of these proposals allow many of these illegals to become legal, thus changing the entire problem, its definition and impact by a change in the law.

Today's illegal alien immigrant can be tomorrow's legal resident and maybe even citizen. That is very possible by Congress changing the law, but is possible even under current law. So stated Justice William Brennan in the 1982 Plyler v. Doe decision by the Supreme Court. It mandated that illegal immigrant children be educated at any public school in the country without regard to their citizenship or legal residency. The decision also defined illegal aliens as "persons" as mentioned in the Constitution's 14th amendment. "Persons" who are illegal aliens, thus, are covered by the U.S. Constitution while they are in the United States. That Supreme Court position takes care of arguments that illegals have no constitutional rights when law enforcement agents take them in custody.

Lastly, Mr. Walker, writes, "This unchecked illegal Mexican assault on our country, our borders, language and culture, is costing us dearly in blood and treasure. Watch as this most serious problem explodes and shakes the foundations of your world." Note he doesn't quantify the loss of "blood" in the form of body counts, of charged murderers, or even of convicted illegal alien felons who kill, maim or otherwise draw "blood." Why doesn't he? Those are public records, public records that, in fact, simply don't substantiate his "costing us dearly in blood..."

All illegals are Mexican; thus all Mexicans are illegal. Some Mexicans commit crimes; thus all Mexicans commit crimes. Some Mexicans cost American society; thus all Mexicans cost us. So declare Anglo-Protestants. Some demand that illegals be shot on sight. Can any of these people spell or define xenophobia (fear of foreigners)? There are college professors who can, and they have now stirred the illegal alien cauldron with feeble "interventions" from the upper reaches of the academy's proverbial "Ivory Tower."

PART ONE

CHAPTER 1

PROFESSOR SAMUEL P. HUNTINGTON
OF HARVARD

The Sky Is Not less Blue Because the Blind Man Does Not See It (Danish Proverb)

Professor Samuel P. Huntington is Chairman of the Harvard Academy for International and Area Studies. He is a cofounder of the magazine *Foreign Policy*, in which a lengthy essay, *The Hispanic Challenge*, was published in the March/April, 2004 edition (www.foreignpolicy.com). Democrat Huntington is a former senior official of President Jimmy Carter's failed and impotent National Security Council. His 1996 book *The Clash of Civilizations and the Remaking of World Order* outlined the current struggle between the Christian West and Islam.

The *New Republic*'s Daniel W. Drezner comments in a March 3rd, 2004 article entitled *Hash of Civilizations*, "If a Nobel Prize in political science were ever announced, Samuel Huntington would undoubtedly be among the initial recipients."

Alan Wolfe writes in the Council of Foreign Relations' *Foreign Affairs* magazine (May-June 2004), "In the course of a remarkably distinguished academic career, Samuel Huntington has demonstrated a steadfast commitment to realism." Scholar Wolfe now writes this about Professor Huntington's newest book, *Who Are We? The Challenges to America's National Identity* (Simon & Schuster): "Gone is the realism that characterizes most of his writing: *Who Are We?* Is riddled with the same kind of moralistic passion—*at times bordering on hysteria*—that Huntington finds so troubling in American Politics." (Emphasis added)

Professor Huntington's words in his article and book from which it comes carefully outline his basic thesis, which is that Hispanics, specifically Mexicans, are not assimilating like past immigrants to the United States, that they don't want to and, that they reject *Anglo-Protestant values*. In Alan Wolfe's view, Professor Huntington, a pillar of Harvard and the Establishment, has written a book that he describes as: *"Who Are We?* Is Patrick Buchanan with footnotes."

Huntington writes: "The persistent inflow of Hispanic immigrants threatens to divide the United States into two peoples, two cultures, and two languages."

Generally, he believes Mexicans are a grave threat, the ultimate threat to the United States. In fact, he declares that the invasion of Mexicans means, "the United States of America will suffer the fate of Sparta, Rome, and other ancient communities."

The numbers, as presented by immigration expert Jeffrey Passel in an article for *Migration Information Source*, are these:

"Mexico represents the largest source of immigration to the United States (In this regard Huntington is right). Of the 32.5 million foreign born covered by the March 2002 Current Population Survey (CPS), 9.8 million or 30 percent were from Mexico; the next largest source, the Philippines, accounted for only one-seventh as many at 1.4 million. The rest of Latin America accounted for 7.3 million, or 23 percent." Thus, Mexicans and other Latin Americans amounted to 53-percent of foreign born, with Asians 10 percent and Europeans and Canadians 5 percent.

Passel reports that Mexicans account for "one fifth" of legal immigrants in the U.S. Many, of these, he writes are a "legacy" of the 1986 Immigration Reform Amnesty that legalized almost three million former illegals. Of new immigrants, about "one in seven are Mexican." In that same March 2002 CPS, there were an estimated "9.3 million undocumented immigrants" in the country. Passel estimates that 5.3 million, or 57-percent were Mexican, with another two million from the rest of Latin America, or "just under 25 percent."

Mexican legal immigration almost doubled between 1990 and 2000. Passel notes that illegal immigration jumped by an estimated 165 percent during the same period. Much of that huge percentage jump can be explained by two events. (1) The economic shock of a huge Mexican peso devaluation at the end of 1994 and, (2) the initial shock of the North American Free Trade Agreement's (NAFTA) impact on Mexican food production that was severely disrupted by cheaper American corn and wheat imports to Mexico. At the end of each Mexican six-year Presidency, it has been traditional that departing Presidents and their "achichinqles" (gophers) rape the government they are term-limited out of everything possible, including cash converted into dollars. The usual and historical result, a huge peso devaluation, and a tightening of imports by high projectionist tariffs. The 1994 devaluation was heavier than normal, catastrophic, in fact.

The new Mexican government of Ernesto Zedillo found itself $50-billion dollars in the hole. A new Republican Congress in Washington immediately responded to President William Clinton's request for a helping hand loan to Mexico. New House of Representatives Speaker, Republican Newt Gingrich and Senate Republican leader Bob Dole pledged their support for a temporary loan to Mexico.

In stepped Pat Buchanan and his congressional friends like Republican Congressmen Duncan Hunter, Dana Rohrabacher and other "conservatives" known for anti-Mexican views. These men called upon a latent anti-Mexican feeling among those who had lost the bitter 1993 NAFTA debate in Congress. This group was inspired by the "Halloween Coalition" led by Pat Buchanan, Black self-anointed "leader" Jesse Jackson, crazy-man Ross Perot and every labor leader in the country. They were successful in blocking a loan in Congress. Nonetheless, the Clinton Administration outfoxed the "Coalition" and found the money needed in funds uncontrolled by Congress.

The second event was the entry of less-expensive corn and cereal grains raised on the most successful (and heavily federally subsidized) farms in the world, those in the United States. Farming became a totally losing proposition for much of rural Mexico. As rural Mexicans fled a 1920s-atmosphere rural Mexico, many bypassed the normal rural to city migration pattern and traveled north to the United States where an economic boom started when Republicans gained control of the Congress and ushered in one of the greatest economic upward lunges in world history.

On the positive side, the Mexican government—led by U.S. educated, doctorate-holding professionals—did not abrogate NAFTA, it didn't slam shut rising imports from the USA, it didn't raise tariffs sky-high, in fact, the Mexican government did not raise tariffs at all. The Mexican government didn't panic. It borrowed $50-billion from the United States and paid the loan off early, paying over $50-million in interest to the United States. Simultaneously, it contained a Communist-led Indian rebellion in the southern state of Chiapas. Almost all Mexicans supported the political and military containment of Indians led by professional Communists trained by Nicaragua's Sandinistas. In economically bursting Baja California, 2,000 kilometers to the north, for example, store and shop owners, factory owners and workers all subscribed to billboards and flyers posted everywhere— *Violencia No!*

The great Mexican Revolution of 1994 did not explode into violence, it did, however, occur—peacefully and out of sight of Americans. In that year, Opposition candidate for Governor in the State of Guanajuato, Vicente Fox, had his obvious ballot victory nullified –stolen—by the ruling party of Mexico. Six years later he would lead the Opposition Partido Acción Nacional (PAN) party to its first ever Presidential victory after a 70-year reign of the Partido Revolucionario Institucional (PRI), a victory that finally unleashed true democracy in Mexico. The Stalinist PRIstas had met their match in the giant cowboy-boot-wearing devout Roman Catholic Mexican politician the people of Mexico wanted to be their president. Credit must be given to PRIsta President Dr. Ernesto Zedillo who made sure of an honest vote count and took to the television airwaves just hours after polls closed to congratulate Vicente Fox in his victory. History will not forget Dr. Zedillo, a true democrat.

The United States needed millions of new workers in the economic boom of the 1990s, many Americans responded and moved into the job market. Mexicans responded also, filling the jobs Americans did not take, or abandoned for upward job mobility. They came without papers and immigration interviews; they came as illegal aliens, millions of them. The booming American economy snapped up the willing workers.

CHAPTER 2

THE TWO FACES OF ANGLO-PROTESTANTISM

Professor Huntington's general thesis is correct in some minor details while totally incorrect in its overview of the problems posed by ten-million illegal aliens and several million legal immigrants from Mexico. He is correct in that the basic foundation of America is Anglo and Protestant. But those two ingredients have been equally problematical and positive for over two hundred years, a fact Professor Huntington totally ignores. He is not alone in ignoring the defects of the American "Anglo-Protestant" culture and way of life.

Both combined, for example, to treat millions of Irish Catholics like disease-ridden dogs for decades. Both combined to permit slavery for over 250 years before the 13th Amendment to the United States Constitution outlawed slavery forever in the United States of America. Both combined to impose the peculiar American racial and political Fascism called "Jim Crow" on many parts of the country. A 100 percent Anglo and Protestant Supreme Court approved the "Jim Crow" policy in 1895 when the court decided the Plessy v. Ferguson case. That court enunciated the policy of "separate but equal" for millions of American-born blacks. They were legally forced to live under this racial fascism for almost 70-years after slavery was outlawed.

Both combined to stifle immigration in 1924 based, not on numbers, but ethnicity (Italian, Greek, Eastern European) and religion (Catholic and Jewish). "Greaseballs" and "Hebes" were to be kept out by all means to keep the country Anglo and Protestant. Both combined to incubate and nurture the Know-Nothing Party (anti-immigrant, anti-Catholic) that won many elections, including governor offices, in the 1840s and 50s.

Both combined to treat Irish immigrant Roman Catholic U.S. Army soldiers like criminals and animals. Both combined to drive these persecuted soldiers to desert the Army during the Mexican War. They joined the Mexican Army and fought in their own San Patricio Battalion. Both combined to find and hang these Irish soldiers who fought against America and did so furtively and quietly so Irish Americans and their Church would not know the truth for a hundred years.

Anglo-Protestants combined to splatter the blood of hundreds of thousands of Americans on the battlefields of the Civil War. Both combined to allow the formation, under English-descended and practicing Protestant Nathan Bedford Forest, of the Ku Klux Klan (KKK). After the Civil War the Anglo-Protestant KKK terrorized blacks, Catholics and Jews throughout the country up to and including the 1990s. Both decided not to punish the soldiers and politicians of the Southern Confederacy, as they should have for rebelling against the Constitution and the Republic. For example, Anglo Protestant Confederate soldiers commanded by General Nathan Bedford Forest, millionaire slave trader before the Civil War, murdered almost three hundred captured Black Union soldiers at Ft. Pillow, Tennessee. People debate the use of the word "massacre" in discussing the slaughter at Fort Pillow, but no one can debate that a war crime occurred and that Nathan Bedford Forest was responsible. He was never charged or tried for the massacre. Instead he served as President of a railroad after the Civil War.

Anglo-Protestants combined to produce the *Grapes of Wrath* that John Steinbeck immortalized in print and on the big screen. Both combined to brutalize the citizens of Los Angeles, Mexican-descended Catholics. They railroaded them into prison on phony charges (The Sleepy Lagoon murder, for example), physically and illegally brutalized ethnic prisoners in the city jails and by segregating those original Angelenos into neighborhoods (barrios) and schools designed and engineered to fail. Both combined to ruin these same neighborhoods by allowing pollution-heavy industries to settle in residential neighborhoods and to pollute them beyond description up to and including today.

Anglo-Protestants combined to prevent the New Mexico Territory from entering the United States as the states of Arizona and New Mexico because too many people were Spanish-speaking—after, of course, three hundred years as Spanish and Mexican territory. The Territory was American territory from 1846 until admitted as a state in 1912. New York Anglo-Protestant newspaper editor Horace Greeley once said of the new Americans of Mexican descent in the New Mexico Territory, they were too "priest-ridden."

We can be thankful to our English-bred and mostly Protestant Founding Fathers for writing the world's finest Constitution, and for the resultant Supreme Court case of Marbury V. Madison. That case truly implemented a check and balance three-part government. We also owe Anglo Protestants the Constitutional provision that black slaves were "3/5ths" of a person. We owe them the perpetuation of slavery until English-descended and Protestant Abraham Lincoln (who won the Presidency with 40% of the vote) put a stop to it with the Grand Army of the Republic. We owe them for "Manifest Destiny" and its implementers that lied about Mexico and provoked a war for real estate in 1846. Manifest Destiny is defined as a simple WASP (White Anglo-Saxon Protestant) plan to grab California (and Arizona, New Mexico, Colorado, Nevada, Utah and parts of Oklahoma, and Kansas) from Mexico because it was ordained by the Almighty that America should be from sea to shining sea.

We owe Anglo-Protestants for a Supreme Court that ruled that Mr. Dred Scott could never become a citizen because he was Black and African. The Anglo-Protestant court also ruled that because Scott had escaped from slavery, he was property and his owner could reclaim his "property." We owe both Anglos and Protestants for ignoring Thomas Jefferson's "all men are created equal" dictum in the Declaration of Independence which, of course, Anglo and Protestant Jefferson ignored also. We owe them for the lynching of dozens of Irish Catholics in Philadelphia in the 1840s because they refused to read from the Anglo-Protestant King James Bible.

We owe Anglo-Protestants for creating the great fiction of "separation of church and state" when, in fact, no such wall was designed by the Founding Fathers in the 1st Amendment to the Constitution. They both combined to build this fiction simply to keep taxpayer money from being spent on superior Catholic schools. In 2003, a diverse Anglo-Protestant, Irish and Italian Catholic and Jewish Supreme Court ruled that government funded school vouchers were constitutional even when redeemed by Catholic parochial and other religious schools. We owe both for Benjamin Franklin, who was both, for observing that German immigrants were "the most stupid of their nation and that few of their children know English." (*Los Angeles Times*, March 11, 2004)

CHAPTER 3

LINGUA FRANCA, SAVVY?

Little has changed since Benjamin Franklin, as the Huntington article seems to indicate. In a *Los Angeles Times* Op-Ed piece (3-14-2004), professor of English and Linguistics at the University of Illinois, Dennis Baron, writes that, "Huntington laments that Latino immigrants retain any of their Spanish and claims that they imperil not just the American language but also American stability."

Baron continues: "Of course, English is associated with representative democracy, not to mention global capitalism and rock 'n' roll. But Spanish and every other language also have words for freedom, business and music. And English, already a global common denominator, has never been the undisputed priority of Anglo Protestants. It began in heathen Europe, traveled to Celtic Britain, was leavened with the Latin of Irish monks, the Norse Vikings raiders and the French of Normans bent on regime change." In other words, English, whole enchilada English, has never been the exclusive property of the Anglo-Protestant, savvy? Savvy, by the way, comes from the Spanish verb—Saber, to know. Savvy? He concludes: "Today, even with ongoing Latino immigration, most native Spanish speakers in the U.S. are losing their Spanish by the second generation. That's *considerably faster than the patterns for earlier groups* (emphasis added)... (Hispanics) object—as all Americans should— (to) such laws (English-only that) translate this Way—'*We Don't Want You Here!*'"

Now, if only the exalted Harvard Professor Huntington had so clearly used definitive words instead of forcing us define his statements and the Professor himself for what he and they truly are. Some might say Huntington was simply issuing a challenge, however, Professor Baron hit the nail with a very accurate hammer.

Professor Huntington was not challenging; he was declaring war on Mexicans and Mexican Americans from his Anglo-Protestant Harvard fortress without proof, evidence or even reason. "We don't want you here" is his message. I reject that message, and so do the millions like me who spoke Spanish before we spoke English.

On balance, then, the combination of Anglos and Protestants has something more than the pure positives Professor Huntington ascribes to them, they both have substantial negatives, historical negatives that we have managed to overcome, but at what price? Here we are 223-years after Mexicans fought for the Americans in their revolt against Anglo-Protestant England (See *Hispanics in America's Defense*, Department of Defense, 1982) and a distinguished American professor is forcefully declaring to millions of Mexicans and Mexican Americans, "We don't want you here." When the Soviets were bogged down in Afghanistan a quarter century ago, a political and military event that helped usher Communism into the ash can of history, Soviet soldiers approached the American Embassy to defect and were willing to spill their military information, secrets and plans to the Americans.

Unfortunately, Professor Huntington's ideal of speaking English-only had bred much of the Russian language out of the American population that less than 8-decades before had welcomed masses of Russian-speakers. The English-only Professor Huntingtons of the country had inadvertently made sure that there were not enough Russian-speakers to interrogate defecting Soviet soldiers. The safety and security of the United States was threatened by this dearth of Russian speakers, but Professor Huntington's desire for a pure English-only speaking America had reached an unfortunate high tide level.

That was a generation ago. As this is written there aren't enough trusted Arab-speaking personnel in the government and/or military to implement our occupation of Iraq and the nation building in progress there. In fact, Americans are dying because there aren't enough bilingual Arab speakers in the service of our troops and effort. Furthermore, as this is written, the *Los Angeles Times* (March 19, 2004) is reporting that "California students who are still learning English have made significant strides in mastering the language for the second year in a row, according to test scores..."

Time's writers Duke Helfand and Jean Merl reported, "Forty-three percent of the state's 1.4 million students who speak English as a second language demonstrated proficiency in 2003 on English tests in reading, writing, speaking and listening skills. In 2002, 34% of such students had reached proficient level, and this figure was 25%, the first year the California English Language Development Test was given." The complete test results are available to Professor Huntington at celdt.cde.ca.gov

Once again, real experience in the classroom makes Professor Huntington's gratuitous assertions meaningless. Facts, Professor Huntington, are very stubborn things.

"The sky is not less blue because the blind man does not see it."

CHAPTER 4

THE NATIVIST AND ROMAN CATHOLICS

Huntington: "Would the United States be the country that it has been and that it largely remains today if it had been settled in the 17ᵗʰ and 18ᵗʰ centuries not by British Protestants but by French, Spanish, or Portuguese Catholics? The answer is clearly no. It would not be the United States, it would be Quebec, Mexico or Brazil."

In an article entitled "Huntington's Unease," Dan Glaister writes in the *Guardian* and in the *Sidney Morning Herald* (Australia-March 17, 2004)) about Huntington's immigration thesis and what the coming of Catholics to America spelled: "…for Huntington, (it means) the end of civilization." The *New York Times'* David Brooks wrote, "Frankly, something's a little off in Huntington's use of the term 'Anglo-Protestant' to describe American culture…There is no question that we have all been shaped by the legacies of Jonathon Edwards and Benjamin Franklin. But the mentality that binds us is not well described by the words 'Anglo' or 'Protestant." Brooks is Jewish and a conservative Republican. Professor Huntington's clear and precise declaration that the answer to his question is "clearly no" stands out in a lengthy essay (or book excerpt) because, as Glaister points out, "The professor assembles an array of circumstantial observations as impending collapse." Glaister notes that the Harvard professor makes "some decidedly unempirical assertions."

Not-so-empirical words and thoughts written by Professor Huntington:

"One might suppose...(2) could, in due course, have significant consequences in politics and government...(3) might have to be fluent...(4) both languages could become acceptable...(5) likely to be..." These words are truly not empirical by definition and certainly would not be accepted by Professor Huntington from any of his Harvard graduate students in written assignments. Andrés Lozano, writing in *La Prensa-San Diego* (March 12, 2004), has this view of Anglo-Protestant Professor Huntington's thesis: "All identity is transitional, progress is nobody's monopoly and change is the only fixed fact of life! Otherwise, we would still be talking in Latin, Greek or Sanskrit. More Hispanics are learning English, mixing and melting in California, Illinois and Texas than WASPs are learning Spanish, mixing frozen Margaritas and melting *nachos*." More pungently, he writes: "Yes, until the mid-nineteenth century the American profile was mainly white, Anglo-Saxon and Protestant, so what? If it remained that way into the 20th Century' he posits, 'America would be like Canada. Go figure how two Canadas could have licked the Kaiser, Hitler and Communism."

The base assumptions of Professor Huntington that this country is what it is only because of an "Anglo-Protestant" founding and "Anglo-Protestant" ideals doesn't work and hasn't since the country was flooded by Irish Catholics followed by waves of Italian Catholics and Eastern European Jews through the early 20th century. Did any of those people make any contributions to the American nation, language or culture? If one believes Professor Huntington, one would "suppose" that they didn't. Oy'veh! One danger in outlining the negatives of the "Anglo-Protestant" heritage Professor Huntington is so enamored with is that some of them also write books. From the rarified racial altitude they operate in, they are not shy about tearing into those who do notice the historical, social and political negatives of the "Anglo-Protestant" history in America and who temper their enthusiasm for that heritage with some cautionary notes.

Nativist white champion ultra-critic of immigration, Peter Brimelow, wrote these words in his book *Alien Nation* (Random House, 1995): "...the factual accuracy of Contreras's argument is not important here (What, facts?). What is important is his profound alienation from America—and his conscious support of immigration as a way of striking back." He previously defined "Alienism" with "...just as everyone has heard of 'nativists' and their dislike of foreigners, so there are also 'aliens' who dislike the natives, and the America that the natives built. To these 'aliens' (who are quite often not immigrants, but disgruntled, 'alienate' native-born) mass immigration offers potential reinforcement and support." Brimelow is an immigrant twice removed from Great Britain, through Canadian citizenship and an immigrant from Canada and, finally, an American citizen. He is a wandering "Anglo-Protestant," if you will. He is among those who, considering the failure of the term "alienist," have begun to use the words "Treason Lobby" against those who disagree with his and their vision of a blond, blue-eyed Anglo-Protestant country that is certainly not the United States of America since World War II.

Brimelow is not the only supporter Professor Huntington has, White Citizens Council syndicated writer, Sam Francis, has jumped into the fray to defend the Harvard Professor. First, Francis claims that Huntington is being smeared because Mexican intellectual, Carlos Fuentes, wrote in the *Los Angeles Times*: "Mexicans in the U.S., according to Huntington, do not live, they invade; they do not work, they exploit; and they do not create wealth, they perpetuate poverty,' spouts Mr. Fuentes." Francis continues: "The rest of his (Fuentes) article is all about how these claims are wrong. Not once does he actually quote anything Mr. Huntington has written, and much of his 'refutation' is no more than the usual cliches about 'traditional values' and all the new business immigrants create." Francis ends his piece with: "Mr. Huntington may not be right about everything he says in either his article (in *Foreign Policy*) or his book, but to judge from the level of discussion so far, he's coming much closer to the truth than his enemies can tolerate."

Surely, White supremacist Sam Francis jests, doesn't he? He accuses Fuentes of not quoting Dr. Huntington, what will Francis say about how much I quote Huntington? Will he accuse me of using nothing but the "usual cliches?" Mr. Francis' defense of Dr. Huntington indicates that Mr. Francis apparently has not yet read Huntington's article in *Foreign Policy* (as of this writing and the publication of Mr. Francis' article in <u>VDARE.com</u>, March 25, 2004). If he had, he would know that Dr. Huntington himself quotes few facts, statistics, official or otherwise, studies by reputable agencies or non-profits in any way, in any form. He simply offers little or no empirical evidence for his anti-Mexican stance. Other observers have commented on that lack of Harvard acceptable evidence as previously noted. Lastly, certainly Dr. Huntington can find someone other than White supremacists like Francis, or Peter Brimelow, to defend him, his scholarship or reputation. As for "name-calling," allow me to laugh out loud. This complaint comes from men who call this writer, the President of the United States and other immigrant and Mexican supporters, the "Treason Lobby."

For all the anti-Catholic rant by Professor Huntington, there is a good response by Alan Wolfe in his article in "Foreign Affairs, "If religion shapes identity, the United States has had many identities because it has had so many religions. Huntington knows all of these things; his command of American religious history is impressive. He just never incorporates them into his argument." In other words, Wolfe diplomatically states that Huntington ignores the facts that Catholics have been involved in the country since it became a country. It has provided the only national religious experience that cuts across ethnic lines, a huge contribution to educating the children of the masses by establishing a national network of parochial elementary and high schools, plus some of the finest colleges and universities in the country.

Further, Wolfe writes, "...Huntington fails to appreciate the degree to which immigrants shaped American culture even as they assimilated. Catholicism was already the largest Christian denomination in the United States by the second half of the nineteenth century, and its distinctive ethos changed the way Americans celebrate Easter, attend school, play sports, and conduct foreign policy. American Jews adapted their faith to American culture, but the paradigmatic embodiment of American culture, the motion picture, was from the early days shaped by a distinctly Jewish sensibility."

CHAPTER 5

THE MEXICANS ARE COMING! THE MEXICANS ARE COMING!

Huntington: "In this new era, the single most immediate and most serious challenge to America's traditional identity comes from immense and continuing immigration from Latin America, especially from Mexico, and the fertility rates of these immigrants compared to black and white American natives." Professor Huntington reminds one of failed politician Ross Perot when he was running for President in 1992. Perot campaigned on a "giant sucking sound" of jobs flushing out of the American economy for low wage Mexico if the then debated North American Free Trade Agreement (NAFTA) proposed between the United States, Canada and Mexico was approved. Mexico, Perot claimed, was the enemy of America, not North Korea, not Iran, not Al Qaeda, not Osama Bin Laden. Perot was joined and one-upped by another ersatz presidential candidate, Pat Buchanan, who chanted that "José" was stealing America from Americans. Buchanan has recently expanded his chant to "José's" invasion is destroying America. He asks, what happened to the 90% white America in 1960 (so does Brimelow, Sam Francis and most immigration critics)? This question, from a man who ran for president of the United States on the NAFTA and job issues while driving a Mercedes Benz.

Perot's "giant sucking sound" turned out to be 18-million new jobs in the United States. NAFTA produced a more stable and democratic Mexico and the displacement of Japan by Mexico as our second largest trading partner, a partner that spends back to the United States 75 percent of every dollar that goes into Mexico for goods and services. For illustrative purposes, The Peoples Republic of China spends less than 10-percent of what it earns in United States in purchases back into the United States. One hears very little Chinese in West Coast expensive theme parks like Disneyland, Sea World or the San Diego Zoo while every other word one hears in those parks is usually Mexican Spanish of tourists from Mexico spending their money in the United States. Maybe we should ask Mickey or Minnie, or even Shamu to help Mexicans assimilate to Professor Huntington's satisfaction.

"Huntington has found the new enemy, and they are arriving from the South," writes Gregory Rodríguez in the *Los Angeles Times*. Wow! – An intellectual Ross Perot parrot! Or, as Ross Perot used to fantasize, *'The Mexicans Are Coming! The Mexicans Are Coming!"*

One side note: Is it not interesting that Professor Huntington mentions "black and white American natives" in the same sentence. His Anglo-Protestant heritage went out of its way to keep slavery American and rebelled against the will of the people to implement Abraham Lincoln's "a house divided, half slave and half free" cannot stand government. Interesting also is the historical institutional Harvard view on blacks (and Jews) that professor Felipe de Ortega y Gasca reminds us of at www.Hispanicvista.com (March 14, 2004). He writes: "So too the science which Harvard geneticist Edward East said would 'redeem man's hope of paradise' did not include a redemption of Black Americans. In 1927 he described Blacks as 'affable and cheerful but subject to fits of fierce passion' ending with the comment that 'we can find no probability that the Negro will contribute heredity factors of value to the white race."

Ah…Steppen Fetchit!

Professor Ortega y Gasca points out that in 1922 Harvard President A. Lawrence Lowell called for his university to participate in a national "quota system" for Jewish students, for "the presence of too many Jews in higher education, he explained, would only add to the rising anti-Semitism of the time." Reminds one of, "We must destroy the village to save it," a policy enunciated by an anonymous journalist in the early years of the Vietnam War. It also reminds one of sheer racist arrogance.

Then, there is the father of Arthur M. Schlesinger Jr., the senior Schlesinger, both of Harvard. Schlesinger Sr. wrote: "The new (1921) immigration from Southern and Eastern Europe, with its lower standard of living and characteristic racial differences has intensified many existing social problems and created a number of new ones." 1921 was a long time ago, granted. However, Junior Schlessinger indicated little had changed in his family, and at Harvard, when his book, *The Disuniting of America: Reflections on a Multicultural Society* (1992), hit the market. It is a negative view of what immigrants were doing in America and the influence they were having on, as Professor Huntington now describes it, the "Anglo-Protestant" culture.

Should Professor's Huntington's negative views on millions of people he seems not to know well surprise us? Should we be surprised that he sees their religion and language as threats to his "Anglo-Protestant" America? No, his views are a continuation of a century of Harvard bigotry. This time, however, there are serious objections being raised by people equipped with intellect and experience to rebut his juvenile thesis.

"Racists," the *Miami Herald* screamed from its editorial page in an Op-Ed piece by Andres Oppenheimer, "Racists in America must be having a field day...At long last they have found a world-renowned intellectual to rationalize their

resentment against America's rapidly growing community."
Professor Huntington is that "world-renowned intellectual" and
he comes from Harvard, a place well-versed in "Anglo-
Protestant" culture. Oppenheimer describes Professor
Huntington's article and thoughts as "...pseudo-academic
xenophobic rubbish." Sam Francis, where are you?

Glaister, in the *Sidney Morning Herald*, "It seems he
(Huntington) didn't even bother to reread his most famous
book *The Clash of Civilizations* before embarking on his latest
tome. In the earlier book, he wrote, somewhat perplexingly,
that 'the cultural distance between Mexico and the United
States is far less than that between Turkey and Europe', and
that 'Mexico has attempted to redefine itself from a Latin
American to a North American identity.'" Nonetheless,
Huntington now writes, "the single most immediate and most
serious challenge to America's traditional identity comes from
immense and continuing immigration from Latin America,
especially from Mexico." In *Clash*, Huntington concluded: "In
the end, Latin American civilization could merge into and
become one sub-variant of a three pronged Western
civilization."

This man appears to be somewhat confused in his
thoughts about the American civilization, an economic
civilization that President Ronald Reagan once promoted as
starting in the Yukon in the Arctic and extending to Tierra del
Fuego at the tip of South America. Before Señor Huntington
is declared St. Huntington of Political Science and awarded a
nonexistent Nobel Prize for Political Science, it must be noted
that not every academician agrees with this obviously confused
septuagenarian. For example, M. Shahid Alam, Professor of
Economics at Northeastern University in Massachusetts,
writes: "The *Clash* obfuscates the realities of unequal power:
in this case, the deepest, most enduring, and widening
divisions between rich and poor countries." He continues, "It
(*Clash*) is carelessly constructed, ahistorical and
contradictory; it is also contradicted by historical

evidence...Apparently, ideologies succeed by appealing to interests, not logic or evidence." Peter Carlson of the Washington Post writes: "The threat (for Huntington) is— Mexicans. Other Hispanics, too, but mostly Mexicans." Shades of Perot and Buchanan. Carlson: "They're overrunning the country, they're multiplying like bunnies, Huntington says, and they threaten our 'Anglo-Protestant culture." Is this an "ideology" seeking "interests?"

Carlson portrays Professor Huntington as a xenophobic clone of Anglo-Protestant Massachusetts Governor Henry J. Gardner who said in 1855 that the Irish Catholic immigrants "swarming" into Massachusetts were a "horde of foreign barbarians." He also equates the professor to H.G. Wells, the British writer and futurist, who warned the United States in 1906 that the continuing influx of Jews, Italians and Eastern Europeans (Polish and Russian) threatened the country with a "huge dilution of the American people with profoundly ignorant foreign peasants." Martin Finucane quotes a fellow Ivy League colleague of Professor Huntington in the Associated Press. Referring to the article in *Foreign Policy*, "The article is 'data free' and unsupported by the evidence, said Professor Rodolfo O. de la Garza of Columbia University...This is really sad because this is the kind of thing we expect from xenophobes. He is a man who's made important contributions to the study of politics in America and abroad,' de la Garza said."

What we have here is a Harvard Professor who appears to have plunged into xenophobia, a disease that equates with the worst racism in American history. Has Professor Huntington taken the traditional anti-Semitic, anti-Black Harvard tradition a quantum leap forward into the 21st Century because he doesn't like Roman Catholics? Or is it because the Mexicans he states threaten the country so, speak Spanish? His views seem to have changed in recent years from when he wrote *Clash*. Any reasonable person must ask why has he changed so much in less than a decade?

Facts: Mexicans brave the desert, elude the Border Patrol, escape the clutches of criminal Mexicans intent on robbing/ killing them for a $20-bill, and find a job in a country that doesn't speak their language. Have we witnessed a fit of personal jealousy on Huntington's part? Are these Roman Catholic Mexicans simply superior in courage and spirit to a tired old "Anglo-Protestant?"

CHAPTER 6

TWO PEOPLES, TWO LANGUAGES?

Huntington: "Will the United States remain a country with a single national language and a core Anglo-Protestant culture? By ignoring this question, Americans acquiesce to their eventual transformation into two peoples with two cultures (Anglo and Hispanic) and two languages (English and Spanish)." Professor Huntington offers not a scintilla of proof to buttress these two assertions. Has the country always been a "single national language" country? Benjamin Franklin, as we have seen, disparagingly remarked over and over that the German immigrants of his day didn't speak, nor did their children speak English. Luckily for the Irish Catholics, their British oppressors had pretty much wiped out the native Irish language, Gaelic, and forced their Irish subjects to speak English. When they arrived at eastern American seaports starting in the 1840s, they understood the signs in "Anglo-Protestant" business establishments that read "Irish need not apply." It does pay to speak English sometimes, ask the Irish. The German immigrants produced children and grand children, who did learn English, as have all non-English-speaking immigrants since.

The Pew Hispanic Center and Kaiser Family Foundation sponsored a 1992 survey that totally disputes Huntington's assertion of "two people, two cultures, two languages" (an assertion for which he provides no scientific evidence in his entire article). The survey concluded that 4% of first generation adult Latinos use English as their primary language; this percentage increases to 46% in the second generation and a whopping 78% in the third generation. The survey also concluded that Spanish was the primary language of 72% of first generation Latinos but only 7% among second generation Latinos and ZERO among Latinos in the third generation or higher. (Emphasis added) The survey concluded that 24% of the first generation is bilingual and that the percentage increases to 47% in the second generation, then falls in the third generation to 22%. To further prove Huntington wrong, 45% of foreign born parents told the survey that their children predominately communicate with their friends in ENGLISH; 32% told the survey that their children use both English and Spanish equally. Only 18% of the parents surveyed stated their children speak only Spanish to their friends.

Keep Professor's Huntington's assertions in mind when reading the studies and conclusions of their conductors. For example, dissect this Huntington statement with the facts as presented here: "If the second generation does not reject Spanish outright, the third generation is also likely to be bilingual, and fluency in both languages is likely to become institutionalized in the Mexican American community." The greatest political scientist in world history, who sits atop the academic world at Harvard, uses these words and expects to be taken seriously: "If," "likely," "likely," in the same sentence, in the same assertion. No proof, just the words "if," and "likely." Terrific scholarship! Terrific empiricism! Where are the studies, Professor? So much for Professor's Huntington's silly proposition that Spanish dominates forever among the growing Hispanic immigrant community. In fact, that very proposition—that is, the Hispanic immigrant community is becoming language dominant, even in the overall Hispanic community—is false, further destroying the Professor's assertion.

"...In the current decade and for the foreseeable future there will be very sizable impacts from the number of native-born Latinos entering the nation's schools and in the flow of

English-speaking, U.S. educated Hispanics entering the labor market. Between 2000 and 2020, the number of second-generation Latinos in U.S. schools will double and the number in the U.S. labor force will triple. Nearly one-fourth of labor force growth over the next 20 years will be from children of Latino immigrants." (The Pew Hispanic Center and Kaiser Foundation Study of 2002; authors, Robert Suro and Jeffrey Passel) In other words, they wrote, "(Hispanic) Births in the United States are outpacing immigration as the key source of growth (in the Hispanic population)."

In what appears to be a prescient assertion that anticipated Professor Huntington's statements, Suro and Passel concluded and wrote, (1) "...the U.S. born children of immigrants (are) emerging as the largest component of that population... (2) Given the very substantial differences in earnings, education, fluency in English, and attitudes between foreign-born and native-born Latinos, this shift has profound implications (3) for anyone seeking to understand the nature of demographic change in the United States."

Et Tu, Professor Huntington?

CHAPTER 7

PROFESSOR HUNTINGTON GETS SOMETHING RIGHT

Huntington: "Mexican immigration differs from past immigration and most other contemporary immigration due to a combination of six factors: contiguity, scale, illegality, regional concentration, persistence and historical presence."

Finally, Professor Huntington makes statements that are correct. Mexico is so much closer to the United States than Czarist Russia, the Duchy of Warsaw or the island of Sicily. In fact, we must congratulate Professor Huntington for recognizing that Mexico is right next door——How perceptive of him. He recognized and wrote that Mexico was rapidly becoming more American than not in his book *Clash*, but seems to have changed his mind in the last ten years. Numbers, yes these Mexican legal and illegal immigrants numbers are record numbers, but as a percentage of the total American population, they don't come close to the percentages of Irish or Italians were of the contemporary American populations in the 19th Century.

Regional concentration: Professor have you not seen the Census Bureau reports that show that Mexican immigrants are moving into all regions of the country? He does mention that Hispanic/Mexican immigrants are moving into areas traditionally avoided by them, yet he still carries on about concentration. The problem is that Professor Huntington once again blends people together who should not be lumped together. For example, though admitting that Puerto Ricans are not technically immigrants, he writes—"in 2003, more than 40 percent of the population of Hartford, Connecticut, was Hispanic." People from Puerto Rico are not immigrants, thus, why mention them in the article aimed by Huntington at "immigrants" and in particular, Mexicans?

At the risk of name calling charges, is Professor Huntington afflicted with "they all look alike to me" syndrome? Methinks he is. When Huntington makes the statement, "The more concentrated immigrants become, the slower and less complete is their assimilation," isn't he just blowing hot air? Where, is his proof? Hartford, where native-born citizen Puerto Ricans now outnumber Blacks? What has Hartford to do with Huntington's general thesis that Mexicans are a threat to the United States of America? He also mentions Miami, pointing out that Spanish-language television outranks English-language television in ratings. He forgets to point out that the Spanish-speaking Cubans arrived in the racially split city, a southern city with no particular economic or political impact on the world and that they did so without ten cents to their collective name. Today, Miami ranks as a capital of trade with Latin America, as home to refugees who have made themselves successful while making their city something other than just another White Southern racist redoubt. This wealth was created by Catholic, Spanish-speaking Cubans.

Better than Miami's Cubans, Mexicans actually make a mockery of Professor's Huntington. A quick look at United States Labor Department reports on labor market penetration expose the dastardly fact that Mexican men and women have far higher labor market penetration than Puerto Ricans do by huge numbers and percentages. Since when is work a threat? Let's look at the South of the United States and Mexican immigrants.

In the *Miami Herald* (3-17-2004) Audra Burch wrote: "In the 1980s, two million immigrants entered the South. Four million came in the 1990s, swelling the total number to 8.6 million—or about 9 percent of the population. Almost two thirds are from Latin America (mostly, of course, from Mexico)." Millions of Hispanics move to the South, many to Iowa and the Midwest, some to New York and Pennsylvania, some even to notoriously anti-Mexican states like Oklahoma and Arkansas. Some pick apples in Washington State and Oregon; some cowboy in Wyoming, some make beds in Las Vegas, some are even moving to Canada, but concentration? No, professor, the days that all Mexican immigrants settled in California or Texas are over.

Since this Mexican Diaspora started 20 years ago, perhaps Professor Huntington missed the change in demographic patterns. Is it possible that Census Bureau studies and statistics of the 1990s and since 2000 have not yet reached Harvard? Persistence— Is that what bothers Professor Huntington? Does he fault individuals for migrating north to a country where they don't usually speak the language? Does it bother him that they keep coming to where most people don't look like them, even when they are brother Indians? Does it bother him that men and women migrate north surreptitiously to where human vultures try to part these people with their labor for little money, or to steal their cash at knife point? Is it foreign to the Professor for men and women to be persistent when a better life is the goal? It must be, for most people consider persistence to be a good quality.

CHAPTER 8

THE PROFESSOR'S LITTLE BIG LIE

Huntington: "...after 1924, immigration was reduced to a trickle (by) the restrictive legislation of 1924." Professor Huntington does not explain exactly why immigration was "reduced to a trickle" for the simple reason that even he has to be embarrassed by what actually happened to cut the flow of immigrants. American Nazi Party founder, Harry Laughlin and his merry band of *scientific eugenicists*, convinced an all-White Congress (including the only non-White congressman, a Black representative from Chicago) to cut immigration severely by using religious and ethnic benchmarks in a very bigoted manner. The technique used was to limit immigration by country to the percentage of the American population the national group had in 1890. In other words, there were infinitesimal numbers of Italians, or Russian and Polish Jews, of Greeks and Sicilians in the United States in 1890. Why? Because they didn't begin to arrive in the United States until *after* 1890 in numbers enough to count. The Congress of the United States, directed by American Nazi Harry Laughlin, skillfully wielded a racial and religious scalpel to eliminate the very thought of more Italian, Sicilian Catholics or Russian or Polish Jews coming to pollute "Anglo-Protestant" America. (*The Nazi Connection*, Stefan Kuhl, Oxford University Press, 1994)

Historical presence of Mexican-origin people in the Southwest disturbs Professor Huntington and is one of the several attributes of Mexicans that he suggest threaten the United States.

CHAPTER 9

THE PROFESSOR FAILS—MEXICANS PASS!

Huntington: "Particularly striking in contrast to previous immigrants is the failure of third and fourth generation people of Mexican origin to approximate U.S. norms in education, economic status, and intermarriage rates." Further, he writes: "In the Southwest, overwhelming numbers of Mexican immigrants have been poor, unskilled, and poorly educated, and their children are likely to face similar conditions."

Lazy, stupid Mexicans... Isn't that what Professor Huntington is saying? Is he right? Are all the critics right? They all parrot Huntington's factless statement, though they usually (as with the Emigration Party of Nevada) do so more crudely and so blue collarish in content and delivery. We've seen those California students with less than perfect English abilities are improving by huge leaps in English and reading proficiency. In test results released by the State of California in March of 2004, "Forty-three percent of the state's 1.4 million students who speak as a second language demonstrated proficiency in 2003 on English tests of reading, writing, speaking and listening skills. In 2002, 34% of such students had reached the proficient level, and the figure was 25% in 2001, the first year the California English Language Development Test was given," reported Duke Helfand and Jean Merl, *Los Angeles Times*.

These children are usually immigrants themselves, or children of recently arrived immigrants. As for the future, the Western Interstate Commission for Higher Education projects the following: "During the early 1990s, underrepresented racial/ethnic groups accounted for approximately 43 percent of all public high school graduates in Texas." This is "projected to continue increasing at a higher rate through the projection period, reaching approximately 63 percent by 2013-14...Hispanics have made up the largest share." "In the 1990-91 (Texas) graduating class, there were nearly 45,700 Hispanics, who accounted for almost 30 percent of the class, their presence increased to 74,489, or 33 percent, in 2001-02. This group is forecasted to grow to 117,500 graduates—about 44 percent of all public high school graduates in 2014." So projects the Western Interstate Commission for Higher Education. Just what do they know that Professor Huntington doesn't know?

Harvard graduate James Crawford observes in his 1999 book on Bilingual Education (*Bilingual Education: History, Politics, Theory and Practice* –1999, Bilingual Education Series)) that in 1908 immigrant children in New York City made no where near the educational level being achieved by today's immigrant Hispanics, mostly Mexican children. According to Crawford, only 13% or New York City's immigrant children at age twelve, studying in *English-Only* classrooms, went on to graduate from high school—while 32% of nonimmigrant Whites went on to graduate from high school.

In April 2003, the Associated Press reported that the Pew Hispanic Center conducted a study of Hispanic high school graduation rates. "The center's analysis of Census Bureau data between 1970 and 2000 found the share of Hispanic immigrants over 25 who graduated from high school increased from 28 percent to 59 percent, while for U.S. born residents it grew from 53 percent to 87 percent." The Public Policy Institute of California reports that, "Mexican youths who arrive in the United States between ages 5 and 15 (graduate at a) 40 percent (rate)." But, "Children who arrive before age 5 do much better. Indeed, their graduation rate is similar to that of U.S. born Mexican Americans, who complete high school at a rate of 70 percent." The report, written by Stephen

Trejo and Jeffrey Grogger, continues: "Second-generation Mexican Americans in California have an average of about four years more schooling and more than 35 percent higher wages than do Mexican immigrants." These people do have a negative lag behind non-Hispanic Whites in the third generation of a year and a half less schooling and earn about 25 percent less income. The report concludes: The experiences of second and third-generation Mexican Americans reveal the long-term economic prospects of the Mexican-origin population, and these prospects are considerably brighter than what is suggested by statistics that do not differentiate between foreign-born and U.S. born Mexican Americans." Better yet, my alma mater, San Diego State University has a student body of over 25,000—25 percent are Hispanic, of mostly Mexican-origin. In my freshman year of 1958, there were fewer than 50 Mexican American students in a student body of 10,000.

Wrong again, Professor Huntington.

Poverty and economics seem to interest Professor Huntington. He declares that Mexicans don't seem to match U.S. standards and norms even after two or three generations. Let's see if they do. Dr. Walter A. Ewing and Benjamin Johnson wrote a paper for the American Immigration Law Foundation (AILF) in which norms and standards were discussed. They state: "While evidence indicates that Latinos are experiencing substantial progress across generations, this fact is lost in the statistical portraits of the Latino population which don't distinguish between the large number of newcomers and those who have been in the United States for generations." Here, clearly, is a message for Dr. Huntington: "Some advocates of restrictive immigration policies have seized upon such aggregate statistics to advance the dubious claim that Latinos are more resistant to upward mobility or 'assimilation' than the Europeans a century ago."

The Rand Corporation's James P. Smith wrote a report in 2003 after studying the California Mexican American population. The Rand Corporation is not chicken liver pate—

it is, in fact, one of the nation's premier think tanks, if not the best. Mr. Smith prefaces his report with these words, words that define Huntington's position even before Huntington articulated his concerns in *Foreign Policy.* "There is concern that Hispanics have not mimicked the European immigrant experience of great generational advance. Reasons for concern vary, but a theme is that Latino immigrants and their kids are less committed to assimilation than Europeans were. Discrimination, adherence to Spanish and frequent trips 'home' due to proximity are said to be the reasons." Smith writes that the first problem is the lumping together of recent arrivals with longtime residents and, in fact, citizens. The methods usually used simply don't produce good information and, in fact, measure much lower or nonexistent progress in the United States. "To correctly evaluate generational assimilation, the data must be realigned to match up the sons and grandsons of the Hispanic population," he writes.

On education, Smith writes: "Latino schooling advances across generations are impressive (Dr. Huntington, are you understanding this?). Consider Mexican immigrants born between 1905-09 with 4.3 years of school. Their American-born sons with 9.4 years doubled their schooling and their grandsons were high school graduates. The average education gain across three generations of Mexican men is over seven years, in contrast to the impression of the cross-section." "Compared to the 1st (generation), schooling gaps of the 2nd generation Latinos has quickened its decline implying that the eventual education gap of the grandsons of Hispanics born in the 1940s would be small indeed," Smith concluded.

As for income, Smith studied income gains that paralleled educational gains as noted. "Mexican immigrants born between 1895-1900 earned 55% as much as native White men over their lifetimes. When their American-born sons competed in the labor market their lifetime their lifetime wage gap averaged 77%. By the time their grandsons worked, the Mexican wage gap averaged 84%." Then Smith writes:

"Adjusting for their own schooling deficits only (less skills, etc.), the wage gap of 3rd generations would only be about 10%."

Comparing today's immigrants to yesterday's leaves something to be desired, so Smith compared the Hispanic population's education and wage levels to today's American-born Black population. "Historical generation data show lower rates of generation transmission for both native-born White and African-American men (see Rand Corp.-James P. Smith, 1986) so that across generations descendants of Latino immigrants achieve schooling gains relative to both groups."

He asks: "Why would schooling transmission be so high relative to native populations?" His conclusion: "The conventional view regarding Hispanic immigrants ability to secure a better life for their kids and grand kids was pessimistic. They were seen as not sharing in the successful European experience, perhaps due to reluctance to assimilate into American culture. These fears are unwarranted. Second and 3rd generation Hispanic men have made great strides in closing their economic gaps with native Whites. The reason is simple—each successive generation has been able to close their schooling gap with native Whites which were translated into generational progress in incomes."

Allow me to bring his closing words to the attention of Dr. Huntington, who, it appears, has never seen a study of Hispanic/Mexican immigrants, ever. "Each new Latino generation not only had higher incomes than their forefathers, but their economic status converged toward the White men with whom they competed," declares Smith after years of study.

Poverty? From the University of Southern California's Urban Initiative, we find a recent report written by Dowell Myers, John Pitkin and Julie Park entitled "California's Immigrants Turn the Corner." "Not only have the sharp increases in immigration of the past few decades leveled off, but fewer immigrants come to California at or below the poverty line and over-all levels of impoverishment amongst the foreign-born in the state have also dropped." "The total poverty of California's foreign-born population also turned downward in 2000, after three decades of increases. The 1970 census showed 14.8% of California's foreign-born population living below the (official) poverty level. The rate grew to 17.6% in 1980 and 19.8% in 1990. However, the 2000 census revealed the first break in this upward trend, dipping to 19.1%. Additionally, the share of foreign born who have incomes more than *Two Times* between 1990 and 2000 above the poverty line also rose 53.9% to 55% (emphasis added). Furthermore, they write, "Evidence shows that poverty rates amongst immigrants fell substantially when they are observed 10 and 20 years after their arrival. For example, in 1980, 27.8% of new Latino immigrants were in poverty, but this fell to 20.3% in 1990, and based on the experience of earlier immigrants was expected to fall to 15.2% in 2000, though the actual poverty rate for this group in 2000 fell only to 16.6%."

One political conclusion that can be reached by this writer about the poverty figures they studied is that Mexican immigrants did exceptionally well under Presidents Ronald Reagan and George H.W. Bush than under eight years of President William Jefferson Clinton and the Democrats that claim so much Hispanic voting support. When Reagan became President, Mexican immigrant poverty was 27.8%. After twelve years of Reagan and Bush, the Mexican immigrant poverty level had dropped by 26.9 percent. After 8 years of President Clinton, the Mexican immigrant poverty rate fell by only 16.7 percent. So much for Democrats doing much for people whose votes they expect as a genetic proposition.

In looking to the future, the USC group writes: "Earnings, homeownership and voting participation all rise markedly with growing length of settlement." Are Smith, the USC group and other scholars and researchers misguided, misunderstood amateurs while Dr. Huntington is the expert in the field? Intermarriage rates? Census reports indicate that the 2nd and 3rd generation Mexican-origin intermarries with non-Hispanics with the best of them. Black/White intermarriage amounts to less than 5%. Hispanics consistently intermarry with Whites at rates that are growing every day. In the second generation intermarriage amounts to more than six times the rate of native-born African-Americans and Whites. Intermarriage, of course, is the ultimate in assimilation.

Wrong again, Dr. Huntington.

CHAPTER 10

HUNTINGTON: POOR BLACKS, STEAMROLLED BY MEXICANS

Huntington: "For the first time in U.S. history, increasing numbers of Americans (particularly black Americans) will not be able to receive the jobs or the pay they would otherwise receive because they can speak to their fellow citizens only in English." Baloney! Pia Orrenius, Senior Economist, Research Department, Federal Reserve Bank of Dallas, in a January 2004 speech said: "Immigration is key to current economic growth. But immigration is also central to future growth, not only because immigration will continue, but because the children of immigrants today are the labor force of tomorrow." She continues: "Interestingly, despite lacking a high school diploma, low-skilled immigrants still outperform native dropouts in the labor market. Low-skilled male immigrants are more likely to work, as shown by their higher labor force participation rates, and less likely to be unemployed." "Because," she says, "of this commitment to work and despite other disadvantages, immigrants assimilate and surpass income levels of like natives after about 16-20 years in the United States."

While Ivory Tower Dr. Huntington laments the plight of people he wouldn't know if he tripped on them, the facts of economic progress and assimilation by those very people he criticizes for not speaking the Queen's English are overwhelming. Sure, they bypass American-born dropouts, so what? They work hard to not just survive but to progress.

If the local native-born can't keep up, so be it. The nation needs hard working people, not sluggards who couldn't even finish a free high school provided to them by hard working, taxpaying people like the immigrants.

Jeffrey Passel of the Urban Institute studied the effects of immigration on African Americans and wrote: "Immigration has no negative impacts for Black workers taken as a whole, according to the evidence." "Native African-Americans in areas of high immigration fared better than native African-Americans in low-immigration areas, however, native African-Americans do not keep pace with the rising wage trends that immigration brings for Anglos and Hispanics. Furthermore, "Immigrants increase the labor market opportunities of African-Americans in strong local economies but reduce them where labor demand is weak." "Selected ethnographic studies find that employers prefer immigrants to native Black workers, particularly in low-skilled jobs (citing Kirschenman and Neckerman 1991)."

The "black" workers Huntington weeps for are subject to basic economic principles: One, they are not preferred hires to begin with; and, secondly, their employment is based on economic and business cycles, period. There is one sociological factor as well: White employers are still White and Blacks are still Blacks, Dr. Huntington notwithstanding, thus employers continue their 300 year old discrimination against Blacks.

Must everyone suffer from the sins of those native-born who have rejected the entire American system of economics and education because they stupidly dropped out of school? I ask the same of Hispanics. Dropping out is a catastrophic mistake and, is in fact, a sin against America. Dropping out is a very stupid thing to do; it is stupid for anyone. One can almost understand the case of immigrants and their children dropping out of school sometimes. They might have language difficulties, or social and economic concerns, but one must wonder at the native-born Whites and Blacks who reject our history, our school system, our social system and just plain good judgment by dropping out of school before graduation.

Poverty is no excuse for anyone, especially native-born Americans to drop out of school. Such Huntington-style laments inch the United States toward total destruction, not from without, but from within by those who didn't finish school and by those who lament their voluntarily achieved status of becoming school dropouts. Immigrants try to work their way up, while Huntington's lamented victims collect government welfare and unemployment checks and have Boston Doctors of Philosophy weep for them.

CHAPTER 11

DUH, I ONLEE SPEEK ANGLO-SAXON

Huntington: "Because most of those whose first language is Spanish will also probably have some fluency in English, English speakers lacking fluency in Spanish are likely to be and feel at a disadvantage in the competition for jobs, promotions and contracts."

Professor, please. Monolingualism is a curse, professor, in a global economy. There are almost half-a-billion Spanish speaking customers from the Rio Grande south to Patagonia. Why would anyone hire an English-only speaker to sell to those hundreds of millions of potential buyers of American goods and services? Why shouldn't someone who does speak two languages earn more money? Where is it written that English-only people are even entitled to jobs just because they are Americans? The Koran, is it Allah's will? It certainly isn't written in the Constitution of the United States.

The global economy and its continued domination by the United States cannot occur if the American work force is limited to English-only speaking workers. Monolingualism, on the other hand, is a destructive force beyond measure in this time and in the future.

CHAPTER 12

MEXICAN OR AMERICAN, CHOOSE ONE

Huntington: "Many Mexican immigrants and their offspring simply do not appear to identify primarily with the United States."

What is the basis of this statement? Where are the studies to back up this silly, if not stupid, statement? He has none, but here are his words: "Anecdotal evidence of such challenges abounds. In 1994, Mexican Americans vigorously demonstrated against Proposition 187—which limited welfare benefits to children of illegal immigrants—by marching through the streets of Los Angeles waving scores of Mexican flags and carrying American flags upside down."

This statement can be challenged without much exertion; an observant 12-year-old could do it before lunch. First, we must challenge the words "anecdotal evidence." When there are millions of people involved, certainly one can quote some scholarly research and not rely on "anecdotal evidence." Such so-called evidence supports any statement by anyone for any topic. Secondly, I was there at the demonstration he mentions. This was the largest California political demonstration ever, in history, dwarfing any the anti-Vietnam War brats had in the 60s. But, his observations that these were "Mexican Americans" is faulty, and in fact, false. While the crowd was mostly Mexican nationals, many were Salvadoran and some Guatemalan. The number of Mexican, Salvadoran and Guatemalan nationals is about 2-million in Los Angeles County. Many were at this demonstration.

The number of bona fide Mexican Americans, that is, American citizens of Mexican-origin was not high, probably not more than a fifth of the crowd was Mexican American. As for Mexican flags, there were Salvadoran, Guatemalan and Puerto Rican flags also displayed by many. As for upside-down American flags, doesn't Dr. Huntington know that an upside down flag is a sign of distress, not of disdain?

Thirdly, the crowd wasn't protesting because "children of illegal aliens" would be denied welfare, they were demonstrating because Proposition 187 was an unconstitutional plunge into a police state designed to smash the Hispanic community with a police state wielded fist. It was also designed to expel from public schools any child regardless of citizenship, American included, who couldn't prove both his parents were legal residents. So that the Harvard professor doesn't misunderstand, Prop. 187 would have expelled American children from school if either or both parents were "suspected" of being illegally in the country. The word "suspected" appeared three times in Prop. 187. Nonetheless, it appears that the Harvard professor was a supporter of this unconstitutional police state measure sponsored by White supremacists. One must wonder why a world famous political scientist would lie with White Supremacists in supporting an overtly racist and anti-child ballot proposition that was unconstitutional on its face, why?

The massive Sunday afternoon crowd on the streets of Los Angeles was right, Proposition 187 was declared unconstitutional by the federal judiciary despite over 5-million people voting in favor of it. 4-million Californians voted no on the obviously unconstitutional offering by the White supremacist community of Orange County, California, on Election Day, joining the 100,000 who protested on the streets of Los Angeles. Within 24-hours of Election Day, seven different California State and federal judges, Republicans and Democrats, enjoined Proposition 187's implementation. Does he rely on news reports from Los Angeles that some "Mexican" nationals booed the American National soccer team in a match between it and the Mexican team? Where these Mexicans even living or working in the United States? Where they just here for the game? Might they have been Guatemalans or Salvadorans, large left-wing and/or Communist populations in the Los Angeles area? Who knows? They do look like Mexicans.

Most reporters who commented or reported on the incident were sports reporters. Sports reporters are hardly qualified to ascertain the nationality, residence and work patterns of people who immigration officials have difficulty even identifying, much less understanding. Perhaps Huntington relies on his own words, "No other immigrant group in U.S. history has asserted or could assert a historical claim to U.S. territory. Mexican and Mexican Americans can and do make that claim." Let us examine the surveys that have been taken of Mexicans Americans on the subject, as we are sure that Professor Huntington did before he made that statement.

Survey number one: _____; Survey number two: _____; Survey number three: _____.

He quotes none because there are none to quote that are of any significance. One survey taken in Mexico alleged that 58% of Mexicans consider that California still belongs to Mexico or should, but that survey was bogus. There are very few American survey firms that can scientifically conduct surveys in Mexico, especially if they have no Mexican partner firms. There are many, many cultural differences between the Mexican and American survey taker, as well as a lack of landline phones in almost all of Mexico. Moreover, there are few Mexicans who still claim Guatemala, Honduras, El Salvador, or Nicaragua as part of Mexico. What? Yes, those countries were part of Mexico when it won its independence from Spain. These countries made up part of the Mexican Empire. California was part of that empire. Few Mexicans pine over the dissolution of the Mexican Empire, even if part of it wound up as the most important part of the United States of America.

For support, he quotes political scientist, Peter Skerry of Boston College. Skerry says: "Unlike other immigrants, Mexicans arrive here from a neighboring nation that has suffered military defeat at the hands of the United States, and they settle predominately in a region that was once part of their homeland. Mexican Americans enjoy a sense of being in their own turf that is not shared by other immigrants." Proof? Neither "scholar" offers any. However, to Huntington's assertion that Mexican immigrants and their offspring don't identify with America, I offer 41 Medal of Honor awards by the United States to Hispanics in the American military who are mostly all Mexican-born or sons of parents or grandparents from Mexico. How many Silver Stars, Navy Crosses, Distinguished Flying Crosses and thousands of other medals have been awarded Hispanic combat soldiers, sailors and Marines?

I also offer the Department of Defense calculation that one in five (20%) of all casualties in the Vietnam War were Hispanics—*read* Mexican—from just five states. Need I point out that none of these five states had any population numbers of Puerto Ricans, Cubans, Dominicans or Hispanics of any sort other than of Mexican origin? These young men killed and wounded came from California, Arizona, New Mexico, Texas and Colorado. Apparently their families conspiratorially congregated among other "separatist" Mexicans so they could deny they were Americans, especially as they bled on Vietnamese soil wearing the uniforms of the American military.

A friendly wager: I'll bet there were more Mexicans and Mexican Americans from Los Angeles, alone, than all Harvard graduates in the Vietnam American forces during the Vietnam

Conflict. There were probably more just in the U.S. Marines than all Harvard graduates in Vietnam, for the entire war.

In the first Gulf War against Iraq, the *Los Angeles Times* ran a story of five, count them, five Mexican boys from one East Los Angeles city block who were fighting in Kuwait. The highlight of the story was the brother of one, who begged his mother for permission to join the United States Marines so he could be the sixth. In the current war in Iraq, one Mexican American Colonel Padilla, A Marine Regimental Commander, was widely quoted when he stated that "We excel at friction," the in-theater word for combat with Iraqis. We should not forget that the theater commander of our forces in Iraq is (at this writing) Army General Ricardo Sánchez. Who identifies more with America, General Sánchez, or the pride of the Ivory Tower, Sam Huntington?

Who has more proof, General Sánchez with the stars on his collar or Professor Huntington with Harvard tenure? In the first few days of the War in Iraq, three of the initial U.S. Marines killed in action were two Mexican-born and one Guatemalan-born Marine who weren't American citizens when they died. I suspect that 99% of all Mexican immigrants and their families were proud of these young men as American fallen warriors, not just as "green carders." One father called his son an Aztec Warrior.

I am not alone in this view, Alan Wolfe writes in his *Foreign Affairs* article, "of the 525 U.S. fatalities in Iraq as of early February 2004, four were named Pérez (Héctor, Joel, José and Wilfredo). By my rough count, 64 of the 525 possessed Hispanic surnames. This is 12 percent of the total, exactly equal to the percentage of the U.S. population that is Hispanic."

Writing of one of those young men, the one who came into the country illegally as a teenager after walking across Mexico from Guatemala, Wolfe writes, bitingly: "Like countless immigrants before him, he assimilated by dying in defense of the society he worked so hard to reach. Indeed, recent immigrants to the United States are more patriotic toward their new home than long-settled Britons toward the United Kingdom, French toward France, or Germans toward Germany. Other countries would be delighted to have immigrants with such assimilationist sympathies."

Wrong, again, Huntington.

CHAPTER 13

THE PROFESSOR'S BLACK HELICOPTERS

Huntington: "Demographically, socially, and culturally, the *Reconquista* (reconquest) of the Southwest United States by Mexican immigrants is well underway."

Here Dr. Huntington displays the most profound ignorance ever manifested by a modern American academic. Perhaps he can produce an inventory of any legitimate Mexican American leaders, politicians, ministers, priests, or business people who have demonstrated for California and/or the Southwest being returned to Mexico. Name one, Professor Huntington. Sure, he can quote some idiotic college professor or Brown Beret, but not one legitimate spokesperson or mainstream Mexican American. There are well over five thousand Mexican American elected officials in the country, how many of them are petitioning for secession? In fact, his statement reflects only fanatical anti-Mexican bigots and their verbal assaults on Mexicans, Mexican Americans and even those who have died in combat as American soldiers. Huntington: "They (Mexican Americans) call attention to and celebrate their Hispanic and Mexican past, as in the 1998 ceremonies and festivities in Madrid, New Mexico, attended by the vice-president of Spain, honoring the establishment 400 years earlier of the first European settlement in the Southwest, almost a decade before Jamestown."

So what, professor? Italian-Americans celebrate Christopher Columbus Day; Irish Americans celebrate St.

Patrick's Day? Communists celebrate May 1st, May Day. Blacks celebrate Junteenth Day. Most of us celebrate the 4th of July. In fact, it is a good thing that many Americans are paying attention to the 5th of May, *Cinco de Mayo*. Why? Because that victory by Mexicans over the French Army delayed the French conquest of all Mexico and its being able to supply the Southern Confederate States with munitions, including cannon, that the South needed to compete with Abraham Lincoln's Union Army. Had the South been able to provide sufficient cannon support at Gettysburg, might they have not won that key battle? We must remember that the Southern infantry of failed General Picket actually reached the Union center lines and engaged in hand to hand combat with Union soldiers still alive because Confederate cannon had not killed them because there weren't enough cannon to kill them. The lack of cannon, however, doomed the Confederates and they didn't have enough cannon power because French "Emperor" Napoleon III did not control enough of Mexico to supply the Confederates until after the Mississippi River and city of Vicksburg's Mississippi River crossing were in Union hands. The Battle of Puebla on Cinco de Mayo was fought on the Fifth of May 1862, a year and two months before Gettysburg. Just think what Robert E. Lee could have done with 500 more French cannon on the 1st, 2nd and 3rd of July, 1863, at a small junction in Pennsylvania named Gettysburg.

Perhaps Professor Huntington isn't aware that Americans a hundred and forty years ago thought enough of Mexicans to enlist in the Mexican Army complete with their official U.S. Army kits and rifles so they could fight the French. These victorious Union soldiers formed the American Legion of Honor. Their officers marched into Mexico City sharing the glory with the Mexican Army after the French were run out of Mexico in 1867. So, if Professor Huntington finds something wrong in celebrating our history in this country, I suggest he acquaint himself with the true history of the United States. He might also ask who was New Mexican Maximiliano Luna, the man Harvard's Teddy Roosevelt appointed to command a company of his famous volunteer "Rough Riders."

CHAPTER 14

DREAM ON, PROFESSOR

Huntington: "There is no *Americano* dream. There is only the American dream created by an Anglo-Protestant society. Mexican Americans will share in that dream and in that society only if they dream in English."

Surprise, Professor, there is an *Americano* dream whether you like it or not. None of his "anecdotal" assertions can be proven or even accepted by rational people. So why should we take his word for anything? We know from all the studies, every single one, that Mexicans and their descendants in the U.S. speak English to one extent or another, usually depending on their length of time in the United States. Only a tiny number live here for any length of time without speaking English more than Spanish. Most of these people are new immigrants in country less than three or four years. Some, like my great-grandmother, tried very hard to learn English so she could become a citizen but, alas, after twenty years in the United States, she simply got so unnerved at test time she couldn't pass the test. Nonetheless, I know how much she wanted to become an U.S. citizen. She never made it, but her love of the United States of America knew no bounds.

This passion for America came from a woman who came to the country after her 60th birthday. It came from a woman who responded to begging peasant soldiers of Emiliano Zapata with food and pesos out the back door of my family's Mexico City house. It came from a woman who witnessed the brigand army of Pancho Villa kick in the front door of our house to loot and pillage. It came from a woman who helped found the political opposition to the long-lived political "dictatorship" of the ultra-left wing, Stalinist-style ruling party of Mexico—the PRI. She, like so many over 60 people, couldn't master English. Nonetheless, she died just five points away from becoming an American citizen. In all other respects, however, she was as American as one might want an immigrant to be. We also know that Spanish has been spoken in the United States since Mexican, Cuban and Spanish soldiers fought in the American Revolution, as has Mexican currency been legal tender in the United States for over half its history.

We know also that the Catholics Huntington so despises were involved in forming this country from the beginning, though the professor declares that the "American dream" was "created by an Anglo-Protestant society" as if they patented it. Does he forget Lord Baltimore and the colony named after the Catholic Queen Mary? Does he forget Spanish-born Admiral Jorge Farragut of the Revolutionary Navy? Does he forget General Bernardo de Gálvez and his critical victory over the Anglo-Protestant Brits at Mobile? Does he forget the battle of outnumbered but victorious Spanish and Mexican militia at what is now St. Louis, at St. Joseph in what is now Michigan, and, at the great battle for the large British naval base at Pensacola and even in the Bahamas? Does he even know that Father Junípero Serra, the Franciscan missionary who founded the 21 California missions, collected a peso from every Indian and two pesos from White men to pay for the troops from Mexico and Cuba, who won those victories of the American Revolution?

Mexicans died for the United States of America before there was a United States of America. For some college professor to now assert that Mexicans are a great threat to America and its Anglo-Protestant culture is more than an insult. Such thinking betrays history; it betrays scholarship; it betrays the very idea of America. It more reflects the "Irish need not apply" attitude of Professor Huntington's forebears. It reflects the massacre of Irish Catholics in Philadelphia because they wouldn't read from Professor Huntington's King James Bible. It reflects the laws that prevented Catholics from voting in parts of New England. It reflects a "Back of the Bus" culture in much of the country that prevented Black Americans from voting, from riding in White buses, from eating at the lunch counter, or from smiling at White women. After all, those dastardly Blacks came as "immigrants" and weren't Anglo-Protestants.

Professor Huntington reflects the philosophy that Blacks nor Jews could own their own houses because some Anglo-Protestants wrote "restrictive covenants" into property deeds a hundred years before the Supreme Court threw them out. Professor Huntington exists in the rarified atmosphere of a very ugly ivory tower. The one positive thing one can say about his writings about Mexicans and Mexican Americans is that he provides an extensive and abundant target rich environment for reasoned rebuttal.

Part 2

Victor Davis Hanson

CHAPTER 15

THE PROFESSOR SPEAKS FROM HIS TRACTOR

Professor Victor Davis Hanson is a Classics professor at California State University at Fresno. He has made his mark as a serious historian of the classic Greek and Roman eras and the wars they fought that laid the foundation of Western Civilization. He caught some attention with his book "An Autumn of War: What America Learned from September 11 and the War on Terror." His fame, however, spilled off of the back pages of the National Review onto the pages of the Wall Street Journal and myriad other publications. His name, voice and visage became ubiquitous in 2003 when Encounter Books of San Francisco published the little book that Roared, the 150 page *Mexifornia: a State of Becoming.* His book is a major seller and has been reviewed and promoted in many venues because he states that, "California is in the 11th hour."

Victor Davis Hanson is not a racist; nor is he a bigot, or is he? That may be irrelevant because he is consistently wrong, in his many unsupported conclusions, no matter how anti-immigrant fanatics, or the National Review Online lionize him. His views about his immediate Selma neighborhood, though pithy and well reported, are wrong and cannot be applied to the general Hispanic population, or to Mexican-origin people of California, nor to the "multiculturalism" he thinks pervades California.

When he observes that many in his vicinity are recent immigrants, he is correct. When he states that they speak only Spanish, he is wrong. When he states that they have no desire to assimilate into American society, he is wrong. He is wrong because those he sees and experiences amount to less than 5% of Mexican-origin people in the Southwest. He basically sees only farm workers who arrive in the Fresno area looking only for work in the fields. Skilled workers go to Los Angeles, Chicago or Houston, not Selma, California. Farm hands do not come for free college education. They do not come to start businesses, though some actually do. They do not come to learn English, or to be multicultural. They do not come to vote in our elections. They do not come to build communities. Approximately 70 percent come to work, then to return home within 7-years according to the Public Policy Institute's studies, as they traditionally have. They come to earn money, to send most home to their families, thus saving the United States billions in foreign aid to Mexico. Certainly, these are factors in keeping Mexico's 50 percent of the population living in poverty from revolting as the Chiapas Indians tried and failed in 1994.

Make no mistake; the worst nightmare the United States can have is a bloody revolution in Mexico. Millions of Mexicans would come as refugees. A Mexican Fidel Castro would take over. His name would be Cuauhtemoc Cárdenas, the son of former President Lázaro Cárdenas, thief of oil wells and elections and unsuccessful protector of Communist philosopher and butcher, Leon Trotsky. As for assimilation, that observed by Professor Hanson in the past –"twenty years" and reported in his book—can't be used by Hanson or anyone. There is no objective standard to use in evaluating rates of today's assimilation because the huge growth in the Mexican-origin population has occurred in just the past few years. The huge jump in population tracked from the 1990 through the 2000 census simply does not allow for good assimilation tracking. Thus, Professor Hanson's perceived lack of assimilation is premature.

Professor Hanson decries a lack of education among the farm workers he sees and among their children. The educational level of farm worker immigrants does leave much to be desired, but can it be applied to 20 million people? However, among immigrant children, educational levels will almost double among them over what their parents experienced. The average farm worker immigrant has about a sixth-grade education and even though an adult, he has never set foot in an American school. Their kids, however, can't even drop out of school until they are 16, thus, even among dropouts, the educational level will almost double parental levels.

Where reality collides with Professor Hanson's views on Mexicans, illegal aliens and multiculturalism is in the heavy border enforcement between San Diego and the Arizona border implemented by President William Clinton in 1993 and 1994. Before the enforcement of Operation Gatekeeper— illegals routinely went home to Mexico when harvests were done, when they had enough money, or for Christmas holiday visits. Some would come back, some wouldn't. Some would come in alternate years. Now, however, the stringent enforcement is forcing illegals away from the urban corridor of San Diego/Tijuana into California's mountains or the Arizona desert. Hundreds are dying in desert heat or mountain winter cold, those that do make it through tend to stay in and around Professor Hanson's small farm town rather than go home. These are the people Professor Hansen sees. He should know that, for he admits to hiring such people over the years on his family farm. He knows what the routine used to be. He was a *patrón*, a boss. The farm workers did what they were told and left when there wasn't work. They stayed out of sight. They can't hide now, for they are too numerous. Perception, thus, and reality contradict each other in Professor Hanson's book. Nonetheless, anti-immigrant fanatics have clutched the book to their bosoms as if it is the second book of Genesis.

Mexifornia is an intellectual panic attack grasped by intellectually challenged anti-immigrant fanatics who can't produce food, goods or a culture of any kind, much less a bilingual one. Professor Hanson sees what he wants to, but reality is something he seems to have not noticed in his intellectual swipe at "multiculturalism." *Mexifornia: a State of Becoming* preceded Professor Huntington's *Foreign Policy* piece by several months. It was, however, just as noticed as Huntington's piece for the simple reason that a college professor with a doctorate was actually criticizing illegal aliens from Mexico in a well-publicized book from a respectable though not-for-profit publisher. His comments and views were devastating to the presence of millions of illegals from Mexico, as well as their being. The fanatical anti-Mexican otherwise deficient bigoted element that is so upset by illegals basked in the publication of this book. His comments were trumpeted from radio talk shows, the *National Review Online*, the *Wall Street Journal* and quoted by every form of critic, legitimate and illegitimate, in motive and technique. Victor Davis Hanson became an instant celebrity exposing an ignorant population to his views, limited in scope and purpose as they are.

Racists throughout the country exulted in Professor Hanson's book. An educated man validated the racists and bigots who live and breathe illegal aliens from Mexico. The professor claims to have Mexicans in his family, he claims he went to school with Mexicans, has hired them, and has observed them all his life from his little family farm in Selma, a tiny town in the fabulously rich Central Valley of California— America's breadbasket. Professor Victor Davis Hanson is not quite the observer he claims to be. His small town background, his limited experience, blinds his view from Selma about people from Mexico. Coupled with his Selma view is his limited view of life in urban California, in urban America. For example, Hanson admits to being part of the old Selma, the Selma of his grandparents, a Selma in which Mexicans weren't very numerous, worked for people like Hanson and owned no businesses. The new Selma,

California has a large Mexican population, though it is not in the majority, it is large and includes many people owning businesses. Several towns around his that have Mexican majorities skew Hanson's objection to Mexican immigrants. Four towns, to be specific: San Joaquin (63 percent Mexican); Huron (56 percent); Mendota (53 percent); and, Orange Cove (52 percent).

Something is wrong, though, with his views as proven by election results of the Special Recall Election in October 2003. Seems those Mexican masses he.looks upon don't think like he thinks they do. Hometown boy Lt. Governor Cruz Bustamante, the first statewide Hispanic to win office in 123 years flopped in Hanson's county. He received only 28.3 percent of the vote while Arnold Schwarzenneger received 51.9 percent of the vote in Fresno County. Moreover, the Recall of Democratic Governor Gray Davis received 66.7 percent of the vote in Fresno County. Even in Los Angeles, the most Mexican city in the world outside Mexico, Mexican American Bustamante received slightly over one third of the vote, 37 percent, while Governor Schwarzenneger received 44 percent of the vote. Those voting for the Recall totaled 49 percent, those against 52 percent. While Professor Hanson is declaring that the Mexicans he sees aren't assimilating and reject American culture, they apparently rejected one of their own *paisanos* and voted against Democratic Governor Gray Davis. Yes, some voted for Bustamante and some voted against the recall, but not very many. Those registered to vote, voted just like the rest of us. That is assimilation.

Hanson has profound defects in his views as expressed in his book *Mexifornia*. He is obviously unaware of the reams of studies that totally contradict his backwoods view of millions of people he claims to know. There are many more statistics than the election results he needs exposure to and needs to understand.

CHAPTER 16

MEXICAN AMERICANS FAIL IN SCHOOL

Victor Davis Hanson: "In my small hometown of Selma in the middle of California's Central Valley, more people now speak Santiago's language (Spanish) than my own. The city's school's are more segregated than when I attended them forty years ago and their scholastic achievement is far lower." Surprise, professor, almost all schools in the United States are inferior today compared to forty years ago. That is particularly true of California schools. As for being more "segregated" than in his schooling days, the professor is unawares, apparently, that there were many forcefully segregated schools in California for many years when his Anglo-Protestants were in charge of schooling. The public schools encouraged Mexican children to learn a trade so they could immediately work to support the family when they reached the legal age to drop out in the eighth grade. The last segregated Mexican school in California closed in 1946. The fact that more Mexican children enter Selma's classrooms than in the past is not news, what is news is that they are in school; the fact they might not do as well as those children forty years ago is also not news.

Classroom teaching is currently deficient in accomplishment not because the kids are too dumb to learn, but because the teachers are too busy being union members and not teachers. One must notice that he doesn't mention whether or not Mexican children in Catholic schools are not performing as well as such children did forty years ago, or whether these children do better academically than those in public school. *The Broken Web: The Educational Experience of Hispanic American Women,* published by Floricanto Press and The Tomas Rivera Center then part of the Clairemont-Mackenna of Pomona College in 1988, revealed that Hispanic students in parochial Catholic schools, including those in low-income neighborhood perform better than all male counterparts, White, Black or Hispanic, and outperform females of any race. Hanson doesn't make such an observation because he can't. He would have to point out that Catholic-school teachers aren't union, thus they are teachers not card-carrying union members. And, he would have to point out that the Mexican children in Catholic schools are the very same children that attend public schools. They come from the same economic level, the same neighborhoods, they speak Spanish, usually, at home and before they start school; they may or may not be illegal aliens themselves and if legal or citizens, they probably are, according to Professor Hanson, children of immigrants.

Are his views validated scientifically? A recent national survey conducted by the Zogby International Hispanic Poll for the *Miami Herald* tells a different story than that related by Professor Hanson. 58 percent of those polled were Mexican American, 10 percent Puerto Rican and 3.4 percent Cuban American. The margin of error is plus or minus 3.2 percentage points. "Of those polled, 67 percent made more than $35,000 a year, 75 percent had at least some college credits, and 64 percent described themselves as moderate to very conservative, with only 30 percent calling themselves liberal to progressive." (Knight Ridder Newspapers, Aril 5, 2004). The Poll also reported that 70 percent of those Hispanics polled speak English at home, with an additional 10 percent speaking Spanish, as well. According to the Poll, only 19 percent speak Spanish exclusively in their homes.

Now, how do those percentages square with Professor Hanson's view that they aren't as academically accomplished as those Mexicans in his day? They don't.

CHAPTER 17

THE ANGRY MEXICAN

Victor Davis Hanson: "There are now more overt signs of material wealth among Selmans—new cars, cell phones, CD players, VCRs, color televisions—but also much more anger that 'aliens,' even if their fortunes have greatly improved in the United States, remain still poorer than the native-born." Anger? What is this man talking about? What study does he quote? None. What interviews does he publish? None. He carries on for a page or two about Mexican gang members and how their existence proves his "anger" point, but it doesn't. He tells us a story of a peach stealer who tells him he can't eat all those peaches so why can't poor people—Mexicans—have the peaches. But that isn't proof. He also neglects to mention that "gangs" are a common historical occurrence in the United States. Millions of words have been written about them and miles of films have been produced, including the *Gangs of New York* within the past two years.

Black gangs, White gangs, Irish gangs, Jewish gangs, Protestant gangs, Italian gangs, Chinese gangs, Polish gangs, even Indian gangs in the South Dakota abound in American history. So now there are Mexican gangs, Salvadoran gangs and Puerto Rican gangs. Anger? No, reasons like poverty, broken families, drugs, working parents, racial profiling by the cops and just plain stupidity cause gangs. Anger about being Mexican or against Americans are not reasons to become a gangbanger.

Victor Davis Hanson: "So are we now a Mexifornia, Calexico, Aztlán, El Norte, Alta California, or just plain California with new faces and the same old customs." Professor Hanson intentionally or unintentionally inflames the question of illegals with his offhanded use of labels used by a tiny number of activists who number fewer than one percent of all Mexicans and Mexican Americans in the entire country, all 19-million of them. I suspect it is intentional, or he would name well-known Mexican origin people who even use those names, singly or collectively. He can't. Anger, Hanson appears to be far angrier than the people he thinks he sees. Victor Davis Hanson: "Charles Truxillo, a Chicano studies professor at the University of New Mexico, for example, promises that some day we will all be part of a new sovereign Hispanic nation called *República del Norte* encompassing the entire Southwest. 'An inevitability.' Truxillo calls it, and it will obtain sovereignty, he warns, 'by any means necessary' as 'our birthright.'" Here, Professor Hanson undermines his entire argument. Where is the list of academics, elected officials, community leaders, Catholic priests, authors, newspaper and magazine writers, evangelical Protestants, union officials, teachers or any people of note who are of Mexican origin who talk like one politically crazy college professor in New Mexico, where?

There is no such list. Mexican Americans have almost a score of elected Congress people in the House of Representatives. None have ever been heard to advocate separatism of any sort, none have been heard calling for a separate *República del Norte*. There are no "Father Hidalgos" screaming "death to Bad American, Gringo Government" from Catholic pulpits. There are no armies of Mexicans demonstrating on the streets against the Gringos, the Anglo-Protestants. There are no Mexican Timothy McVeighs or Terry Nichols running around blowing up megaton bombs killing and wounding hundreds of innocent Americans like these two men did in Oklahoma City. If there were, would a Classics professor have their names and be in a position to publish them for all to see? Of course, this is a noted historian who would publish all relevant facts to buttress his views, if he had them, that is. He obviously has never spoken to "Truxillo," a man who can't even spell his name right. Quoting from some news article isn't sufficient. Why didn't he call his academic colleague and ask him these questions: Who supports your "República?" What do you mean "sovereignty" will be obtained "by any means necessary?" And, what do you mean by "birthright?" Where is the roster of Truxillo's battalions, of his colonels and generals, of his private soldiers? Do they exist? Have the "Brown Berets," a silly Chicano militant group from the 60s, been resurrected? We don't know because Professor Hanson didn't inquire as to their existence. If he did, he neglected to mention them in his 150-page book.

These are simple questions that could have been answered through a phone call. Professor Hanson didn't make that phone call. Perhaps he doesn't want to know the answers or any clarifications that would result from some elementary research. Such might destroy Hanson's assertions. Limp-wristed assertions they are, not conclusions from "scholarly" research.

CHAPTER 18

THE ANGLO-PROTESTANT BOUNTY FOR INDIAN SCALPS

Victor Davis Hanson: "Our immigration dilemma is simple but apparently unsolvable calculus: Americans want the work they won't do to be done cheaply by foreigners who, they wrongly assume, will transform themselves into Americans."

For a historian, this is a comment not worthy of a scholar. First, Americans have always depended on cheap foreign labor, from African slaves to Irish swamp-draining semi-slaves, to Chinese railroad tunnel diggers, to Mexican cowboys and lettuce pickers. Few "Americans" of the Anglo-Protestant persuasion ever expected any foreigner to become an American like them. They usually mistrust foreigners of all sorts unless they look Anglo-Protestant. Example: Until the 1920s several states allowed male white immigrants from Northern Europe vote before they became citizens on the simple promise that they would someday become a citizen. That courtesy was not extended to swarthy-skinned Italians, Greeks, Mexicans and certainly not for any Africans, nor for even white women.

For Professor Hanson to intellectually stumble over historical facts is surprising unless one sees that he has an agenda and facts get in the way of that agenda. For example, his forebears from Sweden united with other Anglo-Protestants to take over California in 1875 after the state elected former Mexican citizen Republican Romualdo Pacheco Lt. Governor.

He assumed the Governor's office when the incumbent resigned when appointed U.S. Senator. It was the Workingman's Party that took over the state. No Mexican American won elective office in California for almost 100 years thereafter. How's that for reverse assimilation? Professor Hanson makes no effort to discuss the political situation of California, nor its history of bigotry, stolen elections (by Anglo-Protestants in Los Angeles) and desire to deny political power to majority populations. The Workingman's Party promptly passed a slew of racist laws. Its government prohibited Mexicans from testifying against White men; it prohibited Mexicans and Filipino men from holding hands with White women; it defined Mexicans as the "issue of Indians and Spaniards," and supported laws prohibiting citizenship and land ownership of real estate by Asians, Chinese and Japanese. They offered and paid "$25.00" bounties for scalps of California Indians, native Americans for the politically correct. That, of course, was before Indian casinos.

This was the state in which Professor Hanson's family built their little family farm, the farm Professor Hanson still works and lives on, with the help of Mexicans, including illegals—by his own admission. Recently, we find the Anglo-Protestant neighbors of Hanson's up to their old political tricks. In Farmersville (such a quaint name) California, we have 8,800 residents of which 33 percent are foreign born and 31 percent poor. The town's majority population is of Hispanic migrant workers—farm workers. The town is 72 percent Latino. In 2000, two Latinos were elected to the local school board for the first time ever. When new school board member Conrado González visited his first school as a school board member, he was refused entry by the principal. In 2003, Blanca Sandoval and Martín Macareno defeated two Anglo incumbents and joined González and Enrique Ramos on the five-member board. Before they could be sworn in, the old Anglo majority voted to extend the contract of Anglo School Superintendent Janet Jones. The two ex-board members defeated by Sandoval and Macareno follow the new members around in an effort to find them doing something wrong like holding secret board meetings. (*Pacific News Service*, January 15, 2004) Hanson, like the defeated Anglos of Farmersville can't give up the power they have had all their lives.

CHAPTER 19

HANSON DOESN'T KNOW
ASSIMILATION WHEN HE SEES IT

Victor Davis Hanson: "Wherever you live, if you want your dirty work done cheaply by someone else, you will welcome illegal aliens, as we (in California) did. And if you become puzzled later over how to deal with the consequent problems of assimilation, you will look to California and follow what we have done, slowly walking the path that leads to Mexisota, Utexico, Mexizona or even Mexichusetts——a place that is not quite Mexico and not quite America either."

"Slowly walking the path" is a complete overstatement when one looks at 2002 Census numbers of the states Professor Hanson mentions. For example, Mexisota, Minnesota for the rest of us, has only 2.9 percent Hispanics. We can assume that of that number, 58 percent are of Mexican origin as they are of the entire Hispanic population. Thus, Professor Hanson frightens his racist supporters with the label Mexisota while only 1.68 percent of Minnesota's population is Mexican. For the Classics professor, that means 16.8 people out of a thousand people. Big deal! Utexico—Utah for normal Americans—has a Hispanic population of 9 percent, of which slightly more than 80 percent may be of Mexican origin—7.2 percent. Mexichusetts—Massachusetts, home of failed President candidates, for the rest of us—has a Hispanic population of 6.8 percent, or which less than a third are of Mexican origin, 2.24 percent. Over two thirds of these

Hispanics are Puerto Ricans, Dr. Hanson. Perhaps it would be more appropriate to call it MassPR.

Mexizona—Arizona—is the only referred to place with a substantial Mexican population. 25.3 percent of Arizona is of Mexican origin. As Arizona is the principal crossing point for many illegals, it is no wonder that many stay in Arizona. Moreover, illegals tend to congregate where there is a good job situation. Arizona is a good job market. Of course, only a few of the one in four Arizona residents are illegal. As professor Hanson states over and over, no one knows how many are here. But we also know that most of the people he fears are actually born in the United States.

***

Victor Davis Hanson: "Immigration, assimilation and the entire dilemma of the Mexican border are insidious problems——a moral quagmire in which any posing as ethical instructors had better take care that they themselves, either implicitly or overtly, do not in some way benefit from the presence of inassimilable illegal aliens." Professor Hanson keeps harping on "assimilation" while providing no proof that assimilation isn't occurring. He doesn't give us a definition of assimilation we can understand so it is difficult to assess assimilation.

First, he can give us no numbers. Is English language usage the only measure of assimilation? After venting his rage at the Catholic Church paragraph after paragraph, is the level of abandonment by Mexicans of the Church a measure of assimilation? (18 percent are Evangelical Christians according to the Zogby Poll) Is high school graduation a measure of assimilation? Is poverty a measure of assimilation? Is use of or no use of public benefits a measure of assimilation? After venting rage at the governance of Mexico for the past 500 years, is divorcement from one's heritage a measure of assimilation? Has he never heard of St. Patrick's Day?

He waxes about the American heritage and history he learned in grammar school as if that which he learned from all-Anglo teachers is the whole story, or even accurate. He mentions President Teddy Roosevelt, but not his Rough Rider Company commander Maximiliano Luna, the Spanish-speaking New Mexican. He does not mention the Mexicans like Juan Seguín who fought for Texas Independence at the Alamo. But, of course, Texans reluctantly mention those facts today and never did until the 1970s. He does not mention the Mexican Americans who helped defeat the Confederates when they invaded New Mexico during the Civil War, nor the Mexican American cavalry that fought the last battle of the Civil War in Texas, of course.

Professor Hanson, when discussing the American War of Independence against England, did your teachers tell you Mexicans, with their Spanish, Cuban and Puerto Rican cousins defeated British troops during the American Revolution. They did so throughout the Mississippi Valley. They also supplied American revolutionaries in the Ohio Valley, defeated the British at Mobile, Baton Rouge and along the Mississippi River before smashing the British at the hugely strategic fortress at Pensacola under General Bernardo de Gálvez with nary a Yankee in sight. He does not mention these things because his teachers didn't mention them, even if they knew this history. They probably didn't because these facts were not taught in American schools or universities by the Anglo-Protestant academy, the same academy that produced Dr. Hanson. Even today, these facts are not taught universally in American schools.

The facts smack of "multiculturalism" in the eyes of these learned men from Harvard and Cal-State Fresno. On the other hand, they, like their Anglo-Protestant brethren, refuse to admit that Mexicans actually fought in the American Revolution. They also ignore that newly minted Americans that became so because the "border" actually did "cross them" fought with great valor in the Civil War.

To his credit, he does mention that Mexican Americans from his hometown served in World War Two, but neglects to mention the three dozen of them who were awarded the nation's highest military honor, the Medal of Honor, in WWII, Korea and Vietnam. Some of these men were born in Mexico and were probably illegal aliens (Hispanics In America's Defense—Department of Defense, 1982). He mentions that an illegitimate Mexican revolutionary government might have conspired with the Kaiser's Germany in 1917 (The Zimmerman Telegram) in a conspiracy many historians doubt actually occurred. Hanson does so to inflame anti-Mexican passions just as some historians are now claiming it was an American conspiracy designed to inflame the American public in 1917 in an effort, possibly, to grab more Mexican real estate. More importantly, as a historian he purposefully ignores the fact that Mexico declared war on Germany, Italy and Japan on its own in June, 1942.

He mentions relatives of his who served in that war and some who did not return, but he does not mention that many Mexican nationals served in the Armed Forces of the United States without being drafted but entirely as volunteers. And, he ignores the facts that Mexico provided fighting men, pilots, to be trained and commanded by the American Army, and that they actually served in South Pacific combat under the command of General of the Army Douglas MaCarthur, Professor Hanson does not inform us well or fairly. The absence or lack of these historical facts in *Mexifornia* cloud and distort his diatribe against Mexico's government, politics, people and religion, to the delight, of course, of his many deeply bigoted supporters.

Certainly, even the professor has to admit that such men, Mexican Americans who numbered in the hundreds of thousands, were assimilated, even to a degree that he can accept. One might suggest that the Mexican pilots themselves might have been assimilated to a high degree. After all, President Harry Truman not only awarded the Mexican pilots a Presidential Unit Citation, he offered United States citizenship to the young Mexican fighting men. In the first few days of the Iraq war in 2003, two Mexican citizen United States Marines and one Guatemalan citizen U.S. Marine were killed in action. Professor Hanson does not mention that fact, nor the 37,000 immigrant noncitizens serving in the 2003 wartime American military, most Mexican, mostly in the army Infantry and United States Marines. Those facts might confuse Professor Hanson's assertions that these men and women reject assimilation.

CHAPTER 20

WHERE IS THE LITTLE RED SCHOOLHOUSE?

Hanson: "As far as I can tell years after their graduation, these young men and women (some illegals from Mexico, the balance—Mexican Americans) left the university to take up productive professional lives while defining themselves as individuals and as Americans, rather than as part of a collective and dependent Mexican underclass." Here Professor Hanson extols the virtues of Mexican American students he knew (and went to school with, in some cases) while jabbing at today's students as if they do not measure up to their predecessors. He is unaware, of course, of the Mexican American experience prior to his recent experience in school.

He does not mention that segregated Mexican schools existed practically up to the minute he was born in parts of California. He does not mention that in 1950, according to Dr. Thomas Sowell, that only 8 percent of California Mexican Americans graduated from high school. Sowell wrote (in Ethnic America): "In 1950, Mexican Americans in the Southwest completed only 5-years of school, compared to eleven for the non-Hispanic white population (and eight for blacks) in the same region. By 1960, this had risen to seven years (a 40 percent increase) for Mexican Americans compared to twelve for non-Hispanic whites and nine for blacks." Obviously, Mexican American educational progress has outpaced that of whites and blacks for several decades and is capped off by more progress even as this is read.

In September 2002, 700,000 Hispanics enrolled in California's public two and four year colleges and universities (according to official enrollment statistics provided by each collegiate and university system on their respective web sites). At my alma mater, San Diego State University, 5000 undergraduate and graduate Hispanic students populate the campus (25%). In my first year (1958) 50 Hispanic students were enrolled out of a student body of 7,000, seven tenths of one percent. Certainly, Professor Hanson's campus, Cal-State Fresno, has experienced similar progress in educating the sons and daughters of the very immigrants he criticizes for not pursuing education and assimilating to a degree he now wishes had occurred in the past two decades. The Gannet News Service reported in June 2003 that, "Many Hispanics counted as high school dropouts are newly arrived immigrants who have never set foot in a U.S. school, suggesting a larger percentage of Hispanics are graduating than previously believed, according to a report released Thursday." "Researchers at the Pew Hispanic Center, a nonpartisan think tank specializing in studies of Hispanics in the United States, found that the dropout rate for Hispanics age 16-19 drops to 14 percent when immigrants are excluded from the data, including them pushes the rate to 21 percent."

Being able to discern non-immigrant Mexicans and Hispanics from immigrant ones seems to be a problem with immigration critics like Hanson. Even among immigrants, however, there are differences that are noticeable to scholars, though not to Professors Hanson and Huntington. For example, Jeffrey Grogger and Stephen J. Trejo, in a report of the Public Policy Institute of California, write, "Immigration plays a tremendous role in the Mexican-white high school graduation gap, even among young adults ages 19-21...Children who arrive before 5 do much better. Indeed, their graduation rate is similar to that of US.-born Mexican Americans..." Explanation: Children who arrive in the United States before they are five from Mexico learn more English than those who arrive later in life and learn it earlier and faster. Television is the primary English teacher of these children.

Television is also the great assimilator, though Professors Hanson and Huntington fail to realize that.

CHAPTER 21

ARE MEXICANS ARMENIANS, ITALIANS OR SPACE ALIENS?

Hanson: "Almost everything stern and uncompromising that for two centuries has helped other immigrants to the United States—language immersion, autonomy from government assistance, rapid assumption of mainstream American culture—has either been discounted as passe or embraced only halfheartedly." Professor Hanson romanticizes the myth that previous immigrants to America dropped their native languages and were speaking perfect English within days after they arrived. He implies that those immigrants promptly assimilated and did so without government assistance. Professor Hanson offers no data to support his sweeping statements. He can't because he has none. In fact, as previously noted, Harvard-educated author James Crawford has written that only 13 percent of non-English speaking immigrant children in New York City managed to not flunk out schools and the rest (87%) never graduated from the city's high schools.

After the Irish rioted in New York in 1863 and killed hundreds, perhaps a thousand or more Black men and women, the city, state and federal governments united to hire as many Irish as they could for government jobs from police officers to garbage men. To this day, urban police departments, fire departments and even the Federal Bureau of Investigation are predominately peopled by Irish Americans. A government check, for make or real work, is still a government check. Perhaps Professor Hanson should notice that almost 20 per cent of Postal Service employees are Black and that Filipinos have entered the Postal Service by the thousands. The old system works today just like it did a hundred years ago. It transfers money from those who pay taxes to others for the fiction of public payroll work.

Moreover, he lionizes his neighboring Armenian people who populated the Central Valley of California after they escaped the Turkish genocide of Armenians. He so admires their progress in California. He also implies that others like the Italians have assimilated. He ignores, however, the fact that it took decades and generations for these people to even be accepted, much less assimilated as Americans. He neglects to mention that an entire new "Maffia" underworld has been created by recent Armenian immigrants in the Los Angeles area (Glendale) who also have created teenaged gangs, drive-by shootings, drugs and other crime he associates only with Mexicans. On the one hand he states that in 1970 there were fewer than 800,000 Mexican Americans in California, out of millions of people and on the other hand he complains about Mexican immigrants who have come since, who are essentially new to the United States. He does not compare time lines to the Armenians or Italians (80 to 100 years), or Japanese immigrants (80-100 years) who have come before the current Mexican immigrant and made it but took generations to do so.

For comparison purposes, the Italian immigration most closely resembles the current Mexican immigration pattern. For example, they are both Roman Catholic; they are both non-English speaking. They were and are both assigned work duties of the dirtiest and hardest nature and both suffered through low wages. Both had significant numbers of single men come and return to their homelands after working for years to accumulate savings. Both had many single men come and work and send home for wives and families. Both had many domestic critics. In the case of Italians, a totally non-Italian American and Anglo-Protestant Congress (with the exception of one Black member from Chicago) cut off Italian immigration by carefully using a congressional scalpel to skillfully discriminate against Italians and Jews in 1924. Today, Congressman Tom Tancredo, buttressed by Professor Huntington and Professor Hanson, is attempting to shut down all immigration, a potential shut down that today mostly affects Mexicans.

One fact seems to have escaped notice of both Hanson and Tancredo—that is: It took the Italians six or seven decades to be classified as assimilated and certainly, due to a lack of entrepreneurial enterprise, didn't enter America's economic mainstream until the 60s and 70s. With the exception of Bank of America, for example, how many big name companies were founded or run by Italians prior to Lee Iacocca's rise in the 1970s. Waving a magic wand does not create big companies, they arise from small businesses that grow.

The other facts that escape notice is that since the cohort of Hispanic and Mexican immigration has doubled and tripled, the number of businesses formed by the Hispanic community has outstripped the general population's business formation pace by three and four to one. The number of Hispanic businesses has increased by a third since President George W. Bush was inaugurated and appear to have increased the pace of new business formation even faster than in the previous record setting decade. Even during the recession years of the late 1980s and early 1990s, Hispanics, according to the Labor Department, formed businesses at breakneck speed. That pace has continued to the point that Hispanic businesses far outnumber those of American-born Blacks, for instance, while the number of professionals, lawyers, doctors et al who are native born Hispanics is rapidly increasing, much to the chagrin of Tom Tancredo, Professors Hanson and Huntington.

There is one more similarity between the Italian and Mexican immigrations—organized crime. It was the Italian that created the drive-by shooting, the Mexicans who perfected it. It was the Italian that organized against Anglo-Protestant alcohol prohibition and it was the Mexican who developed a wide open border town to satisfy the needs for alcohol, women and gambling of America's royalty, Hollywood, in Hollywood South, Tijuana. In recent years, it was the Italian that developed a pipeline to supply white suburban America and urban Black America with heroin from the Middle East and Southeast Asia. It was the Mexican who introduced the sweet weed Mary Jane. And, as the Italian gangster dies off some Mexicans are filling the void left behind by the passing of an era of Sicilian and their Anglo-Protestant bankers.

Professor Hanson neglects to mention this unique contribution to America, the MAFIA. Nor does he recount how these unassimilated Italians corrupted and molded the entire American population and local and state governments by corruption, some of which persists to this day.

CHAPTER 22

HANSON VENTS HIS PERSONAL RAGE

Hanson: "Embittered Californians decline to challenge the therapeutic bromides offered to Hispanics in their schools and state agencies—but then go quietly to the polls to vent their rage by ending what they see as special concessions to those who broke the law in coming here."

What hogwash! When someone steps forward to positively comment on progress of Mexican Americans in our society the critics rise up with their emotional attacks that are rarely sustained by facts and scientific data. Those things simply don't matter. Neither the complainers who are "embittered" nor their academic spokespersons like Hanson produce objective data to support "the therapeutic bromides" that are producing record numbers of Hispanic graduates and college students, they simply gratuitously assert fantasies and urban myths. Professor Hanson criticizes the number of Mexican American students at Cal-State universities and the University of California who must take remedial English courses, as if this is the exclusive property of these students. He ignores the fact that these courses were called "bonehead" English in my collegiate days and that almost 100 percent of those who had to take and pass "bonehead" English were people with names like Smith and Hanson. I didn't have to take those courses, and I didn't speak English when I entered school. What "bromides?"

He, of course, criticizes bilingual education that didn't come about by politics, but by experience and necessity at the local level long before the experts in state capitols took over. Harvard graduate and ersatz California politician Ron Unz used every argument against bilingual education there is and convinced those "embittered" ones to vote against bilingual education, no matter the fallout. They passed the Unz prohibition, but failed and bilingual education still exists in every single school district and still does the good it was intended to do, to teach children to read and write in their first language, Spanish, then to convert them to English. In fact, if one compares two school districts in California, one that tried to outlaw bilingual education in its entirety and one that still permits it, Oceanside and Vista schools, one finds some startling information. Oceanside has terrible SAT scores, far below the national average, while Vista has far higher scores. The student bodies are both 50% minority, mostly Mexican. The proof is in the SAT scores. Vista, 528 verbal, Oceanside, 495 verbal, period, end of argument. The graduation rates of these children is far higher than, say, those non-English speaking children the New York schools flushed out of their English-only system a hundred years ago. No matter, Hanson and the other "embittered" still whine about how taxpaying Hispanics demand their tax money be spent on their children.

CHAPTER 23

LIVING OFF THE PUBLIC

Hanson: "Yet more skeptical statisticians employing different models reach a radically different conclusion that aliens cost the United States over $40-billion a year, and that here in California each illegal alien will take from the state $50,000 more in services than he will contribute in taxes during his lifetime."

Rubbish. Different models based on different assumptions produce different conclusions. Recent (March 2004) legitimate studies, however, debunk Professor Hanson's juvenile statements which, of course, he doesn't back up with scholarly researched conclusions. In a paper entitled *California Immigrants turn the Corner* by USC's Dowell Myers, John Pitkin and Julie Park, we find the "poverty rate for total foreign born in California" to have peaked in 1990 and dropping since. The poverty rate has dropped even for recent immigrants. They write, "Evidence shows that poverty rates amongst immigrants fell substantially when they were observed 10 and 20 years after their arrival. For example, in 1980, 27.8% of new Latino immigrants were in poverty, but this fell to 20.3% in 1990 and, 16.6% (in 2000)." In total contrast to Professor Hanson's unsubstantiated statements, these researchers conclude that, "Earnings, home ownership and voting participation all rise markedly with growing length of settlement."

As to the claim that illegals will draw $50,000 more in services than they will pay in taxes during their lifetime, Hanson offers no specifics. In a report from the Public Policy Institute of California by Deborah Reed in February 2004, we find these words that might apply here, "For low-income families, income from government transfers contributes 13 percent of family income. The largest sources of government transfers are social security (which illegals cannot collect), supplementary security income (which illegals cannot collect), public assistance (which illegals cannot collect) and unemployment compensation (which illegals cannot collect).

So much for an assertion Hanson cannot prove, nor even cite by source for fear that he will be laughed out of the academy.

CHAPTER 24

THE WELFARE MYTH

Hanson: "We are told that blanket amnesty and legal status will ensure assimilation and prosperity; but statistics reveal that after twenty years, Mexican immigrants who have obtained legal papers still double the welfare rate of American citizens."

Let me repeat facts researched by real scholars. In a paper entitled *California Immigrants turn the Corner*, by USC's Dowell Myers, John Pitkin and Julie Park, we find the "poverty rate for total foreign born in California" to have peaked in 1990 and dropping since. The poverty rate has dropped even for recent immigrants. They write, "Evidence shows that poverty rates amongst immigrants fell substantially when they were observed 10 and 20 years after their arrival. For example, in 1980, 27.8% of new Latino immigrants were in poverty, but this fell to 20.3% in 1990 and, 16.6% (in 2000)."

In total contrast to Professor Hanson's unsubstantiated statements, these researchers conclude that, "Earnings, home ownership and voting participation all rise markedly with growing length of settlement." From the *Wall Street Journal Online*, February 29, 2004, we find more comments from Dowell Myers, Pitkin and Julie Park; to wit: "According to 1970 Census data, 17.7% of immigrants (mostly Mexicans) who arrived in California in the 1960s were living in poverty. Ten years later their poverty rate had dropped to 12.2%. By 1990 it has fallen to 9% and in 2000 it was 8.7%. The trend held true for immigrants who arrived in the 1970s, '80s and '90s." The article continues, "Among Latinos who arrived in the 1960s, he (Myers) found that 68.1% of those age 60 and older owned their own home by 2000. Younger Latinos own homes at a slightly lower rate—67.2% for those in their 50s and 61% for those in their 40s. California's overall homeownership rate is 56.9% and nationally it's 66.2%." The article concludes: "The number of new immigrants arriving in California has leveled off over the past decade and the number who arrive poor has dipped (according to Census statistics). If those trends continue, then California will be collecting more in taxes from the immigrant community just as the percentage of immigrants who need government services is shrinking."

Poor, poor Professor Hanson...His statement may be true that long resident immigrants may collect welfare by 2 to 1 over native-born, but so what?

Native born are mostly white, better educated, and have had better economic circumstance because of the preeminent social place whites have always had since the days Anglo-Protestants organized the society to their advantage. That said, so what, professor Hanson?

Twenty years, let's see what those years might bring. In a recent study (October 2003) from the Pew Hispanic Center, *The Rise of the Second Generation: Changing patterns in Hispanic Population Growth*, edited by Robert Suro, formerly of the *Washington Post*, and the Urban Institute's Jeffrey S. Passel, we see some projections that are earthshaking. What can we expect? Suro and Passel write: "(Hispanic) Births in the United States are outpacing immigration as the key source of growth. Over the next twenty years this will produce an important shift in the makeup of the Hispanic population with second generation Latinos—the U.S. born children of immigrants—emerging as the largest component of that population." They continue, "Given the very substantial differences in earnings, education, fluency in English and attitudes between the foreign-born and native-born Latinos, this shift has profound implications for many realms of public policy…"

CHAPTER 25

NUMBERS, WHERE ARE HANSON'S NUMBERS?

Hanson: "...the invisibility of intermarriage, the inability to count illegal alien populations, and the tendency of many Hispanics to list themselves as 'white' on surveys rather than check the box that makes them officially a 'person of color.'"

This Hanson fallacy is easily dispatched with these words from *Second Generation*: "Intermarriage: First generation Latinos, like immigrants in general, tend to marry within their ethnic/racial group. That is not true of second and third-plus generation Latinos. According to recent estimates (Edmondston et al., 2003) only 8 percent of foreign-born Hispanics intermarry, compared to 32 percent of the second generation and 57% of the third-plus generations." What is Professor Hanson smoking? Maybe he should contact the Urban Institute to ask for a copy of *Immigration and Ethnicity: The Integration of America's Arrivals*, by Barry Edmenston and Jeffrey Passel, Editors, the Urban Institute Press, 1994. Maybe someone can tell Professors Hanson and Huntington what the word "integration" means.

Hanson: "Almost one-quarter of California's inmates are from Mexico, and almost a third of recent drug-trafficking arrests involved illegal aliens." Professor Hanson is now becoming tiresome and boring. What are his sources for those figures? The only possible source is the California

Department of Corrections and it reports different figures than Hanson makes up. Yes, makes up. To make his point he grasps at urban myth figures and statements:

25 percent of California inmates are not from Mexico!!!

As of March 31, 2003, the Department reports that 162,120 inmates are incarcerated in state prisons. Of those, 17,893 were born in Mexico—*11 percent, not 25 percent.*

He also misstates that a "third of recent drug-trafficking arrests involved illegal aliens." Where, Professor Hanson are these arrests, in Selma, in San Francisco, in Pacific Palisades? Or, are they arrested on the border where almost every single smuggler of drugs or anything else is a Mexican national?

Hanson:…."some studies indicate that the presence of plentiful foreign laborers in the 1990s reduced the wages of unskilled workers by 5%." Wrong, again, Professor Hanson. You forgot to mention the study by Bean-Lowell-Taylor that stated, "The magnitudes of the effects are hard to interpret but the authors refer to them as 'not very sizable. The concern that *undocumented immigration may be depressing the earnings of native-born workers does not appear to be borne out by these results.*" (Emphasis added) In a review of effects on aggregate earnings by immigration, Jeffrey Passel of the Urban Institute concluded: "Immigration has no discernible effect on wages over-all. Wage growth and decline appear to be unrelated to immigration—a finding that holds for both unskilled and skilled workers (1994). Better yet, former University of California, San Diego and current Harvard immigration critic, an immigrant himself, George Borjas, the most quoted anti-immigrant academic prior to Hanson or Huntington, has an even better view. In 1990 he wrote: "The empirical evidence indicates that immigrants only have a minor effect on the earnings and employment opportunities of natives" About illegals in particular, he wrote, "There is no evidence…that illegal immigration had a significant adverse effect on the earnings opportunities of any native group,

including Blacks." These quotes can all be found at http://
www.cato.org/pubs/policy report/pr-imearn.html

Hanson: "Wages to illegals are often paid in cash, which is a bargain for everyone involved." If one of Professor Hanson's classics students wrote these words in a blue book essay, Hanson would grade the student down severely. Where is the data that proves illegals "are often paid in cash?" The federal government has contracted for many studies made up of interviews with thousands of illegals in custody. The interviews occurred at the Otay Mesa Border Patrol facility in San Diego while the illegals were awaiting deportation. The studies concluded long ago that 75 percent of them were paid with regular payroll checks in which all deductions were taken by the employer for Social Security, and state and federal taxes. Hanson simply reinforces the popular myth that all illegals are paid in cash. That is not true and he should know better than to feed this myth without a study to back him up.

CHAPTER 26

AMERICANS BY CHOICE, NOT ACCIDENT

Hanson: "Even legal immigrants from Mexico rarely become citizens: of all those admitted legally to the United States since 1982, only 20 percent had become citizens by 1997." Hanson: "Consequently, even after twenty years, 8 of 10 never become naturalized American citizens..." Wrong! Starting in 1995, the number of Mexicans who have naturalized has increased by leaps and bounds thanks to Governor Pete Wilson, Professor Victor Davis Hanson and Proposition 187. For accurate statistics we go to where Professor Hanson has an aversion to, the facts. In *Trends in Naturalization* published by the Urban Institute in September, 2003, and written by Michael Fix, Jeffrey Passel and Kenneth Sucher:.

Mexicans who naturalized in 1995 numbered 19%. That grew to 34% in 2001 and has continued to grow since to over 40%. Other Latin Americans naturalized at a 40% rate in 1995 and grew to 58% in 2001. (Source, *Census Bureau Current Population Surveys, 2001*). Apparently, Professor Hanson doesn't have access to the Internet so he can find these statistics in two minutes flat.

Hanson: "So what accounts for the stubborn resistance to assimilation, besides the increases numbers and our own lack of confidence in the melting pot." If there were any truth to this dumb statement, it might be worth exploring. But the statement is too dumb to comment on as we have seen from empirical evidence presented here from unimpeachable sources. Hanson: "In sum, that racism has been a factor in the Mexican experience is indisputable; that in the present world of integration, intermarriage and government subsidy it still largely explains the disappointment and failure of millions of aliens is false." Another dumb statement from noted historian Dr. Victor Davis Hanson. As we have seen from information from unimpeachable scholarly sources, there is no lack of "integration" or "intermarriage." And, "government subsidy" plays little part in the rush of Hispanics and Mexicans, specifically, to create new businesses and companies.

Hanson: "Supporters of financial bailouts (of Mexico, 1995) and unrestricted immigration perhaps err when they claim such engagement is necessary to prevent a Mexican catastrophe." In another part of this work, I discussed the Clinton Administration's help in the form of a $50-billion emergency loan to Mexico in 1995. The loan was paid off early and the USA made a profit of $50-million. Why shouldn't the USA help its second largest trading partner, its next door neighbor and original homeland to millions of its citizens? President Roosevelt ignored if not broke law to help Great Britain in 1940 with a "Lend Lease" program that helped arm Great Britain for its survival against Nazi Germany.

Hanson: "Within twenty years the poor, brown Indian alien could enjoy a material existence in America superior to that of the upper class white Mexican in Mexico City." How uninformed is this statement? Hanson and others constantly complain about Mexico's upper classes. He denigrates them and their standard of living by suggesting that the illegals he hires to work on his farm can economically overtake these people with a finer standard of living. That standard will only get better as Mexico continues on an economic path making it a larger industrial and petrochemical power. Hanson: "...whether you believe that we are all going to be fine because an illegal alien becomes valedictorian of his high school class, or that none of us will have a future when almost four out of ten Hispanic students—natives, resident aliens and illegal immigrants alike—are believed never to finish the twelfth grade."

Hanson: "…According to some studies, almost 40 percent of both Hispanic aliens and Hispanic citizens of immigrant background do not graduate from our state's high schools within the normal four years, while 90 percent of Mexicans of all statuses have no B.A. degree." Hanson: "Three decades after the rise of the new militancy and separatism, along with unchecked immigration, Hispanics have the highest dropout rates from high school and the lowest percentages of bachelor's degrees of any ethnic group in the state."

Three very stupid statements that are debunked by real research and facts as previously noted. One must ask this man just how he dismisses the 700,000-plus graduate and undergraduate students in California's public colleges and universities, just how? Cannot this man simply look up the web site of his own employer, the California State University, the largest public university in the world, to see how many Mexican Americans there are debunking his *very ignorant* statement?

CHAPTER 27

AMERICANS BY THE CONSTITUTION

Hanson: "Equally bizarre is the American policy of granting instant citizenship at our hospitals to infants of illegal aliens. We see pregnant women with no cash, no husband, no English and no papers who rush to the local hospital at the last minute to bring forth a United States citizen." Hanson: "The birth is a miraculous event indeed, for in theory the infant instantaneously can anchor a new American existence for a full array of parents and assorted relatives of illegal aliens. How surreal! How surreal!"

Bizarre? Again, what is this man smoking? Whatever it is, it isn't very good. It muddles the man's mind beyond description. Citizenship by birth in U.S. soil is the Constitution's mandate. Now, what is really surprising is that the man claims to be a Roman scholar. It was Roman law, the foundation of our civilized legal system—which was imposed upon the Anglo-Saxons by the Normans—that created three basic principles of acquiring citizenship: These were by way of blood, soil, and law. The Romans established *Jus solis*--the right to Roman citizenship of someone who was born on Roman soil. As opposed to *Jus sanguini*, the right to Roman citizenship based on the "blood," or Roman parentage, regardless where you were born. Finally, the Roman Senate promulgated laws (*leges*) granting citizenship to all foreigners living in Rome, and later the Italian Peninsula. Most western societies follow these three principles to grant citizenship, including the U.S. European legal tradition incorporated these principles into their legal system, and constitutions. How surreal is that Hanson, now is showing incompetence in his own field to justify his prejudicial statements.

It is not "policy" Dr. Hanson; it is a Constitutional mandate clearly defined in an 1898 Supreme Court case (Wong Kim Ark, 169 U.S. 649), and long established in Western Law. Mr. Wong Kim Ark was born in San Francisco of Chinese citizen parents living in San Francisco. He went to China and was not allowed back into the United States. He petitioned the court to allow him back into the country because he was a natural born U.S. citizen and the government could not keep him out. The government argued that the Congressionally passed Chinese Exclusion laws did not allow his entry into the U.S. even though he was born here because he was a "Chinese" person. The court went back to English common law, the Calvin cases of 1608 to discuss what the 14th Amendment meant. In the case, we find these words: "…and therefore, every child born in England of alien parents was a natural-born subject, unless the child of an ambassador or other diplomatic agent of a foreign state, or of an alien enemy in hostile occupation of the place where the child was born." Quoted also is "U.S. v Rhodes (1866), Mr. Justice Swayne, sitting in the circuit court, said, 'All persons born in allegiance of the king are natural-born subjects, and all persons born in the allegiance of the United States are natural-born citizens. Birth and allegiance go together. Such is the rule of this country, as well as England."

After 600,000 people died to perfect the Constitution in the Civil War, America redefined the Constitution. The 14th Amendment to the Constitution was ratified by the states on July 9, 1868 after two years of debate, debate that was highlighted by the U.S. v. Rhodes case in the middle of the debate. The 14th Amendment that is applicable here: "All persons born or naturalized in the United States and subject to the jurisdiction thereof, are citizens of the United States and of the State wherein they reside…" Notice that Congress was very careful to use the word "persons" and notice that it used the word "all," all persons means all persons. The thrust of the Amendment, of course, was to wipe out the fateful Dred Scott case of 1857 that declared that Black slaves were "property," and as Africans could never be citizens because they were not "white."

There is no question that the amendment had Black men, women and children in mind when Congress debated the issue, but there was mention on the floor of Congress of the "strangers among us," aliens, if you will, legal or illegal. This subject was covered in the Slaughterhouse cases (1873) 16 Wall. 36, 73. Mr. Justice Miller wrote: "We do not say that no one else but the Negro can share in this protection. Both the language and spirit of these articles (13th, 14th and 15th Amendments) are to have their fair and just weight in any question of construction." He continued for the majority, "And so, if other rights are assailed by the states, which properly and necessarily fall within the protection of these articles, that protection will apply, though the party interested may not be of African descent." "It is only necessary that he should be born or naturalized in the United States to be a citizen of the Union," Justice Miller wrote, ending forever the question of whether babies born to illegal aliens are citizens.

So, the question Hanson tries to raise in such a juvenile way was established over two thousand years ago, and settled in the U.S. well over a hundred years ago punctuated by the deaths of over 600,000 people. As to his assertion that these are "anchor babies" that can themselves bring in all sorts of relatives legally to the United States is stupid and merits little comment. No child under 18 (in some cases, 21 years of age) can bring in family members and many times whole families are deported when the parents are illegally here and their child or children are American citizens.

As for Wong Kim Ark's case, the Supreme Court determined that a: "child born in the United States, of parents of Chinese descent who, at the time of his birth, are subjects of the Emperor of China, but have a permanent domicile and residence in the United States, and they are carrying on business, and are not employed in any diplomatic or official capacity of the Emperor of China, becomes at the time of his birth a citizen of the United States." The parents could not become citizens of the United States at the time, but no matter, Wong Kim Ark was born here and he was a citizen, period. The same is true of any children born of an illegal alien mother or father, period. Hanson knows that. If he doesn't, his ability to teach young people in college should be denied.

Chapter 28

Hanson v. Huntington: Florida

Hanson: "Florida, a long peninsula with an inhospitable climate, was settled and its swamps drained as it became a successful multiracial state; Baja California, about the same size and shape and also blazing hot, until recently remained mostly a parched wasteland."

Has there ever been a dumber statement by an educated person than this comparison of Florida and Baja California? Professor Hanson ought to get out of Selma some time. His attempt to demean Mexico as a country is transparent with this statement. Florida had some swamps that were drained; Baja California is almost all desert, pure rainless desolate sandy desert. Nonetheless, the Mexicans have transformed the previously desert wasteland of the Mexicali Valley into one of the most productive agricultural locales in the "Third World." In fact, the loud whine one hears from Florida tomato growers is about tomatoes from Mexico, some from the Mexicali Valley. Tijuana is the third largest city in Mexico. The city abounds with hundreds of factories and thousands of well-paid workers. They manage to spend $2 billion dollars a year in Southern California that generate millions of sales tax dollars that more than pay for medical care for Mexican nationals, Illegals, in many cases, in the single public hospital in the city of San Diego.

Florida was nothing until the railroads were built into it. Miami was a racist backwater southern city with nothing but a few beaches until the Cubans arrived in the early Sixties. Comically, Professor Samuel Huntington laments the Miami experience of becoming a "Hispanic" city where the number one television news program is in Spanish and where the city's power structure is not "White," it is Hispanic. This, while Professor Hanson extols Florida. He did forget to mention that Anglo-Protestants raped and pillaged an all-Black Florida town and killed dozens of Blacks for the crime of being born Black. Florida's Anglo-Protestants were, in fact, some of the most vicious racists in all of American history.

Hanson goes out of his way to dismiss American racism many times in his book, but he cannot be allowed to extol the development of a place like Florida with its serious racist background and a place in Mexico that politically has lead the country out of one-party dictatorship, led the country in modern industrialization, and has a higher percentage of home ownership than most European countries and a per capita income that most probably exceeds Mississippi.

CHAPTER 29

RACE, TRIBE AND RELIGION

Hanson: "Few Mexicans could ever be accepted as full citizens in China, Japan, Zimbabwe or Saudi Arabia—in other words, in many places of the non-Western world that define their citizenry by the criteria of race, tribe and religion."

Professor Hanson lacks Classical scholarly judgment. He fails to understand that the Roman principles of citizenship are Western concepts, thus by history and culture do not necessarily apply to non-Western nations. .He also seems to indulge in the same Anglo-Protestant fetish as Professor Samuel Huntington. This statement very clearly puts the United States of America into the same category as Japan, Zimbabwe and Saudi Arabia. Certainly Professor Hanson wrote these words with something else in mind. At least we hope he did for those countries are racist and severely bigoted in how they view Whites and non-Muslims. However, these words in combination with his and Huntington's views and fantasies about Mexicans not willing to become "Americans" and not willing or able to learn and use English, imply that Mexicans cannot be accepted into the United States. Reason: The same racism and bigotry of those three countries is prevalent in this country and, apparently, meets with the approval of these two professors, or, these two indulge these passions in their own minds and actions, certainly their words indicate that is true.

"Race, tribe and religion" seem to be at the core of the positions taken by these two academics; that is, the American Anglo "race" and "tribe" and Protestant "religion."

PART 3

TOM TANCREDO AND HIS RACIST ASSOCIATES

CHAPTER 30

WHO IS TOM TANCREDO?

Before we examine Colorado Congressman Tom Tancredo's views and actions on immigration, legal and illegal, we should know what his true character is. This article from the Rocky Mountain News is reprinted by permission. State Treasurer Coffman apologized to Tancredo according to the News after the event reported here. He shouldn't have.

"March 27, 2003

Coffman Left Rally to Protest Tancredo. Lawmaker Supports Iraq War but Didn't Fight in Vietnam

Author: John J. Sanko, *Rocky Mountain News*

State Treasurer Mike Coffman confirmed Wednesday he walked away from a pro-war rally with Congressman Tom Tancredo because of questions about Tancredo's failure to serve in Vietnam. Coffman, a former Marine who saw action in the first Persian Gulf conflict more than a decade ago, left the Colorado Capitol stage in what he described as a personal protest. But Coffman said he warned his fellow Republican ahead of time that he would not share the platform with him. Coffman made no public statement at the time and confirmed the action only after asked about it by a reporter. "I didn't make a statement about it publicly," Coffman said. "I never intended to do so. You guys found out about it – I don't know how. "I just didn't feel (Tancredo) had the moral authority to send other young people off to war when he was not willing to go himself." When asked about the Sunday incident, Tancredo issued only a brief statement from his Washington, D.C., office.

"If Mike Coffman left early, I am disappointed," Tancredo said. "My first comments were those of praise for him and for others in attendance who had served." Lara Kennedy, a spokeswoman for Tancredo, said he would have "nothing further to say at this point in time." Last year, it was reported that in 1970, after Tancredo's student deferments ran out, he appealed his 1-A draft status, which would have put him at the top of the list for draft eligibility during the Vietnam War. Tancredo said he didn't remember it that way. But he said he was given a 1-Y status, which put him at the bottom of the list, when he reported that he had been treated for mental illness as a teenager. Tancredo said he was diagnosed with depression when he was 16 or 17 and received medication for five years for panic attacks and bouts of anxiety and depression. Because of Tancredo's draft record, Coffman said he specifically asked organizers of the rally whether Tancredo would be speaking. "It was only after they told me he was not scheduled to appear that I agreed to be a speaker," Coffman said. "When, much to my surprise, I then saw Congressman Tancredo in the audience, I privately informed him that I was not comfortable appearing with him. "The congressman angrily told me to do whatever I thought was right, and (he) added that I was wrong about the circumstances regarding his deferment from the draft." When Tancredo came on the stage to speak, Coffman walked up the Capitol steps to go back to his office. Coffman, whose father served in the military in World War II and Korea, admitted he did not have an objective view of the situation. "I grew up at Fitzsimons seeing casualties from Vietnam on a daily basis," said Coffman, who worked among the injured then as a volunteer. "I know what the sacrifices are like that are made by our people in the military."

Coffman, now 48, served in the Army, enlisting when he was 17 in 1972. He later joined the Marine Corps, serving from 1979 through 1982, and was called into action for Operation Desert Storm in 1991 when he was a state legislator. He retired from the service as a major. "As a young soldier, I was taught, and it was later reinforced to me as an officer in the Marine Corps, that you never order a subordinate to do something that you yourself would be unwilling to do. "Consequently, I have difficulty sharing a platform with someone who publicly advocates sending our young men and women into combat while he sought a mental deferment to avoid military service during time of war. "There are a broad number of issues on which I agree with the congressman and would be glad to appear with him. However, this is one issue where I cannot." Coffman and Tancredo also have clashed over the issue of term limits. Coffman criticized the congressman last year for abandoning his term-limits pledge. Many observers assumed Coffman would run to succeed Tancredo in 2004. But Tancredo's reversal clears the way for the incumbent to run again in the heavily GOP district." Tancredo is not only a draft-dodging escapee of military service, he also supports international terrorism, specifically, he supports Iranian terrorists guilty of murdering Americans. What kind of man is this Tom Tancredo?

Here, from a Rocky Mountain News editorial:

January 18, 2003, "...Why is Congressman Tom Tancredo actively supporting the national Council of Resistance of Iran— a fanatical front organization for the People's Mujahedin of Iran, which the State Department classifies as a terrorist group supported by Saddam Hussein? Since its founding 35 years ago as an anti-American, Islamic-Marxist alternative to Shiite fundamentalism, the Mujahedin has murdered U.S. military personnel and civilians, bombed U.S. business offices, supported the taking of American hostages in Iran in 1979, and engaged in fraud, smuggling and money laundering on U.S. soil." The editorial continues: "...Only this week, his (Tancredo's) photo appeared in a full-page advertisement in the New York Times that noted his signature on a recent

Congressional 'Iranian Statement' supporting the Mujahedin
a 'legitimate resistance movement."

On January 27, 2003, the Rocky Mountain News followed
up with another editorial that proves beyond doubt that Tom
Tancredo is an ignorant man who takes positions he cannot
back up legitimately with proof and facts. His support of
murderers of American and terrorists is beyond belief. If he
supports murderous Islamo/Fascist terrorists, killers of
Americans, how can we trust anything he says about
Mexicans, Mexicans who, unlike Tom Tancredo, have fought
in the American military and alongside it in the War on Japan,
the Korean War, Vietnam, Kuwait and now in Iraq, how? The
Rocky Mountain News: "First, Tancredo's assertion that the
State Department blacklisted the Mujahedin "several years
ago" as a sop to Iran is a tired falsehood (Lie). Iran itself was
also designated in 1996 by the State Department as a sponsor
of terrorism." Moreover, "both the Reagan and Bush
administrations had denounced the Mujahedin. In 1991,
Clinton's State Department strongly condemned it." The White
House said of the Mujahedin: "Iraq shelters terrorist groups
including the Mujahedin-e-Khalq Organization (MKO), which
has used terrorist violence against Iran and in the 1970s was
responsible for the killing several U.S. military personnel and
civilians."

What prompted the editorial outcry of the Rocky Mountain
News was a full page advertisement in the January 15, 2003,
New York Times that declared "support" for this terrorist MKO
group by "150" congress people, including Colorado's Tom
Tancredo. Actually, the ad listed only six Congress people by
name. Tom Tancredo was one. Mysteriously, California
Democratic Congressman Bob Filner, who rejects claims that
Iraq was a terrorist state and opposed the war with Iraq,
supports this same terrorist group. A Vietnam War draft-dodger,
military shirker and supporter of terrorist Iranians who have
murdered Americans, is Tom Tancredo.

So much for Tancredo being a super-American patriot, a
believable trustworthy American patriot. Lacking any originality

or imagination, Tom Tancredo simply mimics Pat Buchanan's ethnic hatred of Mexicans that was, of course, rejected by the American people in 2000 when his campaign for President managed less than one half of a percent of the national vote. Buchanan watchers can point out that Buchanan's views were not new on the subject of people he calls non-White. As a young man, he was fond of throwing rocks at Black–only Washington D. C. buses. He and his friends delighted in garden hosing down his family's Black maid. Buchanan was expelled from Georgetown University after being found guilty of attacking a D.C. police officer. The officer was hospitalized for the serious injuries street tough Buchanan inflicted on the man by kicking him in the groin. Only a financial contribution, AKA bribe, by his father to Georgetown University allowed expelled Patrick Buchanan back into school. Later, he was yanked off speech writing for President Ronald Reagan on any subject relating to minorities, civil rights or foreign policy relating to Mexico and Latin America. Why, because his speech writing work was antithetical to President Reagan's feelings and policies of equal rights and opportunity for all. Reagan confidantes say that Buchanan's work was pure racist drivel and not worthy of any President of the United States.

The difference between Buchanan and Tancredo is that Tancredo is an elected official, a Congressman from Colorado, while Buchanan is a nonelected commentator and worked on staffs of elected officials. There is one more similarity between the two, Buchanan, like Tancredo, evaded serving in the American Military by conjuring up a suspicious knee injury that his doctor, I repeat, his doctor diagnosed. He claimed that the knee would not permit Buchanan to serve in the Army. That knee didn't stop Buchanan from playing basketball. The result, neither super patriot Congressman Tancredo or super patriot "commentator" and former presidential candidate Buchanan has ever served the United States of America, unlike the thousands of immigrants, noncitizen immigrants, who presently serve the United States as soldiers, sailors and Marines.

Of Tancredo's associations, especially noteworthy is that the Southern Poverty Law Center has labeled—after careful and clearly documented research and observation—several of the groups with which Tancredo associates, as "racist groups." In particular, they so labeled the California Coalition for Immigration Reform (CCIR, Barbara Coe) and, AmericanPatrol.com (Formerly Voice of Citizens Together, Glenn Spencer). Tancredo has spent time with these people and helped CCIR raise money. Interestingly, one candidate Tancredo endorsed in one of the most Republican legislative districts in the country, Jim Gibson, former Marine and a businessman, ran a poor third in the Republican primary for California Assembly District shared between Orange County and Northern San Diego County. Tancredo's coattails appear to be as short as his truthfulness.

In an early 2004 flap, the California chapter of the National Republican Hispanic Assembly awarded Tancredo a Certificate of Achievement for his stand on "protecting" America's border, then withdrew it when they researched the Congressman's public positions on Mexicans, Mexico and illegal aliens. The Assembly was unaware of the Congressman's association with "racist" groups and his broad support among the most racist elements in the country. The group was profoundly embarrassed by this incident and proves that every group must thoroughly research people who claim to "protect" the country. In their simple way of looking at the problem of illegal aliens, the Tancredo/Spencer/Coe cabal asks, simply: What part of illegal don't you understand? To these people, the very presence of illegal aliens will end the United States of America, as we know it. To these people, illegal aliens are the worst problem in American history. Certainly, they think, illegal aliens are the worst American problem today, despite the attack on the United States by Arab Muslims on September 11, 2001. These people equate September 11 with illegal aliens from Mexico who come to work and produce. Mexicans, Arabs, can't they tell the difference? To these people, "they" all look alike. This socially and racially myopic view is what makes these people so dangerous. Despite the fact that the illegals who applied for Ronald Reagan's amnesty in 1987 came from 150 different countries, these people charge that illegals are all from Mexico and that they are sent here by the Mexican government to steal America from its rightful owners, pure European Protestants. Excuse me, the Anglo-Protestant.

Thus, their conspiratorial beliefs lead them to look at any Mexican-origin person, even if a natural born United States citizen as a 5th Columnist traitor more loyal to Mexico than the United States. They classify the Mexican American as an enemy and traitor to the United States. They call Mexican Americans and their friends and supporters, including the President of the United States part of the "Treason Lobby." Tancredo does not object to such characterizations or to the words "Treason Lobby" even when applied to the President of the United States. Example: Glenn Spencer, founder of Voice of Citizens Together and Americanpatrol.com, produced a video tape in which he calls Mexicans a "cancer" in America and blames them for ruthlessly trying to take over the country with drugs.

Like all fanatics, he declares that Mexico is behind the drug problem in America. Like all Mexican haters he charges without acceptable proof that Mexicans are the drug problem. What he does is use a White Iowa farm boy's drug addiction as proof, that it was Mexicans who addicted the poor little 18-year old to drugs. Never does he or the fanatic Mexican haters blame the boy, the junkie. It is this junkie and the millions of junkies in this country, mostly White and not poor, who cause the drug problem. The others simply supply the junkie. Supply comes to demand. The demand looks far more like the Mexican haters than it does Mexicans.

Of course, most marijuana sold in the United States comes from Northern California, Hawaii, Oregon, Canada and

Kansas, according to the Drug Enforcement Agency of the federal government. Further, 95% of heroin used in the United States originates in Afghanistan, Turkey, Lebanon, Pakistan or Southeast Asia. Less than 5% comes from Mexico. This fact doesn't stop the fanatics from calling Mexico a "narco-republic" and blaming Mexico for all of America's drug usage. Tom Tancredo is one of these fanatics. More than one of these people advocate machine gunning Mexicans as they try to sneak across the border, just as Communists used to shoot to kill East Germans attempting to leave Communism. Tom Tancredo does not repudiate these statements thus, logic decrees that he must also believe them. Silence is consent, according to legal theorists.

White Citizens Council columnist Sam Francis typifies this kind of so-called American. At a meeting in New Orleans he declared that the "Governors of Arizona, New Mexico and Texas should be tried for treason for meeting with Mexican President Vicente Fox." So quotes Heidi Beirich and Mark Potok in an article they wrote for the Southern Poverty Law Center's "Intel Report." They also quote Francis as stating non-White immigrants can be compared to "foreign colonizers, like space aliens." Tom Tancredo does not repudiate these statements. Silence is consent. Ross Perot, the supreme Mexican hater of his day, for example, once loudly proclaimed that the Army National Guard should surround Mexican neighborhoods in Texas and that police should search each house door to door for drugs and guns with no search warrants, of course. Presidential "candidate" Perot denied ever saying such a thing when he was running, but the reporters who heard him say it restated that they did hear him make such a statement.

Like Patrick Buchanan, Ross Perot was humiliatingly defeated in his quixotic two runs for President. He was squashed like a bug. The only thing he accomplished, besides embarrassing himself and his barber, was to hand the 1992 election to William Jefferson Clinton. Is it possible that Tom

Tancredo, who is touted as a Presidential candidate by some of the fanatics, realizes that his position is so fringed-out that he skipped running for an open Republican Senate seat created by Senator Ben Nighthorse Cambell's retirement? Is he that much of a political coward? Probably, as he proved beyond all doubt that he is a personal coward during the Vietnam War. Additionally, one must question his political wisdom and judgment when one sees that Tancredo supports international terrorists who have killed Americans. Racial profiling and an unconstitutional trashing of the 4th Amendment to the Constitution (Search and Seizure) are just two ways these people would violate the 38-million or more Hispanics of America. They, like Tancredo, are cowards of the worst sort, racist cowards. The bunk and bogus information these people live and breathe by amazes reasonable people. Reread the Walker letter in the Introduction to see how ignorant bigots think.

Let us look at Tom Tancredo's own words to try and understand him.

Chapter 31

Fanatic Anti-immigrant Tom Tancredo

Republican Congressman Tom Tancredo represents a Colorado suburban area –the infamous Columbine area, actually, that is safe politically for any Republican and contains few Hispanics of any kind, from any economic class. The constituency being almost all White, Tancredo feels free to run amok in his fanatical attacks on the very people who put food on his table. Moreover, when the former teacher who makes more money as a Congressman than ever in his life, spent over a $100,000 remodeling his Denver suburb house, illegal alien workers did the work. Unfortunately for Americans who have read and understand the Constitution of the United States, demagogue Tancredo appears to have never read the foundation document of our entire system and government.

Tancredo leads a small group of congressmen in proposing a gigantic constitutional usurpation that signals a new fascist paradigm that cannot be ignored. Fascist is the correct word to use when discussing Congressman Tancredo. The Tenth Amendment to the United States Constitution reads: "The powers not delegated to the United States, nor prohibited by it to the States, are reserved to the States respectively, or to the people."

Mr. Tancredo and a handful of fellow fascist-wannabes have introduced a bill (Fall, 2003) in Congress that would punish the State of California for violating the Tancredo view that

California cannot issue driver's licenses to anyone it wishes to, especially to anyone not in the country legally. Specifically, he would deny federal highway funds to California. Another Tancredo bill would prohibit airlines from accepting a California driver's license as proper identification to board an airliner in the United States. Perhaps it is possible that Tancredo doesn't know that the legal ability to issue driver's licenses is and always has been a state responsibility.

The issuance of driver's licenses is not a power or duty "delegated to the United States" as explicitly stated in the Constitution in its itemization of federal government powers. It is not prohibited by the Constitution to the individual states. So, how can Tancredo propose an unconstitutional punishment by the federal government against a state exercising its own constitutional responsibility? To properly examine Congressman Tancredo's thinking one only has to examine his own words. One must notice that Tancredo obviously believes that anything he says must be accepted as fact and the truth. He rarely uses objective data or research to buttress his positions on issues. He appeals to simpleminded airheads who believe anything they hear or see about Mexicans, true or not with anything to rely on but his words and opinions that are anything but shortsighted, gratuitous assertions.

Here are segments of speeches delivered to empty chambers of the House of Representatives by Colorado Congressman Tom Tancredo. Though the congressional chamber was empty each time, these speeches were cablecast by C-SPAN throughout the country. Interestingly, the man is such a bald-faced liar that he recounts conversations that never took place, complete with content of those alleged conversations that he fantasizes in his own mind. He doesn't produce tape or video recordings to prove the statements he alleges, nor proof of any kind. Tancredo sees conspiracy behind every cactus. Tancredo sees millions of armed Mexicans lurking at the Border, carrying backpacks full of drugs. Tancredo seems to be unaware that the bulk of all illegal drugs enter the United States by ship, plane or automobile. Every knowledgeable person over 12 years of age knows that heroin from Asia comes by ship. Once, Chinese triads attempted to smuggle in hundreds of kilos of heroin that had been mixed with other materials and inserted into the wheels of power lawnmowers. The triads are Chinese Mr. Tancredo, not Mexicans walking across the border. 12-year-olds also know that cocaine from South America enters by planes or boats, in bulk, and not by backpack.

As only 5% of all heroin used in the United States is Mexican, Tancredo focuses attention away from the real smugglers and on to a patch of desert that is used by minor league drug smugglers. 100% of all cocaine comes from South America; it is chemically manufactured from coca leaves into cocaine with American and German chemicals, chemicals manufactured by brand name companies, so why does Tancredo yell about Mexicans? They don't grow coca leaves, nor process the leaves into cocaine, or into "crack." Why doesn't Tancredo pass laws making the manufacture and sale of chemicals in Colorado and Texas needed to process cocaine illegal? That logic and solution escapes Tancredo. The man is not only anti-any-kind-of-immigrant, but he is viciously anti-Mexican. He proves his deep-seated bias by not attacking American chemical companies that make cocaine possible while attacking Mexican "mules" for carrying drugs in backpacks, even though most of those "drugs" are marijuana, not cocaine.

Here are segments of speeches made by Tancredo for the C-SPAN cameras that none of his congressional colleagues heard or watched. So that the reader understands, let the reader know that Congressman Tom Tancredo may be a Republican, but he is not welcome in the White House of a Republican President. The most recent Republican National Chairman labels Tancredo as a "crazy man." Former Chairman Mark Racicot so declared to me personally. We know that Tancredo manipulated the Selective Service System by claiming Student Deferment status to avoid serving in the United States military. Then, when he ran out of student deferments, he claimed the most cowardly method and manner of avoiding the draft and avoiding service during the Vietnam War—he claimed mental depression and that he had been prescribed drugs. A real man would have served. He did not make this claim when he turned 18-years of age; he only made it when his student deferments ran out because he deliberately overstayed his college attendance time of 8-semesters. In other words, while American men were fighting and dying, Mr. Tancredo was a professional college student enrolling every semester just to avoid serving the United States of America.

During his draft-dodging days as a professional student, one would think that Tancredo would have learned proper English. One would also think that his congressional staff could speak proper English, as well. Such is not the case.

CHAPTER 32

CONGRESSMAN TOM TANCREDO SPEAKS

THE WORDS OF CONGRESSMAN TOM TANCREDO (MY COMMENTS ARE IN *ITALICS*: HOUSE OF REPRESENTATIVES – JULY 14, 2003, [PAGE: H6698]

Tancredo: "Maybe it is something that we cannot avoid that we will be forced, that all American workers will be forced to lower their wages, lower their standard of living to meet the competitors around the word who are competing for these jobs. If that is it, I want somebody who believes that to stand up and tell the American people that is where we are going and they will have to take less money for what they are doing, what they want to do for the rest of their lives, the jobs they are involved in, or become underemployed or unemployed. Maybe they have to sell their homes and get a smaller house and their whole standard of living has to change because of this whole New World economy."

RLC: *Tancredo offers no proof that immigrants are driving the standard of living down. Personal income is up and it is up every year. Consumer spending and confidence is reaching all time highs. The "whole New World economy" is caused by the spread of free enterprise. One must look with askance on a so-called Republican who rejects the free market philosophy that has raised the United States to economic levels never seen on the planet Earth. One must also ask what is wrong with trading with China and India so that those countries, the two largest in the world, can become more and more capitalist and less and less socialist or communist.*

Will American's have to sell their houses because Chinese are making more money, or Indians answering our calls to our credit card companies? Of course not; A rising tide lifts all boats.

Tancredo: "It is pretty simple to understand that if you bring millions of people into this country every single year who have very few skills, that they are going to compete with other low-skilled, low-wage workers in America. And these are primarily recent immigrants. But even those people who have been here for many years because, unfortunately, many times people who are in the minority communities who are stuck in these low-wage jobs, they are the most negatively affected by massive immigration because it is their jobs that are at risk, and it is their wages that go down. It is a cheap labor policy."

RLC: Apparently, Congressman Tancredo hasn't seen the previously quoted studies that disprove that the "minority" community—Tancredo means Blacks, a group he is so concerned about—isn't much affected at all by immigration as a whole. Blacks who have little schooling are affected. But, it is not because immigrants take jobs or keep wages down, but because many Black young men won't work when it is available, or suffer from the crime of being Black in an employment market that has double Black unemployment over the more favored White unschooled worker. The prison system is full of such young men.

Tancredo: "Yet we hear from both sides of the aisle how we need to encourage this phenomenon. From the Democrats who are petrified of actually impeding the flow of illegal immigrants into this country, or legal immigrants, for fear that their voting constituent rolls would be impaired negatively, that the numbers would not be rising as quickly as they would like of potential voters for the Democratic Party, because they fear that political outcome and because a significant chunk of their supporters come from immigrant groups and immigration groups that want to expand immigration into the country, because that is the case, they will do nothing to impede this flow."

RLC: One of the most persistent myths promulgated by people like Tancredo is that Democrats need more immigrants so they can eventually become Democrats when, in fact, Hispanic immigrants usually register 60-40 Democrats and Republicans, not as all Democrats. Besides, Democrats have outnumbered Republicans for generations and have still managed to lose most national elections. Since 1952, Democrats have won in 1960, 1964, 1976, 1992, 1996, five times out of 13 elections conducted since 1952 while Republicans won the other 8-times.

Tancredo: "On my side of the aisle there is this desire for cheap labor. We want to respond to the needs of corporations in this country that have lobbied so hard to get cheaper labor. Well, both of these agendas I think are unworthy of our efforts. Both sides of the aisle should think about something that is far more important than the immediate political future of either party, and that is the effect of this kind of massive immigration, legal and illegal, on the people of this country."

RLC: Wrong, Tancredo. "Desire for cheap labor" doesn't compute with the statement "immediate political future of either party." The country was built be cheap labor, including the labor of Tancredo's Sicilian immigrant grandparents. Cheap labor, as he calls it, contributes to greater productivity because someone must pick up the trash, or do the lettuce picking while others create the Apple Computer in a garage.

Tancredo: "Is it right and proper that our own Nation's borders should be porous so as to allow the flow of millions of people into this country to take the jobs of American citizens, to force people either to work for less money than they were working for just a few years ago or be unemployed, in order to achieve these political goals that I have just described, cheap labor and greater political benefit, greater potential voter pool? I think it is despicable..."

RLC: "To force people to work for less money...?"Are you kidding us, Tancredo? Who is forced to work for anything in this country? In fact, the prisons are full of people unwilling to work at all, much less forced to work. More importantly, the illegals do not take jobs from Americans; they take jobs no one else wants, or wants for a market set wage. No amount of whining by Tancredo or the antis can ever prove that illegals freeze Americans out of jobs of any sort on a massive basis.

Question: How many Americans, white or black, are willing to get on their hands and knees to pick strawberries for a ten-hour shift? Answer: _____(fill in the blank).

Tancredo: "How can we explain the fact that maybe 70 percent of the population consistently tells pollsters that they are in desperate need and they have a great desire for control of immigration, for securing our borders, for even reducing the amount of legal immigration so we can actually integrate those people, the millions that have come in the recent past?"

RLC: Baloney. "Desperate need?" "Reducing the amount of legal immigration so we can actually integrate those people, the millions that have came in the past?" What a liar! That never happened, as we have seen. The shutting down of immigration came only because the Anglo-Protestant rejected Tom Tancredo's grandparents, the ills of Catholicism and the Mafia they brought with them from Sicily. Those Anglo-Protestants who manipulated the Congress also abhorred Jews.

His on-point "70 percent" reflects only on the stupid question pollsters ask, pollsters who predetermine the answers they want by crafting the stupid question. For example: Would 70 percent agree with this question: "When the number of workers supporting Social Security drops below two to one, do you support slashing Social Security benefits to keep it from going bankrupt? Yes or no...

Suppose, then, that the answer is 70 percent no.

The next question—"Rather than see the workforce suffer from old age and a lack of new young workers, should the economy shut down while benefits paid for by taxes be slashed? Yes, or no...

Suppose, then, that the answer is 70 percent no.

The next question—Rather than see Social Security and other tax-paid benefits, such as Medicare, slashed for lack of revenue, would you welcome more young workers into the economy to do the work needed?

Wouldn't 70 percent, or something like that percentage, answer yes? Of course, Americans aren't stupid. They can see that Japan and Germany are rapidly approaching the day when their populations will no longer support their economies, causing, both countries to melt away as economic powers. Does anyone want America to follow their path into economic oblivion? I'll bet 70 percent don't. I'll also bet that Tom Tancredo would argue with me that such could happen, even as the United States native born are approaching 40 years of median age with Baby Boomers rapidly approaching retirement.

Tancredo: "In this Nation's past we have had periods of high immigration, but we have had periods of very low immigration. It has been cyclical. It has not been a constantly increasing pattern since the day the Nation was founded. There are many decades with low-to-almost-nonexistent immigration in terms of the ratio of people coming and leaving, and yet the economy actually grew. In the late 1940s and early 1950s, immigration was a very small percentage of the population growth of this country, and yet we had an enormous growth rate in the productivity of the country and in the economy itself."

RLC: This man certainly does not know his history. First, he is wrong to attribute the economic growth of the 1940s and 50s to a lack of immigration.

The economic growth of the 40s was related to the War and to the lunge in economic growth after the War. Contributing also was the presence of thousands of legal Mexican agricultural workers called "Braceros." The 50s growth came from the burst of energy unleashed by WWII veterans coming out of college and their new families and activities put on hold during the war, by the war. It should also be noted that present in the United States in the 50s were thousands upon thousands of legal and illegal Mexican workers.

There are no decades of low immigration prior to the huge restrictions placed on immigration in 1922 and 1924. Once the Irish Catholics started coming to the United States in the 1830s, immigration grew and grew until the 1920s. Tancredo isn't telling the truth.

Tancredo: "We do not need massive immigration to fuel economic growth. We can point to the areas, as I say, the times in the past where this economic growth has been achieved without massive immigration. We need a time-out. We need some time to actually in a way, if you will, digest the massive numbers of people that have come in and to help them get integrated into this country. That has been the process in the past. But we are abandoning that for the political goals that I have identified here. We are suggesting that we can keep the doors open forever, that our borders can and, in fact, should be erased."

RLC: Borders erased? What an ignoramus! We don't need immigrants for economic growth? Does he think an aging White and Black population will produce economic growth? How do retired baby-boomers produce economic growth on the golf course and on Medicare? How does a shrinking aging work force produce economic growth?

A "time-out," what is this man thinking? Does he think China is taking a time out? Germany, Japan and Italy are taking times out, that is, they have no population replacement by births or immigration working for them, thus these countries are shrinking and will lose their economic power base because they cannot produce growth, nor maintain their current production. Countries that suffer from no population replacement will sink into history as has-been countries that could not survive in the 21st and 22nd Centuries. History will treat them like it does the former Soviet Union.

Tancredo: "Mr. Speaker, I believe with all my heart that massive immigration into this country will not only determine what kind of a country we become, that is divided, Balkanized or united, it will determine whether or not we will be a country, a nation, at all. There are folks who want us to simply be a place on the earth that has residents, not citizens. The whole concept of citizenship is under attack every single day."

RLC: This statement proves exactly what a fanatic this man is. This bilge from a man who opposes the President's suggestion that we legalize workers so they don't have to hide in the shadows and work illegally. The concept of citizenship isn't under siege, most people who come here to work would be happy to become bona fide citizens if given the chance. The concept is fine what needs fine-tuning is naturalization and labor law.

Tancredo: "Constantly, we are seeing proposals, especially on the other side of the aisle but not uniquely from the Democrats, something from our side, too, proposals to have amnesty for people who are living here illegally, proposals to extend all kinds of benefits to people who are living here illegally, proposals to give people who are living here illegally, who have violated the laws of the land to come in, proposals to say to them, we not only will teach all of your children in K-12, we will teach them in higher education at taxpayers' expense, that we will give you driver's licenses, that we will give you social service benefits, and that we will in fact even let you vote."

RLC: Again, what a fanatical speech by a whacked out fanatic. Amnesty? What's wrong with amnesty? As this is being written a taxpayer's amnesty is going into effect in California that allows tax cheats and tax-filing criminals to pay up with immunity from prosecution. As this is written, murderers are walking the streets because they were given immunity from prosecution so they could testify against coconspirators. Millions of reckless and speeding drivers are turned loose every day to threaten the general public with death, as are drunk drivers. And this man complains about giving legal status to working men and women.

As for his gratuitous assertions about "teach all your children" and a "higher education at taxpayers' expense" let me say this: What kind of idiot is this man? K-12 education? The Supreme Court ruled a generation ago that all children be educated regardless of immigration status. Don't their parents pay taxes? Of course they do. Aren't many of these children Tancredo hates American citizens? Of course they are. Taxpayers paying for higher education? Of course, but illegals are taxpayers also, much to Tancredo's chagrin. So, since when do we deny taxpayers benefits they pay for?

The college education Tancredo used to keep out of the military was paid for by, among others, illegals, even if he attended a private college, for they are taxpayer subsidized as nonprofit institutions.

When a child walks into school, no one asks him if his father is a murderer in prison, or if his parents are married, or if his parents are legal residents if he is White. So why even discuss children at all? As Justice Brennan wrote in Plyler v. Doe, 1982, he asked a timeless and Biblical question—should we punish children for "the sins of their fathers?" Or better yet, "We do not punish sons for the sins of their fathers!"

Tancredo: "There are places called sanctuary cities popping up all over the country, and they are telling their police forces in these cities that they are not to cooperate with the INS in any way, shape or form. They are telling people in the community that they can come and vote if they are simply residents of the community, not citizens of the United States but simply residents of a community."

RLC: What an idiot. Police don't want to be immigration officers; they want to fight crime. Ask them. Actually, many chiefs of police oppose laws mandating that their officers become immigration officers. Moreover, where would the money come from to train police to be immigration sleuths?

These cities want their police to police and protect, not to waste their time racially profiling men, women and children.

As for voting, obviously Tancredo is no student of American history. Until 1922, over half of the states permitted noncitizen immigrants to vote by simply declaring that they would become citizens some day. Of course, that privilege was reserved for White men only, not women or Blacks, Mexicans, Japanese or Chinese immigrants.

Tancredo: "We have got to think about what is the effect of the elimination of the concept of citizenship. What does it mean when a nation abandons its own borders? What does it mean when it tells people by the millions that they should attach themselves not to the principles of the United States, the principles of western civilization but they should actually hang onto the political and cultural heritage that they came with and that they came from, they should keep it, and they should keep the language, not become immersed in an English language, not become part of the American mosaic but stay separate and distinct. How does that benefit us if our goal is to create a continuing American society revolving around the ideals on which this Nation was founded?"

RLC: Here we go again, they aren't assimilating. Where is his proof? He has none, because there is none. Most if not all, of the relevant empirical evidence proves just the opposite of what this Congressman is trying to peddle as truth.

Tancredo: "And that is important to understand, that this country uniquely was founded on ideas, nothing else. No other country has that distinction. Ideas are the only thing that holds us together here. It is not culture, it is not language, it is not habit, not custom, none of those, not the color of our skin, not our ethnicity, none of those things do we have in common in this Nation. What holds us together is an adherence to principles."

RLC: This from a man who evaded the Vietnam War by sobbing that he was depressed. Tancredo supports international terrorism in the form of a certified terrorist group in Iran. Principles, he has none. He proved that while millions of us managed to serve the country.

Tancredo: "Mr. Speaker, I think that western civilization is superior. I do. I believe it is superior. I think it has at least as much to offer, and if you do not want to buy that, then consider it has at least to offer as any other culture in the world. There are many things that we should be prideful of, there are many things that are part of western civilization and American culture that we should try to hang on to and fight for. It goes back to that first discussion we had tonight. It is very hard to make sure that you can do that if your own society is being torn apart, being cut up into little pieces, everybody is put into victimized classes and told that whatever culture they came from was better, was superior and they should hang on to it; politically, hang on to it; ethnically, hang on to it; linguistically, hang on to it."

RLC: This ignorance is not backed up by anything other than this man's ignorance and bigotry. The fact he mentions ethnicity and linguistics proves he is a bigot. His declaration that people claim their cultures are superior to America's is as dumb as he is. If those people thought that, they would stay home. I see few demonstrations by such people. I see more demonstrations by Americans against the War in Iraq and from people protesting the current administration than any against the American culture.

Most revealing in these words is what a hypocrite Tancredo is, by his own description; to wit: "...There are many things that are part of western civilization and American culture that we should try and hang on to and fight for."

"Fight for...?" Tancredo escaped serving the United States of American during a shooting war by claiming he was mentally ill, depressed and on medication. Some fighter!

House of Representatives – June 04, 2003, [Page: H4881]

(Mr. *Tancredo* asked and was given permission to address the House for 1 minute and to revise and extend his remarks.)

Tancredo: "Everything has changed on the border. The government of Mexico has decided to move as many people into the United States as possible, as I was told by Juan Hernández, who was the head of something called the Ministry for Mexicans Living in the United States, a newly-created ministry in Mexico. He was at that time the minister, and when I asked him the purpose of such an agency, I had never heard of such an agency before, he said, well, no, it is new, and I am the first minister, and the purpose is essentially to increase the flow of people into the United States from Mexico. I said, why do you want to do that? And he said there are several reasons."

RLC: This is a blatant lie. Tancredo has no witnesses, no tape recording, nor any published statements from this United States citizen working for the Mexican government. If he had never heard of this new Mexican office, he probably didn't know that Juan Hernández is an American citizen and a college professor in his own right.

Are we supposed to take Tancredo at his word that an important government minister would say such stupid things to a wacked out congressman? We can assume, can't we, that minister Hernández was thoroughly briefed by his staff as to who this congressman was and is and what he thinks and says about Mexicans?

Tancredo: "He was very, very candid. I must tell my colleagues I was astounded by how candid he was when he said, well, the reason why we are trying to get as many people into the United States as possible is so that eventually we will be able to affect American policy vis-à-vis Mexico just by the number of people who exist there."

RLC: Again, another blatant lie. No witnesses, no tape recording, no published accounts of such statements by this American citizen named Hernández.

Tancredo: "They have a huge unemployment problem and they have lots and lots of very young people who are unemployed, and as certainly we know, what that means throughout anywhere, any country, it means instability. And so they want to move these people out of Mexico and into the United States."

RLC: Again, a blatant lie. No Mexican public official would dare say this in public and certainly not to an ignorant politician who forgot to mention that this Mexican official is an American citizen with a doctorate and speaks English better than the Congressman.

Tancredo: "Some people would even suggest that there are other reasons, that term "reconquista" is more than just an idle phrase; that people actually believe that they can reconquer that part of the United States, the southern part of the United States, by simply moving people into it."

RLC: Here we go again, Tancredo uses the terms of the fanatics to describe something no responsible Mexican American, or immigrant believes or is working towards. Where are the names of responsible people in the community who speak of "reconquista?" There aren't any. There are a few whacked out militants, a couple of college instructors, but no numbers that are relevant. Tancredo buys into the fanatic Mexican hater "reconquista" myth and it does not accrue well to his intelligence. He, of course, joins the famous Harvard political scientist, Dr. Huntington, in perpetuating this lie.

CHAPTER 33

AN AMERICAN YUPPIE SWALLOWS THE PROPAGANDA

Tancredo's bigotry and lack of true information is obvious, but he is not alone. Similarly, one otherwise bright and educated young man carried on about how tired he is paying for people who don't speak English. He is tired of paying for schools for illegal aliens. He is tired of paying for medical care. He is tired of them taking jobs from Americans. He is tired of ballot information in Spanish for people who shouldn't be voting anyway. How unfair is it to millions who patiently wait through the legal process of immigration, he asks, as if he really cares, this accidentally born U.S. citizen. He believes this is all a zero sum game. He said all this at a large Republican fundraiser. The chocolate-dipped strawberries he consumed with such gusto were, of course, picked by the very illegals he complained about. So were the guacamole's avocados. So were the grapes, the celery sticks, the broccoli, and the cauliflower/carrot medleys scattered throughout the party. The California wines, including champagne-sparkling wine, were made from grapes picked by illegals. Even the tiny filet mignon steaks served with pineapple from Thailand were processed by illegals in Omaha or Iowa, as were the piles of "Buffalo Wings" served to these super-affluent Republicans.

This otherwise bright young man is living in a victim-hood that doesn't exist. If all people are as uninformed as he is, the country is in real trouble. Unfortunately, many Americans are ignorant of the real facts involved with illegal aliens, illegal immigrants, or as the politically correct say, undocumented workers. Surveys constantly show that over two-thirds of Americans are "incensed" about illegal aliens. Of course, few of these "incensed" know how many illegals are in the country, or how much they really cost taxpayers, if anything, or how much they pay in taxes. In reality, they are "incensed" at the word "illegal," not the people themselves, for if they all hated the people, as the anti-illegals do, they would have to hate many people and the many products they produce we all enjoy and eat. Certainly, they eat the food illegals produce, pick and place on America's tables, including those of the people who hate them so much. One must laugh when one considers that if the illegals disappeared tomorrow, food prices would substantially increase.

In Greater Los Angeles alone, food prices could go up in excess of $500 per family, per year, totaling over $2-billion dollars annually in just five counties. This information is based on studies done by the Los Angeles Economic Development Corporation on the impact of the introduction of Wal-Mart Superstores into the City of Los Angeles. Those studies conclude that with a decrease of approximately 5-10% of area-wide food prices caused by competition between Wal-Mart and existing food markets, Los Angeles' families would save $529 per family. Thus, if prices increase by the same percentage, multiply that estimate by 4000 counties and one sees billions of dollars of higher food prices, higher food prices that equate to a horrible regressive tax, the worst kind of tax there is in the system. Even fanatics admit that food prices will increase. They quote studies from the University of Iowa that predict a 3-5% increase in food prices. Those percentage increases may look small and reasonable, but translated into $500 or more per year, per family, and we are talking a giant regressive increase in the nation's food prices. Of course, the Iowa professors have no clue about exactly what will happen if all illegals disappear from our agricultural fields, chicken plants, slaughter houses, mushroom caves, fishing boats, furniture factories, carpet factories, et al. They only work with computer models, not actual experience. So, if one changes just one element of the model, one achieves different results. In other words, I can take their models and show food price increases of 10-15 or 30 percent by a simple tweaking of the input.

What is revealing about wide spread ignorance of illegal aliens is how the masses spout off about illegals not realizing that this isn't a problem just along the border. William F. Buckley has recently written that if one wants to see the illegal alien problem, just look around, for they are everywhere. The illegals aren't all Mexican, Buckley and other informed observers point out to "incensed" people. Noteworthy here are the recent raids by federal Homeland Security officers of various Wal-Mart stores across the country that netted over 300 illegal immigrant workers, most of whom were from Eastern Europe. Isn't that interesting? Most of the busted illegal alien janitors were from Eastern Europe, not Mexico.

PART 4

CHAPTER 34

AN AMATEUR IS PUBLISHED:

Illegals: the Imminent Threat Posed by Our Unsecured U.S. –Mexico Border, by Jon E. Dougherty

This book is promoted with these words on the dusk jacket: "America is under siege, facing a hostile invasion on its own soil that most of its citizens know nothing about: the invaders are illegal immigrants, their battleground is the U.S.-Mexico border, and what's at stake is the money, security, and freedom of all Americans." It continues: "…This book shows definitely how illegal immigration costs taxpayers greatly and threatens the lives of all Americans, native-born and otherwise. It also proves once and for all that our government is doing nothing to stop this ever-growing crisis." "This is the untold, unnerving story of life on the U.S. Mexico border—how illegal immigration is quickly making us all strangers in our own country."

Wow! Can all this be true? Is there a qualified investigative, well-educated, deeply experienced writer who can present this case as described on the dust jacket?

From the dust jacket: "Jon E. Dougherty is an investigative reporter and author of WorldNetDaily.com's special report *Election 2000: How the Military Vote Was Lost. Before joining WND,* Jon published and edited a daily web-based newspaper, *USA Journal,* and worked as an associate producer and on-air personality for *The Derry Brownfield Show,* a top-rated talk radio program. Throughout his remarkably varied career, Jon also spent fifteen years as a paramedic, was a corpsman for the U.S. Naval Reserve and the Marine Corps (Reserve), and served as a flight medic for the Missouri Army National Guard."

Let's ask some questions. How many people read his web-news paper, *USA Journal,* or even ever heard of it? An associate producer for a radio show is usually a board operator or coffee gofer, isn't it? It is not like being a movie producer who puts up the money and runs the show. On-air personality, please. The Derry Brownfield Show is top-rated where? As for his experience, we have these facts: He worked as a paramedic and served as a corpsman in the Naval Reserves and Marine Corps Reserves. He worked as a medic in the Missouri Air National Guard. He is, or was, a weekend warrior. What university did he attend? What newspapers has he worked on? Besides passing out pills for headaches in the Reserves, did he do intelligence analysis, or military operations? Has he served in a law enforcement capacity anywhere? Was he a "spook" for the CIA, or Customs, or the Border Patrol? As a Navy corpsman, what schooling did he have in military weapons, American or otherwise?

Now, let's look at the book.

CHAPTER 35

DOUGHERTY SAYS...

The notes to his Chapter 6, Incursion! – are fascinating. Of 39 notes, we find 9 from an article from a John Birch Society publication. Three are from his employer WorldNetDaily.com. 13 are from articles he wrote for WorldNetDaily.com. Three are from *Human Events*. One from Sam Francis (of the White Citizens Council); Two from the Associated Press; One from the *San Diego Union-Tribune*; One from the *Miami Herald*; one from the *Arizona Star* and two from the Gannet News Service. An objective observer might note that his sources are rather weak and look like they might barely support a 10th grade term paper. In Chapter 9: Bad Apples, we find these notes: 14 notes are labeled "Interview with author." Tom Tancredo press releases are quoted twice. Two of the notes are from FAIR, the Federation for American Immigration Reform, an anti-immigrant front group founded by John Tanton with money from the Nazi-founded Pioneer Fund. Two of the notes are from the Border Patrol Agent Union, the same union that held up the organization of the Homeland Security Department so Border Patrol agents could maintain their union status. There are 36 notes for this chapter, 20 of these notes are from suspect sources. We can conclude, therefore, that Mr. Dougherty's sources are weak and back up few of his assertions with real facts. A 10th grade English teacher would have serious problems with the substance of the notes and how they do not back up his serious allegations. In fact, the notes would simply not be acceptable.

On page 6 we find this: "In June 2000, Fox News reported that the violent assaults against federal agents along the southwest border increased from 156 in 994 to 500 by 1999." Notice he quotes Fox News, not the Border Patrol or any other government agency, why? Because if he had gone to the Border Patrol he would have discovered that the statement is not true. During those years, the Patrol labeled anything on the Border that involved an agent an *incident*. That incident might be a gun shot, a rock thrown, a yelled epithet through a chain link fence or a middle index finger extended by a child in the agent's direction. There is no breakdown in the number of *incidents* by definition. Thus, to use the words "violent assaults" is inaccurate. A real reporter would have found that out. He writes, "Fortunately, it isn't every day that a U.S. agent or, for that matter, Mexican authorities, are killed by incidents (the correct word) that occur along the southwest border." True statement, for only two U.S. agents have been gunned down on the border since anyone can recall. Some have died in car or van accidents and one by drowning in the Colorado River, but only one Park Ranger and one Border Patrol agent has been killed by a Mexican.

How do these words from Dougherty read? Are they original? "One side of the political aisle seems too eager to cater to illegal immigrants and their families for votes, while the other wants to exploit them for cheap labor as favors to corporate donors and sponsors." Where have we seen these words before? The words certainly don't come from an expert analysis by Jon E. Dougherty, a man trained at the University in Political Science. Here he quotes a front man for nationally known bigot John Tanton who funded FAIR, the virulent anti-immigrant and anti-Mexican group. He also funded the anti-immigrant and anti-Mexican Center for Immigration Studies (CIS). He also funded the publication, *Social Quarterly* that was edited by Mr. Roy Beck, the man Dougherty quotes. "Roy Beck, executive director of the policy group NumbersUSA," an anti-immigrant and anti-Mexican group, is quoted as saying, "September 11 was caused in part by our huge immigration system, our system of allowing and encouraging and winking at illegal immigration..." Dougherty uses this quote without a shred of skepticism. How many of the September 11th murderers were illegal aliens from Mexico? None were. How many were even illegally in the country? Two? How many spoke Spanish? Facts are stubborn things, aren't they?

How's this for a reasonable observation: "While America is being overrun by illegal immigrants it can't absorb, it is also being swamped by a sea of drugs for the same reason: Because, critics contend, the will does not exist in Washington to enforce America's legitimate borders." Don't you know, Mr. Dougherty, that most illicit drugs don't come from Mexico? The DEA knows that, where is a quote from the head of the DEA? Despite the well-known facts that most illicit drugs come from South and Southeastern Asia and South America and, recently, Canada, we find this Dougherty statement: "U.S. officials estimate that about half of the $65-70 billion in drugs bought by Americans annually comes through Mexico." That is a blatant lie. What U.S. officials—What are their names-What are their positions—exactly which drugs is he writing about—cocaine, heroin, marijuana, methamphetamine? One more question, how do drugs that do cross the border, or come in by ship, or air, make it through the United States, across thousands of miles of streets and highways, under the very noses of cops and prosecutors, American cops and prosecutors? How, without a pot-full of bribes paid to those who are paid to serve and protect? Does the name Ramparts Division of the Los Angeles Police department mean anything to Mr. Dougherty? How about the French Connection in New York City?

How about this statement: "Joe Guzzardi covered such a case on Vdare.com—a respected immigration and commentary Web site published by Peter Brimelow's Center for American Unity." "...respected immigration and commentary" site? Does this "author" know that Vdare.com is listed by the Southern Poverty Law Center as a hate site? As this is only one of several references to the Southern Poverty Law Center, it must be noted that there are people who reject the Center as a nothing but an ultra-pro civil rights organization. They charge that it does nothing but witch hunt Whites and that, in its history of winning many lawsuits against the Ku Klux Klan and other white racist groups, such activity on behalf of individuals is sheer socialism and radical socialism at that. The claim is that the Center's leader, Morris Dees, is a communist Jew. The illogic of such a position is prima facie evidence that most critics of the Center are bigots and racists themselves. There are few, if any legitimate people and organizations that criticize the Center. The Center, for example, targets another quoted "expert" by Dougherty, Glenn Spencer of Arizona, formerly of California and formally a well-observed target of law enforcement agencies in California.

Here he quotes his own publication and then the famous Glenn Spencer, Mexican hater supreme, a man who speaks at racist gatherings sponsored by American Renaissance and burns a Mexican flag in front of the Mexican Embassy in Washington, D.C. Interestingly, while Spencer, the Mexican hater, was scheming, like Tom Tancredo, to not serve in the American military, to be exempted from all military service by hook and crook, three Mexican citizens had already been awarded the Medal of Honor. Why, for fighting above and beyond the call of duty (Silvestre Herrera, Army; Macario García, Army; and José Francisco Jiménez, Marines).

"...A radical Hispanic movement's dream to retake the southwestern United States is becoming a reality with the aid of Mexican and U.S. policies, according to some immigration watchers," is from WorldNetDaily.com. Immediately following this opinion presented as fact, we have this: "Glenn Spencer, head of American Patrol, a border control group advocating reduced immigration and beefed up border security, says a massive influx of illegal immigrants is 'importing poverty' and growing an ethnic community with greater loyalty to Mexico than the U.S. 'Unless this is shut down within [a few] years, I believe that it will be irreversible, and that it will most certainly lead to a breakup of the United States. I don't think there is any doubt about it."

Neither Spencer nor Dougherty back up these silly statements with any evidence that any such movement can be documented. Of course, they manage to point the finger at another college instructor wacko as proof.

CHAPTER 36

DOUGHERTY'S COMING MEXICAN REVOLUTION

Dougherty writes, "Prominent Chicano Activist and University of California at Riverside professor Armando Navarro says he believes secession of a state or states in the U.S. is very possible if immigration levels continue at a rapid pace." That is not what Navarro says, even in the quote. Read on. "If in fifty years most of our people are subordinated, powerless, exploited and impoverished, then I will say to you that there are all kinds of possibilities for movements to develop like the ones I have witnessed in the last few years all over the world, from Yugoslavia to Chechnya, he (Navarro) said." What he actually does say is that there are "many possibilities" if certain conditions exist in "fifty years." However, those conditions do not exist now, so why would a better educated, better skilled people, many of whom will be intermarried and the children of intermarriages, have cause to secede? Navarro's statement might be visionary or correct if the United States looks like the America of the movie *Blade Runner* and the population is an easily identifiable 25 percent Hispanic population in dire poverty, but chances are that will not happen.

Consider that for every Professor Navarro or Truxillo or even the total of self-identified Chicanos, there are tens of thousands Hispanic-Mexican American business and professional people. They are marrying non-Hispanics, making money, educating their children in massive numbers in

California public colleges and universities, alone (700,000 enrolled in the Fall of 2002). The number of Hispanics in poverty drops every day, even among recent immigrants, as we have seen in previous chapters. Dougherty continues to quote Navarro, "A secessionist movement is not something that you can put away and say it is never going to happen in the United States. Time and history change." Navarro simply has to look at the History of the United States to make this statement. George Washington faced rebellion in his first term of office and had to raise an army to fight it off. Need anyone be reminded that half the country (Anglo-Protestants by the way) rebelled and attempted to secede because the Anglo-Protestants wanted to continue owning slaves?

Dougherty then returns to Glenn Spencer, who says, "...Navarro believes that the ultimate goal for Hispanic immigrants from Mexico is to repopulate and annex 'Aztlan'— the mythical birthplace of the Aztec Indians (California and the entire Southwest). 'I see that as the overreaching goal of the Mexican government and many Mexicans who want self-determination." Has anyone noticed that among Professors Huntington and Hanson and this amateur Dougherty, they can manage to quote only two people, both college teachers, as sources for their dire warnings about "secession" and "self-determination?" Where are the published quotes of Mexican officials, elected or otherwise, who declare their intention to "repopulate" the Southwest? Where are the petitions signed by hundreds of thousands of Mexican Americans and Mexican immigrants demanding secession and "self-determination?"

Considering that there are thousands of elected Hispanics serving at the local, state and federal levels, including mostly Mexican origin office holders, where are the quotes from any of these? Certainly many of them represent constituencies that are entirely Hispanic, thus they are safe for re-election no matter what they say or do. Dougherty actually tries to create the impression that Spencer's non-documented assertions are fact, not opinion. They are opinions only, they are opinions of the two whacked out college teachers and of Glenn Spencer, who has recently been arrested and charged with serious felony charges in Arizona. Take this Navarro quote: "One could argue that while Mexico lost the war in 1846, it will probably win it in the 21st Century, in terms of numbers…But that is not a reality based on what Mexico does, it's based on what this country does." Dougherty then writes, "That rings true. In fact, there are already entire sectors of America that are little more than extended enclaves of Mexico. Spanish is the primary language; 'Anglos' speaking English are sometimes shunned or ignored, even in restaurants or entirely 'American' businesses like Wal-Mart, K-Mart and other outlets." "True," that "rings" true? What an amateur! How does it ring true? Where exactly are the "entire sectors of America that are little more than extended enclaves of Mexico?" Where are they, Mr. Dougherty? East Los Angeles, the Rio Grande Valley, Selma, California, North Las Vegas, New York City, San Francisco, Reno, Where, Mr. Dougherty?

"Spanish is the primary language" where, Mr. Dougherty? Show us the schools where Spanish-only is used. Show us a place where every single newspaper, magazine or television station or cable channel is in Spanish. Even in Mexico all cable channels aren't' in Spanish. In Puerto Vallarta, there are 70 cable channels of which ten are in English or are American. Show us, Mr. Dougherty, be specific as to exactly which Wal-Marts and K-Marts use Spanish-only and ignore English speaking customer. Inquiring minds want to know. At the Puerto Vallarta (Mexico) Wal-Mart Superstore most employees spoke enough English to communicate with English-speaking customers and went out of their way to be helpful to their foreign visitors.

Are we now to believe Mr. Dougherty that Spanish-speaking American Hispanics working for Wal-Mart make up their own customer relations rules so they can ignore "Anglos?" I don't think Bentonville, Arkansas, headquartered Wal-Mart executives would permit such a thing from happening, Mr.

Dougherty. Here he quotes another anti-immigration fanatic, Robert H. Goldsborough, and tries to legitimize the man and quote by identifying him as the "president of the immigration think tank Americans for Immigration Reform."

"The Democratic/Republican sellout to illegal immigrants is pure insanity," states Goldsborough. Which brings us to a definition that everyone must understand; i.e.: the words "immigration reform" are code words for bigoted, prejudiced, anti-immigrant, anti-Mexican groups, organizations and foundations. Immigration reform means no Mexicans, even legally entered Mexicans.

Dougherty actually thinks he's so believable that he writes: "Indeed, criminal activity along the U.S. Mexican border in San Diego County led local officials in the 1980s to conduct a study of arrest rates according to legal status. In the City of San Diego, 26 percent of all burglary arrests and 12 percent of all felony arrests involved illegal aliens, who are estimated to comprise less than 4 percent of the total city population..." The source is one Carl F. Horowitz from the Center for Immigration Studies (CIS) the anti-immigrant and anti-Mexican "think tank" funded and founded by Michigan bigot John Tanton. Superficially, then, the quote is suspect because the source is suspect. On the one hand, the fanatics claim the country is being overrun by illegal Mexican aliens, then states that "less than 4 percent of the total city population (of San Diego, a city of 1.3 million people, immediately adjacent to Tijuana, Mexico)" is illegal. The Center contradicts itself in the same sentence. More importantly, the information they try to pawn off on America through Dougherty is false. It is in fact a lie.

Most Mexican nationals arrested in San Diego are, in fact, legal. The survey that was conducted was of Mexican nationals, there was and hardly ever is a breakdown by legal residency. Determination of nationality is made by a booking clerk at the county jail (the City does not maintain its own jail), not by a sworn officer, or by a federal immigration officer. There is no way to determine legality at that level. The question asked at booking is: "Where were you born?" In fact, of the average daily 5000 county prisoners in jail or in honor camps run by the Sheriff of San Diego County, according to Sheriff Bill Kolender, only an average of ten percent of his jail population are illegals, per day. That would be 500 illegals. At the state level only 12.5 percent are illegal aliens from all countries, according to the California Department of Corrections (March 31, 2004).

So, while it may be true that 26 percent of burglary suspects and 12 percent of suspected felons are Mexican born and, who may be the same people in many cases as burglary is a felony, there is no way to determine their legal residency, period. One must notice that no city official was quoted, nor was any high-ranking police officer, or even a police rookie. Maybe they should refer to a report from the San Diego Association of Regional Governments (Sandag) released as this was written (April 2004). According to this official source, violent crime is down again. In 2003, 4.7 violent crimes per 100,000 people occurred, down from 2002's 4.8 violent crimes per 100,000. Violent crime is what the CIS quote tried to refer to when it stated that 12 percent of all felony arrests were of illegal aliens from Mexico. That was a misrepresentation, which is a diplomatic way of stating the CIS lied, Mr. Horowitz lied.

One must notice also that the statement referred to an alleged study done 25 or more years ago. That's an effort to deceive by Mr. Dougherty. Mr. Dougherty continues quoting fanatic anti-Mexican and anti-immigrant groups and people rather than official statistics from the government or even private nonprofit study groups such as the Rand Corporation. When he does, he misinterprets what they say. For example, he quotes a 1995 study by the National Bureau of Economic Research Study: "Immigrants arriving in the past decade or so are earning less compared to native-born Americans than immigrants who arrived in earlier decades." He forgets to point out what is pointed out in other parts of this book that studies conclude that immigrant-native born comparable wage levels have been widening for almost one hundred years. There is nothing new in the statement quoted. Not quoted is the fact that Mexican immigrants who came to the USA two or three decades ago have higher home ownership rates than the rest of the United States. What is Dougherty's explanation for that fact? He, nor any of the critics, has an explanation for such a phenomenon.

CHAPTER 37

DOUGHERTY SPEAKS WITH FAIR

He then uses other numbers from FAIR (Federation for American Immigration Reform). The Pioneer Fund organization provided John Tanton one million dollars to start FAIR. American Nazi, Harry Laughlin, founded the Pioneer Fund in the 1930s. The numbers are not proven or documented by any legitimate research. Note true science can replicate any experiment or study if legitimate scientists or statisticians use scientific methods.

Here are some of the unproven, phony figures. More important than exposing these propagandists for what they are—liars, is to expose how they mix and mingle legal immigrants with illegal immigrants. Why, because FAIR is against any immigration to the USA by Roman Catholics, Jews, Blacks or Asians. FAIR wants nothing but Anglo-Protestants to come to America, such as English soccer hooligans. From page 71—FAIR "The cost of educating legal and illegal immigrants, aged K-12, in the nation's public schools is more than $20-billion."

Recently, FAIR has issued estimates that illegal immigrants and their children cost $7-billion to educate. There appears to be some disconnect among FAIR estimates. First, why don't they separate out American citizen children from the alleged spending on immigrants? Of course, the most glaring omission in this silly statement is where is the statement and calculations of immigrants paying taxes, the very same taxes native-born American pay, as do illegals. Thus, educational costs must be declared as gross costs from which taxes contributed must be deducted or whatever figure is used is inaccurate and/or misleading. Thus, the claims that immigrants cost $20-billion, or $7-billion, to educate are untrue unless balanced off against what immigrants pay in taxes and how many are United States citizens. The question should be, after deducting school and property taxes immigrants pay from the actual costs of educating K-12 children, do immigrants cost us more than they pay to educate.

Also, what income and tax projections can we make for the future that these educated people will earn and pay in taxes? The other question one must ask—is such a calculation even proper? It is not. FAIR: "Immigrants collect more than $26-billion in Social Security benefits annually. One, that is untrue. Secondly, where is the amount of payroll taxes these people and their employers have paid into Social Security? Also, how much is in old age benefits, and how much in SSI, a fund only administered by the Social Security Administration. Again, FAIR misrepresents. So does Dougherty by publishing these numbers.

FAIR: "Immigration costs local governments $20-21 billion annually." Another FAIR misrepresentation...What governments, for what benefits and costs? Are we to take FAIR's word for it? FAIR: "Nearly $7-billion is spent on immigrants annually in the form of Aid for Dependent Children (ADC) and food stamps."

Another FAIR misrepresentation...ADC is only available to American citizen children, as is the case with food stamps. It may be that parents are immigrants, but the probability that $7-billion is spent on immigrants is not possible, especially when one deducts the taxes paid by these people. This is not a zero sum situation. FAIR: "Between 40 and 50 percent of wage-loss among low-skilled Americans is due to the immigration of low-skilled workers. Some native workers lost not just wages but their jobs through immigrant competition.

An estimated 1,880,000 American workers are displaced from their jobs every year by immigrants; the cost for providing welfare assistance to these Americans is over $15-billion a year."

We obviously are not privy to where FAIR gets these numbers from because they, or Dougherty, don't say. Who can prove that "40 to 50 percent of wage-loss among low-skilled workers" is attributable to immigrants? Some researchers make that claim, but those claims are suspect for when they can't prove it, they simply state that illegal aliens are the cause. Who estimates 1,880,000 American workers are "displaced" from their jobs "every year?" If we don't have 1,880,000 immigrants of working age come in every year, how could that exact number of American workers be displaced? They can't for several reasons: One, there aren't 1,880,000 immigrants, legal or illegal entering the country every year. Americans who won't work are a problem, yes. But immigrants don't necessarily displace that number of American workers. If so, how is it that Orange and San Diego Counties in California, two heavily illegal immigrant counties, officially have less than 3-percent unemployment as of March 2004?

One does not see illegal or legal immigrants flooding into the Rust Belt, or taking over industries at the executive level so they can shut down factories in Ohio or Indiana. No, one sees Harvard-educated Anglo-Protestant MBAs shutting down nonproductive factories thus displacing low-skilled American workers, or sending jobs overseas because America can't afford low-skill factory jobs any longer when more modern and robotics plants in China can out produce the American high school dropout by a profitable mile.

As tiresome as Dougherty is in quoting illegitimate sources, he does so throughout the book. For example, "Immigration is a net drain on the economy, corporate interests reap the benefits of cheap labor, while taxpayers pay the infrastructural cost,' says an analysis by the Colorado Alliance for Immigration Reform." Where is the proof that immigration is a "net drain" on the economy? Where is the proof that corporate interests reap the benefits of cheap labor, while taxpayers pay the infrastructural cost?" And, what qualified people conducted this so-called analysis? We must remind Mr. Dougherty and the "experts" of the Colorado Alliance for Immigration Reform that immigrants pay taxes and that there is no proof that they are a net drain on the economy when one adds up the taxes they pay and the productivity they are responsible for in the individual work place or in the entire national economy.

One must be reminded that any group that uses the words "Immigration Reform" is a fanatic anti-Immigrant group that is not legitimate, reasonable nor qualified to make any intelligent analysis, without exception.

CHAPTER 38

THERE MUST BE A PONY IN HERE SOMEWHERE

Ronald Reagan used to tell the story about the optimistic little boy who went to the barn to look for his Christmas present. A quick cursory look didn't reveal his wished for pony. So he started digging into the horse manure furiously. His father asked what are you doing? The boy responded, I know there's a pony here somewhere. There is no pony in this book. This 282-page book –*Illegals: the Imminent Threat Posed by Our Unsecured U.S.-Mexico Border* by Jon E, Dougherty, overflows with anti-immigrant, anti-Mexican drivel.

The fact that Dougherty managed to write several thousand silly statements and words does not qualify him as a trained experienced observer, for he obviously lacks the experience to properly discover and interpret real facts and to document the opinions of himself and others with objective, scientific substance. The question also must be asked, is this book nothing but a racist screed, tract or piece of propaganda? The only correct answer comes in this quote in the book from an anonymous source, a source that claims to be a man:

"Our borders will never become secure so long as we have Hispanic Border Patrol agents more interested in protecting their people than doing their jobs', says one Caucasian border resident. There are also too many Hispanic politicians meddling in this process and protecting the illegals too."

The only rebuttal necessary here is to note that 37,000 noncitizen immigrants are serving in the American Armed Forces, and that most of them are Mexicans, almost all Roman Catholics. They are the very antithesis of Anglo-Protestants. Most of these immigrants serve in the Army Infantry and the United States Marines. Many successfully fought their way across Afghanistan and Iraq. In the words of one U.S. Marine Colonel Papilla, they did so because they "excel at friction." That is, friction with enemies of the United States of America, the land they have sworn to defend.

Mr. Dougherty, the top echelon of FAIR or the Colorado Alliance for Immigration Reform, Glenn Spencer, the Border Militias, or the anonymous "Caucasian border resident" cannot claim that distinction.

PART 5

CHAPTER 39

Black Xenophobia and Mexicans

Contrary to the myth of a "Rainbow Coalition" promulgated by Jesse Jackson and left-wing Chicano Mexican Americans, Blacks and Mexican Americans have little in common with each other. Black critics of immigration and illegal aliens are numerous and very vocal. This situation is most evident in Los Angeles. One needs to remember that Presidential candidate Pat Buchanan chose as his running mate in 2000 a Los Angeles Black woman who was a member of the notorious John Birch Society, one Ezola Foster. Her candlepower was demonstrated at a congressional committee hearing when a fellow Black woman, a Congress person from Houston, innocently asked Ms Foster if she had attended a segregated by law all-Black college in Texas. Ms Foster couldn't or wouldn't answer the question. She only wanted to talk about the criminal Mexicans who have crossed the border without permission. No wonder one-note Buchanan chose her.

Many Blacks in Los Angeles think that illegals are shoving them aside for entry level jobs and forcing them to move out of homes and neighborhoods they have lived in since the 1920s, where they were segregated by evil White bigots. The word "segregated" is important here because the Los Angeles White power structure strictly segregated housing and employment in Los Angeles through and including the 1960s. The Blacks complain that illegals are allowed to buy homes when they aren't. The truth is that Hispanics, legal Hispanics, are buying up the old houses of south-central Los Angeles by pooling their resources and buying the homes because they believe in home ownership, in contrast to the normal South-Central Black. The truth is illegals can't buy homes with loans from bona fide financial institutions. A further truth is that many Hispanics have high home ownership, especially if they are over 50 years of age, thus fueling the myth that Blacks are being shunted aside in favor of Mexicans.

A buyer must have a legitimate Social Security number just to get a credit report—illegals can't have legitimate Social Security numbers that belong to them. California homebuyers must have a picture ID issued by the state or federal government. California buyers must have active bank accounts, which until recently, an illegal alien couldn't have because he needed a Social Security number and a driver's license to open such an account. Blacks have all these things and still many don't buy homes. Nonetheless, they whine all over Los Angeles about illegals buying homes Blacks have lived in and could have bought for $10,000 twenty years ago.

It should be noted that the Government reports that a record 68% of all Americans own their own homes. Recent studies by California researchers conclude that Mexican immigrants who have been in the United States 20 years or more easily surpass the California average of 56 percent and match the national record of 68%. One Mexican-illegal alien Black critic, Terry Anderson— a mechanic—claims on a radio talk show that young Black males can't get jobs in fast food restaurants because all those jobs are taken by "illegals." He claims he knows one young man who was refused a job because he couldn't speak Spanish. He claims the boy told him the restaurant manager told him that and that his presence would be disruptive among all the "illegals" from Mexico working there. I'm sure the restaurant manager declared that his entire staff was in the country illegally to a stranger. I'm sure Anderson is telling the truth. I'm sure because we all know that not a single Black works in Los Angeles fast food places—not a single one. I guess my eyes lie to me when I'm in Los Angeles.

The problem with Anderson and people like him is that many in the Black community actually believe the drivel coming from the mechanic. His financial support comes from followers of Glenn Spencer with whom Anderson has been allied for several years. One must admit that the scene of Anderson addressing audiences dressed in blue farm yard overalls and whining about Mexicans who he claims are getting ahead of Blacks in Los Angeles is rather funny. He, of course, forgets to tell people that Blacks in California rarely exceed 5% of any county's population, thus are and have been on the very short end of the social and economic scale for generations. Now, instead of blaming the white political infrastructure where the blame belongs, he looks around and blames Mexicans because some are here illegally and he can't tell the difference between legals and illegals, thus, that all Mexicans are to blame. Talk about adopting the master's ways, Anderson is the quintessential plantation man.

Despite the cries of Tancredo, the people who believe in him and his paranoia, and some Blacks of Los Angeles, the coming and presence of illegal aliens is not the worst problem in American history—not even close. Tom Tancredo, the Federation of Americans for Immigration Reform (FAIR), the California Coalition for Immigration Reform (CCIR), Americanpatrol.com and the otherwise bright young man at the Republican fundraiser, notwithstanding, there are many problems in the United States of America, what with almost 290-million people living within our borders.

Illegals are nowhere near the most serious problem in the country.

CHAPTER 40

ILLEGAL IMMIGRANTS, SERIOUS PROBLEMS?

A huge battle is being waged throughout the United States between a small but vocal hysterical clique of anti-immigrant, anti-Mexican people and reasonable people. Though the anti-immigrant clique's immediate targets are all immigrants, legal and illegal, they concentrate their ire on the Mexican illegal alien.

The battle involves a tiny number of people led by columnists and writers not renowned for racial tolerance such as, Pat Buchanan, Georgie Anne Geyer, Sam Francis, Peter Brimelow, VDARE.com's Steve Sailer and numerous web sites such as Americanpatrol.com, FAIR.com and that of California Coalition for Immigration Reform (CCIR), HumanEventsOnline.com, *The New American* (a John Birch Society publication which is on the stoptheftaa.org). Sam Francis, for example, works as the editor of the newspaper of the historically racist white supremacist Council of Conservative Citizens. That group's web site recently described Blacks as "retrograde species of humanity." Brimelow's Vdare.com site has been classified by the Southern Poverty Law Center IntelReport as follows: "Based on evidence compiled by the Intelligence Report, the Southern Poverty Law Center is adding VDARE to its list of hate sites on the Web."

A small number of Congressmen also stir the anti-immigrant cauldron. There are 40 to 60 congressmen that subscribe to anti-immigrant rhetoric who are led by the aforementioned Colorado Republican Congressman Tom Tancredo. None are Hispanics; all are pure White stock, usually from rural or suburban areas. Hispanic Republicans avoid this group; the Hispanic Republican Caucus includes one Texan, three Floridians and one Californian. In fact, only 23 Republican congress people (one woman and 22 men) signed a letter to the Speaker of the House in January, 2004, protesting President Bush's call for immigration reform and legalization of illegals. This is Tancredo's cabal and it numbers but 10% of the Republican majority in the House. In a phrase, they are no big deal. They represent the knuckle-dragging element within the Republican Party that behaves like the Democrats in Congress during the 50s and 60s. These Republicans are like those Democrats who fought against desegregation and insisted on continuing the bigoted Jim Crow laws that they created and nurtured for a century.

Most of the time, the Tancredo-led immigration-reformists try to expound various excuses for limiting immigration. Most simply don't hold water. Rather than have some of these people hide behind the lie that they are for limiting immigration so recent immigrants can assimilate, or that we are becoming too populated, they must be exposed for what they are, uncompromising bigots. They are against all immigration, period, as long as immigration comes primarily from Mexico and the Philippines. They say and write so. These people lay before the public urban myths that are untrue. Example: Illegals from Mexico commit so many crimes that there is a huge crime wave; that welfare offices are choked with illegals claiming benefits; that schools are overcrowded by illegal alien children; and, that, California has collapsed economically because it is so full of illegal aliens.

Crime: Writer Heather MacDonald writes in the Manhattan Institute's *City Journal* that, "Police Commanders may not want to discuss, much less respond to, the illegal alien crisis, but its magnitude for law enforcement is startling. One example: In Los Angeles, 95 percent of all outstanding warrants for homicide to (which total 1,200 to 1,500) target illegal aliens. Up to two-thirds of all fugitive warrants (17,000) are for illegal aliens." Shocking! The only problem with Ms Heather MacDonald's words is that they aren't true. According to the Los Angeles Police Department on March 23, 2004, there are 748 outstanding murder warrants in the City. In the County of Los Angeles (population-9-million) there were 262 outstanding murder warrants in the 6-million person county outside the City with its 3-million people. My calculator shows that there are 996 outstanding warrants, 33 percent fewer than Ms MacDonald claims. Oops!

Moreover, both the Sheriff's Department and the LAPD state there is no way of knowing how many of these are for illegal aliens. That is not known until they are booked in jail and even then there is no certainty in the classification. Ms Heather doesn't know what she is talking about on homicide fugitive warrants. Her claim that "up to two-thirds of all fugitive warrants (17,000) in Los Angeles (city or county, or both) are for illegal aliens" is simply untrue. In the entire county there are, according the both departments, 18,000 such warrants on March 31, 2004, and that maybe 60 percent are for people with Spanish-surnames. That amounts to 10,800 not 17,000. Moreover, both the Sheriff Department and the Los Angeles Police state that before anyone is apprehended, there is no way to discern the legal status of anyone. Thus for Ms McDonald to flatly state that these fugitives are illegal aliens is not factual, for she has no way of knowing who with a Spanish-surname is legal or not legal. Unless, of course, her view from Manhattan is that they all look alike to her. She may assume that if someone has a Spanish-surname they are here illegally. She also assumes whoever told her the fantasy numbers about illegals is accurate.

Lastly, she states that police commanders will not talk about these numbers. Really, I had no trouble. I made two phone calls and sent two e-mails to retrieve the correct information.

Perhaps she should call the office of Sheriff Leroy Baca for information. Oops, I forgot, he is a Mexican American with a Spanish surname, thus she will classify him as a high ranking illegal alien. Ms Macdonald apparently would rather deal in fantasy numbers than the truth. Here, then, Ms MacDonald exposes herself for what she is—She is, in fact, an uninformed, factless, bigot. Ignorants like Ms MacDonald aside, one must grant that of the many problems in the country, the presence and growing population of illegal residents, AKA illegal aliens, is one, but certainly not the largest, or most important.

Chapter 41

Serious Problems, Illegals Notwithstanding

Of the many problems our huge country has, most have far more serious consequences than those caused by illegal aliens, to most sensible people, that is. An example of such a consequential problem is that there are over 40-million people without private health insurance coverage of some sort. For those who are unaware of true facts on health, however, everyone can get medical treatment and some government health plan or another covers everyone. Some people might consider that to be of far more importance than a quarter of that number being in the country illegally. Sometimes, those problem people are one and the same. Legal residency, thus, might solve some of the non-health coverage problem in a two-fer solution as legal employees might qualify for employer supported health insurance.

Certainly, for example, a poverty population that numbers almost 35-million people is more important than the presence of a few illegal aliens who mostly work and are productive. Deducting out illegal aliens under the poverty line, one would still find that well over 12% of Americans are mired in poverty, as they always have been. One must take notice that among the large numbers of homeless on the streets of our major cities, most are desperately poor and pretty much contaminate everything and every place they touch.

One must notice also that during the eight years of the Clinton Presidency, there were homeless, there was poverty, there was heavy duty racial discrimination in hiring and firing, and that Black unemployment was always twice as high as White unemployment and always higher than among Hispanics. Clinton left millions in poverty when he left office, a multimillionaire. He also left dead bodies of Mexicans scattered throughout the Southwest deserts with his unleashing of the Border Patrol in California and Texas.

How does the presence of working illegal aliens keep Appalachia's Whites and Blacks in the perpetual poverty that they have experienced for decades if not for a century? How do working illegal aliens contribute to the homeless problems when everyone knows most homeless won't work and won't even sleep in shelters because it "infringes" on their "freedom?" It doesn't and they don't, and no one believes that it does except for the anti-Mexican immigrant fanatics and some social workers. There is a possibility that one of every 29 people in the United States of America is living in the United States illegally. That is: There might be one illegal in 29 people in the United States, one only. The mathematics of this situation is astounding in view of the emotional highly charged atmosphere so many are foisting on our 292-million people.

Here enters the Pioneer Fund funded Federation for American Immigration Reform (FAIR) a front group for bigot John Tanton, former president of the Zero Population Growth movement. In a report released in April 2004, FAIR claims that, "if legal immigration is not substantially reduced and illegal immigration curtailed, this nation will continue to see a precipitous and continual decline in its middle class—arguable the cornerstone of American democracy." (Http:// www.fairus.org/news/NewsPrint.cfm?ID=2417&c=55)

FAIR's paid researcher Jack Martin says that immigration is killing the American middle class, especially illegal immigration. He tries to prove that by using statistics that show, (a) the wage gap is increasing between poor and not poor Americans; (b) the number of middle class families is declining in areas of high immigration and stabilizing in areas with low immigration. His conclusions: "The analysis and the earlier study of 1990 Census data indicate that the trend of a decreasing share of middle-income households is likely to continue as long as mass immigration and lax immigration law enforcement continue." He writes: "In a society that continues to espouse egalitarian principles and hold upward mobility as an opportunity for all, a growing abyss between the shibboleth and the practice of upward mobility may led to growing increasing resentment and frustration. The growing settlement of foreign newcomers who compete for job opportunities with earlier immigrants and others in the nation's most disadvantaged segment of the population, increased social tensions and conflict mat be expected."

Is any of this true? No. Martins/FAIR's conclusions are dictated by their paid for bigotry mandated by Dr. John Tanton founder of FAIR (with Nazi Founded Pioneer Fund dollars). These intellectually vacuous people of little science have read the script of the Michael Douglas movie "Falling Down" and have projected that fantasy into their reality. We know that scholars Michael Fix and Jeffrey passel concluded that "Immigration has no discernible effect on wages overall. Wage growth and decline appear to be unrelated to immigration—a finding that holds for both unskilled and skilled workers."

Harvard's George Borjas, the Crown Prince (paid by Tanton' Center for Immigration Studies (CIS)) academic of anti-immigration fanatics, writes, "The empirical evidence indicates immigrants only have a minor effect on the earnings and employment of natives." On illegals, he wrote in 1990, "There is no evidence that illegal immigration had a significant adverse effect on the earnings opportunities of the native group." Scholars LaLonde and Topel conducted studies on immigrant earnings and their effect on natives in 1991 and concluded:

"...The entry of Mexican-born illegal aliens barely affects the earnings of natives. A 10-percent increase in the size of the Mexican illegal-alien population reduces the earnings of Mexican-American men by .1 percent; does not change the earnings of black men; reduces the earnings of women by .2 percent. There is no evidence, therefore, to suggest that illegal immigration had a significant adverse impact on the earnings of any native group, including blacks (1990). Http://www.cato.org/pubs/policy report/pr-imearn.html

Martin's thesis does not hold up when compared to studies conducted by James P. Smith of the Rand Corp., perhaps the country" preeminent think tank. One might observe that the quality of Rand Corp. research is somewhat higher than Dr. Tanton's achichinqles (gofers) at FAIR. In a paper prepared for the American Immigration Law Forum (http://www.aistagnationlf.org/ipc/policy reports-2003 succesorstagnation.asp) Dr. Walter A. Ewing and Benjamin Johnson report: "In a 2003 study by the Rand Corporation, economist James P. Smith finds that successive generations of Latino men have experienced significant improvements in wages and education relative to Anglos." They continue, "According to Smith, 'the reason is simple: each successive generation has been able to close the schooling gap with native whites which then has been translated into generational progress in incomes. Each new Latino generation not only has had higher incomes than their forefathers, but their economic status converged toward the white men with whom they competed."

Later in their report, they refer to economists Jeffrey Grogger and Stephen J. Trejo who made the same conclusions as Smith after studying the Mexican American population for the Public Policy Institute of California in 2002. "Smith, Grogger and Trejo reach a number of similar conclusions. They find that 'Mexican Americans experience dramatic gains in education and earnings between generations. On average, U.S.-born Mexican Americans have three and a half years more schooling and at least 30 percent higher wages than do Mexican immigrants." The Grogger and Trejo conclusion is: "...that the 'experiences of second and third generation Mexican American reveal the long term economic prospects of the Mexican-origin population, and these prospects are considerably brighter than what is suggested by critics using statistics that do not distinguish between foreign born immigrants and U.S. born Mexican Americans."

So, who are we to believe, a paid researcher paid to conclude the worst about immigrants, or honest objective researchers writing for nonpartisan think tanks?

Martin's thesis simply doesn't hold up. It might be true that some income gaps have occurred in some areas and that coincidence might explain those gaps. But, in-depth research concludes that (a) the Hispanic population is now weighted by native born, not by immigrants. And, (b) the research clearly shows that native-born Mexican Americans are better educated and make more money than their own immigrant parents. And, (c) we know that immigrant incomes improve with time and that after a dozen years, or so, immigrant incomes bypass native born with similar education.

The most bruising blow against FAIR's Jack Martin comes from Deborah Reed's study for the Public Policy Institute of California, Recent Trend in Income and Poverty report in February 2004. Her conclusions: "The sustained economic growth period from 1993 to 2000 brought substantial income growth for families at all levels of income, but growth was faster at the bottom of the distribution. Even in the recent downturn, the poorest families experienced only small income losses. As a result, poverty in California was much lower in 2002 than it was ten years ago. Moreover, the income levels of low-income families show more growth in the last decade than do income levels of high income families, and income inequality was substantially lower in 2002 than in 1993."

Another factor that leads to a larger gap between the rich and the poor is that the number of millionaires in California has mushroomed in the past decade for the simple reason that the world of hi-tech, of modern and future technology, is headquartered in California. More rich people means fewer middle class for the middle-class is where the rich come from. Significantly, the Census Bureau reports in its 2002 CPS, Current Population Survey) most people in the Mexican American and Mexican communities are not poor (78.2), they are in fact middle and upper class. The poverty figures used by even the paid prostitutes at FAIR show this to be a fact. If they aren't using the 21.8% calculation in the 2002 CPS, that documents the truth, then what are they using? The CPS concludes that 30.2% of all Hispanics are lower-middle class, which leaves a whopping 50% of all Hispanics earning better than 200% of the poverty level, which, by the way, is higher than among the Black population of the country.

As usual, FAIR falls short in presenting studies it claims back up its position that all immigration should be curtailed and especially that of illegal aliens. The questions that beg answers are (1) What are FAIR and Martin thinking and, (2) in what universe do these Klingons live?

FAIR is totally disreputable and has yet to ever tell the truth in any of its studies. Is it $20 billion, or $7 billion that illegals cost us in school costs? Are all Hispanics, Mexicans, in poverty, or are they doing better than the Black population of the country, or even the White population that FAIR says it represents in Appalachia?

CHAPTER 42

ON AMNESTY

Every day 100-million or more drivers violate speed laws in each and every state causing death and destruction in the thousands and costing billions of dollars in damage. Drunken or speeding American drivers slaughter over 20,000 people a year on our roads and highways. Generally these killers are drivers who have been convicted of drunk driving, DUI— Driving Under the Influence, or speeding more than once in our courts but permitted to continue driving. Nonetheless, Tancredo, Francis, Brimelow and their ilk are apoplectic over one in 29 people who might be in the country illegally.

That calculation is drawn from guesswork by Northeastern University academics that think there are 10-million illegals in the country. No one, however, knows how many illegal immigrants there really are in the country. If most of the illegals are from Mexico, as claimed, then we can posit that one in 40 people in the country is illegally here from Mexico. One in 40, yet the fanatics, including the Harvard and Cal-State Fresno professors are frantic that America's White Anglo-Protestant culture is being assaulted and destroyed.

Wildly higher estimates of illegal alien numbers abound in the netherworld of anti-immigrants. Here, for example, are the words of a Mr. William Norman Grigg in the John Birch Society publication, *The New American*: "...the current illegal alien population, which is commonly estimated to be 6-12-

million (but may be 20 million or more)." Notice no source is quoted for the 20-million figure, just the writer's statement. That is how some in the country get information—un-sourced wild-eyed statements by people like this writer (Grigg) and Fox News Channel's Bill O'Reilly, CNN's Lou Dobbs and previously noted Doctors Huntington and Hanson and (probably only a) high school graduate Jon E. Dougherty. Twenty-million? That coincidentally is slightly below the approximate 26-million people in the USA of Mexican descent. In other words, it might be that Mr. Grigg and his ilk can't tell the difference between legal residents, American citizens of Mexican descent and illegal aliens from Mexico. We've seen that even the Pride of New York, Ms Heather MacDonald, who can't seem to tell the difference between Mexicans, Mexican Americans and 100% legal "Green Carders." Or, is it possible that they don't want to know that there is a difference between native-born American citizens of Mexicans descent and illegal aliens from Mexico, isn't that possible?

Of course, as retired career Foreign Service officer Francis Gómez recently wrote in the *Hispanic Link*, there may be up to ten million more Hispanics than the Census thinks. That, for the simple reason the census admits it is never accurate and that its error might be up to 5%. So, the Hispanic population is somewhere between 38-million and 48-million. Mr. Gómez is correct about the total number of Hispanics; probably more correct than the professors from Northeastern who admit to guesswork even worse than that of the Census Bureau. But might these additional Hispanics be illegal, probably not.

Of the element in the country that is anti-immigrant to begin with, there is a vehemently anti-illegal immigrant element that is vocal far beyond its numbers. All one has to do is listen to any radio talk show to hear these people. While not numerous, they are ubiquitous, particularly on the Internet and on talk radio. A small group of them in the state of Nevada has even organized themselves into the "Emigration Party." It numbers four score and 15 people; at least that is how many they claim receive their e-mailed newsletter.

Pithy quotes from these "educated" Nevadans are found elsewhere in this book, the quotes in which they suggest shooting to death people looking to bus tables and pick lettuce.

CHAPTER 43

1994, THE WATERSHED YEAR FOR PARANOIA

In 1994, the anti-illegals and anti-Mexicans scored an electoral victory with California's Proposition 187 in a viciously racist campaign that sickened over 4-million people who voted against Proposition 187. 5-million voted for it, however. Though the courts squashed Proposition 187, these people continue to bemoan that the court "overthrew" the wishes of the people by declaring their pet Proposition illegal. Now, they point to the Recall of California Governor Gray Davis as a furtherance of their electoral ability to chase away illegals. They claim that the recall turned into a referendum on illegals because so many opposed Governor Davis because he signed into law a bill allowing illegals to get California driver's licenses.

It is true that 70% or so of Californians disapproved of the driver's license bill, including 40% of the state's Hispanics. Nonetheless, it was legal for illegals to get driver's licenses for 65 years before the Democratic legislature made it illegal in 1993. Hispanic disapproval of the Governor's action was because he had vetoed similar bills, stronger bills, in fact, twice before, as late as last year when he was running for reelection. Hispanics frowned on the Governor's blatant and obvious prostitution because, as one told the *San Diego Union*, "does the Governor think we are stupid?"

Despite the revolt that threw Governor Davis out of office, his replacement, Republican Governor Arnold Schwarzenneger upon being sworn in immediately started negotiations with Democratic Senator Gil Cedillo to write a new license law that he can approve of and sign into law. While it may or may not come to pass, as an issue it isn't important while new Governor Schwarzenneger struggles to restore fiscal sanity to the state run down by the Democratic Party. Shocked by Governor Schwarzenneger's outreach to Senator Cedillo, the antis continue to beat the drums with petitions, numerous web sites and a massive misinformation campaign designed to demonize these people who, as a rule, come looking for and do find work. They are trying to place a similar to Prop. 187 bill on the Arizona ballot (Protect Arizona Now—PAN), despite knowing ahead of time that the state cannot control immigration in any way and can't deny anyone rights and benefits they are entitled to legally, including the right not to be hassled, questioned or arrested because they appear Hispanic.

The Arizonans who are spearheading Protect Arizona Now have been circulating petitions for six months as of this writing and have less than 10% of the signatures they need to qualify for the November ballot. PAN's making the November ballot is a real longshot by any observation. Recently, the proud sponsors of Proposition 187 have come back and circulated a new petition to place a Son of Proposition 187 on the 2004 November ballot that will require the state to "verify" the legal residency of any and all people in California when they *(1) Apply for Any State Service, or (2) Apply for a California State Driver's License.*

There are, of course, very few state services like, say, a hunting or fishing license, that are not funded in part by the Federal government. Thus, there are few people who would actually be affected by intrusive state employees, unqualified to check legal residency. That, of course, is because this proposal could not apply to any service funded in part by the

Federal government as it and it only can verify legal residence. The rub in this proposal comes in the driver's license. There are more than 22-million California licensed drivers of which one sixth, or so, must renew every year. That is, almost four million licensed drivers would have to go through the verification system each and every year. The proponents haven't calculated how much that will cost and who must pay the enormous costs, the taxpayers or the applicants. One thing we know, the cost would amount to hundreds of dollars per license, far more than the $15 fee currently charged.

Estimates by the California state government are that this proposal would cost the state more than a hundred million dollars annually. Observers noted that the 590,000 valid voter signatures necessary to qualify the initiative for the ballot would be hard to come by with a handful of volunteers. These same sponsors would have never made the ballot with Proposition 187 in 1994 if the California Republican Party had not spent $300,000 on professional signature gatherers. To qualify almost 600,000 valid signatures would require the gathering of 800,000 or more signatures and cost at least a dollar per signature.

Ron Prince was the leader of this effort. He declared in Bankruptcy Court in 1995 that he did not work, did not have any income, did not own any property, did not own a car, did not pay rent and lived in a house with a male friend who gave him spending money. In 1994, he told my radio audience that he took up Prop. 187 because he was a tired taxpayer, tired of supporting illegal aliens. Just one more lie from the biggest liar of 1994. One must doubt that Mr. Prince, a bankrupt Ron Prince, can afford to pay a dollar a signature to qualify his petition for the ballot. Unless, that is, his current benefactor is giving him a larger allowance than he received in 1994. As of April 29th, the deadline for signature submissions, the Prince effort fell 200,000 signatures short of the number of valid signatures needed to make the November ballot. Prince failed, again.

Fortunately for American society, the anti-immigrant coterie seldom has money. The very foundation of the movement is peppered with people like Barbara Coe who was a civil service clerk, or Glenn Spencer who raises money to fight illegal immigration, but spends the money on his own living expenses. Then there is the perpetually unemployed Jack Foote of Texas and his quintessential poor White Border Militia.

CHAPTER 44

THE BORDER MILITIAS

Of late, there has risen a number of "militia" groups that are almost all-White, almost all dysfunctional ne'er-do-wells, who have enviable unemployment records that have cost taxpayers and American businesses millions in unemployment compensation and welfare dollars. These brave men have taken up arms, dressed in camouflage, bought Radio Shack walkie-talkies and hit the desert trails of Arizona and Texas. These border militias strut around "arresting" illegals as they cross from Mexico. That act is illegal on its face, except on private property by property owners.

Of late, however, many of them have been arrested themselves by real law enforcers for attacking, assaulting, falsely imprisoning people and, in some cases, violating federal laws on federal property and, of all things, trespassing, the very crime they accuse illegals of doing. They are almost all convicted or pleading guilty because they are guilty. If their claims of an "invasion" were true, they wouldn't have the opportunity to plead guilty for they would be dead in the desert, shot to death by highly motivated trained military "invaders." Let me repeat, if the illegal border crossers were really "invaders' they would wipe out these incompetents in minutes after any confrontation. Instead, we have illegal border crossers that professional Border Patrol agents admit are usually docile and follow orders by agents almost without exception 100% of the time. When a Border Patrol agent or two come across a group of illegals, they simply order the illegals to sit on the ground while the agent radios in for transportation to deport the men, women and occasional child. They do this without drawing their pistols, without, as a rule, carrying rifles or shotguns. Their authority is simply badges and their orders in Spanish. These vigilantes are around and get much publicity in Arizona newspapers, fortunately for all of us; however, there are few of them. Every day, week and month, more of them are going to jail for breaking myriad laws. With some luck, some might even get real jobs.

The Tucson Citizen reports (February 14, 2004), "The Next time a Mexican soldier sets foot on the small chunk of border property owned by a Ranch Rescue Member group, members plan to open fire, their leader said." "Two in the chest, one in the head," warned Jack Foote, president of Ranch Rescue, a civilian group that patrols in search of illegal immigrants and drug smugglers. He said his group is "protecting the rights of property owners." Foote has recently been expelled from his own group and is suing them to recover his "goods" as the hobos of our past used to refer to their possessions.

The "Mexican soldier" reference is to Tom Tancredo's declaration that "200 to 250" Mexican military incursions have occurred on the border. Tancredo and the militias claim that these are deliberate incursions by the Mexicans as part of their attempt to take back territory. Most of the reported "incursions" are not witnessed by anyone but the reporter, certainly not by two or more witnesses. Usually, they are reports from one person, usually a Border Patrol agent who claims to have been shot at but cannot produce any evidence such as shell casings, footprints or any forensic evidence whatsoever. Generally speaking, Border Patrol agents report "incursions." However, union officials only report these alleged incursions. These same union officials decry any patrol agent working alone. In other words, they wanted more agents so the union could have more members. The world is still waiting to see video tape of Mexican Army troops on the American side of the border. Considering there are thousands of miles of poorly marked borders, one wonders how there might not be some incursions.

One famous incident was photographed in San Diego that showed a United States Border Patrol agent chasing a Mexican looking man back across the border into Mexico and, after catching him, dragging him back across the border, slightly mistreating him in the process. Nothing happened to the agent, despite the photographic evidence. To the best knowledge of most border observers, no video or photographic evidence has ever been presented showing Tancredo's "250" Mexican military incursions into the United States. The Border Patrol union officials are now a dying breed because the agents no longer have to belong to a union, under the Homeland Security Act. Given that fact, the *Tucson Citizen* newspaper reports "four" reported such incidents since 1997 in southern Arizona. Since October 2003, however, Border Patrol spokesperson Gloria Chávez reports seven confirmed incidents along the Arizona border with Mexico. No pictures, no video. Facts, then, undermine Congressman Tom Tancredo, again.

Back to Foote, who told the *Tucson Citizen*: "We choose to fight. We're not going to run away." Just before he was expelled from his own group, Ranch Rescue, He told the Tucson Citizen: "Mexican drug smugglers. Mexican Army. Pretty much the same thing. We're in a border war." In a paper delivered to the Center for Comparative Immigration studies at the University of California-San Diego in October 2003, militia observer Robin Hoover made these observations about the "vigilantes" on the border:

"Vigilantism is ephiphenomenal of the embedded social and cultural elements of racism, bigotry, resentment, and indifference."

"Civil Homeland Defense is run by Chris Simcox…Border patrol intelligence reported to me (Hoover) that Simcox has had some funding from an 'outside' group. Simcox has federal charges pending."

"American Border Patrol is run by Glenn Spencer. We Arizonans certainly want to thank Californians for showing him the highway. This man is, in my opinion, *the most dangerous of them all, because he is a cultural warrior* (emphasis added). He sees things from a Michael Savage point of view: everything is borders, race, language, culture, the whole mess."

Joining Robin Hoover and the *Tucson Citizen* in exposing the Border Militias is the Anti-Defamation league (ADL). In the Spring of 2003, the ADL released a report entitled *Border Disputes: Armed Vigilantes in Arizona.* In the release press release, Bill Straus, ADL Arizona Regional Director, says, "The Arizona border has become the flashpoint for America's far right anti-immigration movement. Anti-immigration groups are engaged in a campaign of vigilantism and intimidation, and their ideology has all the hallmarks of the hateful rhetoric promoted by anti-Semites and racists. We are greatly concerned that the collusion of anti-immigration groups and their extremist sympathizers is contributing tot he growing climate of intolerance, lawlessness and violence along the Arizona-Mexico border."

The report states, "Historically, hate groups and other extremist groups have tried to exploit immigration, legal and illegal, as an issue to gain support and publicity. Anti-Semite and former Klansman organized Klan border patrols in the late 1970s. In the early 1980s, White supremacist Louis Beam conducted paramilitary activities to intimidate immigrant Vietnamese fishermen in Texas. Beam, then head of the Texas Knights of the Ku Klux Klan, urged Klansman to reclaim their country by 'blood.' More recently, New Jersey white supremacist radio talk show host Hal Turner encouraged his shortwave audience to 'kill every single one of these invaders."

On the September 11 attack, the report states, "Racist groups such as the Council of Conservative Citizens blamed the attacks on a lack of American vigilance against immigrants." It includes: "In March 2003, a number of white supremacist groups, including White Revolution, the National Socialist Movement, Aryan nations, the Celtic Knights of the KKK, and the Creativity Movement (formerly World Church of the Creator), joined to hold an anti-immigration rally in San Antonio, Texas, to speak out against 'the tide of illegal brown wretched refuse steadily darkening our land."

"Several extremist groups are spearheading an effort to mobilize armed vigilantes to 'patrol' the Arizona border and stop what they view as a Mexican 'invasion," the report states. The groups: American Border Patrol—Glenn Spencer that the report states, "Spencer did not target immigration so much as he targeted Hispanics, particularly those of Mexican origin, regardless of whether they were immigrants or not (like many anti-Hispanic activists, Spencer rarely differentiates between Mexicans and Americans of Mexican descent).

The report states what this book is all about: "Many anti-Hispanic haters fear, above all, a loss of cultural dominance to people who look different, perhaps speak differently, and who are likely to be Catholic." Does that sound like professors Samuel Huntington and Victor Davis Hanson? Group two-Ranch rescue, Jack Foote's former group. Enough said.

Group three—Civil Homeland Defense. Chris Simcox, a former "teacher" in California, moved to Arizona and has formed an armed group to patrol the border. "Preying on post-911 fears of terrorism, Simcox described illegal immigration as an 'invasion' and part of a larger conspiracy against American security.... There's something very fishy going on at the border. The Mexican army is driving American vehicles (Hummers)—but carrying Chinese weapons. I have personally seen what I can only believe to be Chinese troops." Never having served in the United States of America military,

Simcox has problems identifying the American M-16 rifles used by the Mexican Army or the Belgian automatic rifles they use as automatic weapons. More interesting is how Simcox can't tell the difference between Mexicans and Chinese. Most other people can. The federal government charged Simcox with violating federal weapons laws.

On April 30, 2004 Simcox was sentenced to two years probation by a federal court after being found guilty of two federal misdemeanors. He was also fined $1000 and prohibited from owning or carrying any firearms during his probation.

CHAPTER 45

HOW MANY MAKE IT, ILLEGALLY?

Immigration, legal and illegal, has big numbers, but, while we have a handle on legal immigrants, we have no idea how many illegals come into the United States across the border on foot, or how many simply overstay their legal visas. No one knows. Anyone who states unequivocally that they know how many illegals there are in the country is simply misstating the facts, for there are no real numbers, only guesses. Nonetheless, based on apprehension statistics of the old Border Patrol, we can posit that approximately 10,000 people a day used to try to slip into the country across the Mexican border. The Border Patrol reported that they apprehended about one in three people who attempted to cross the border. The Public Policy Institute of San Francisco estimates that about 300,000 illegals who cross every year stay, while 700,000 return home to Mexico or Central America. In other words, about a million illegals cross into the United States in a year, not millions as the antis claim.

The Public Policy Institute guesses a million and that estimate has been recently supported by a study conducted by the Mexican government itself. As we shall see, however, there are people who wildly exaggerate the number of illegals.

PART 6

Chapter 46

Fantasizing Fanatics on the Internet

Here are two articles from the PhoenixNews.com website (reprinted by permission) and some posted responses that clearly expose most anti-immigrant, anti-illegal fanatics for what they are, exaggerators of small kernels of truth, liars and true believers in urban myths. These are the same myths believed by academics Dr. Samuel P. Huntington and Dr. Victor Davis Hanson, which demonstrates how ridiculous these two so-called educators are in scope and intellectual development. In the words of my long-departed hero admiral, a man is judged by the company he keeps or keeps him.

My comments are in *italics*. By permission from PHX.COM—Immigration reform bill a necessity. Posted by PHX – U.S. Rep. Jim Kolbe on Thursday October 30, 2003 at 11:36 pm MST

The nation could be significantly relieved of the financial burden incurred while caring for illegal immigrants if a bill I have recently introduced along with two other members of the Arizona congressional delegation is passed. The Border Security and Immigration Improvement Act deals with very complicated issues. However, it has come at an appropriate time: Last month, the number of illegal immigrant deaths in Arizona in 2003 surpassed last year's record of 145. This is a sobering statistic and adds urgency to our fight to reform our current immigration system. There are three main reasons why I have introduced this bill:

First, each year the federal government uses enormous amounts of resources to attempt to prevent the border crossing of hundreds of thousands of illegal immigrants. The fact is, the vast majority of those crossing the border are merely seeking a better life for themselves and their families.

We need a legal structure for those who wish to enter the U.S. to work at jobs that no American wants. Such a system will shift 99 percent of the crossings from everywhere along the 6,000- mile northern and southern land borders to a few ports of entry, where they can be managed and screened. This change in policy would allow the Border and Transportation Security Directorate to focus its border resources on criminals and terrorists, dramatically improving the security of our nation.

Second, we will face a very serious labor shortage in the future. As baby boomers get older and Americans become more educated and skilled, fewer people will take on manual or unskilled jobs such as dishwashing or house cleaning. We as a nation need to recognize that it is difficult to find Americans who are willing to do these types of jobs that are vital to the health of our economy. This is where a temporary worker program comes in. Unfortunately, with the exception of a small number in the agriculture industry, we have been haphazard in the way we use these programs. Third, any immigration reform bill must deal with the illegal immigrants currently living in the United States. Those who are not public charges, do not have a criminal record and are not terrorist suspects must be offered an incentive to seek a legal status – both for the security of our nation and to ensure that they are not exploited by their employers.

To address these realities, our bill creates two new visa categories. The H-4A is for foreign workers currently outside of the country who wish to work within the United States. This process begins when an employer posts job openings on a newly created Electronic Job Registry. The listing of an individual job is open to U.S. workers for only two weeks, and if no qualified U.S. worker has expressed interest in that time, the listing is then opened to foreign workers. If a foreign worker is interested in the job and is qualified, the employer can pay a fee and petition for that foreign worker to be brought into the country on an H-4A visa. The visa is valid for three years, and may be renewed one time, for a total of six years. After three years in the program, the worker may petition for legal permanent residence. At the end of six years, the worker must either be in the process of applying for permanent status or return to their home country.

The H-4B is a vehicle by which illegal workers who entered the U.S. before Aug. 1, 2003, can obtain a legal status through a penalty period and the payment of a fine. The H-4B immigrant worker must pay $1,500, which goes to offset the costs of implementing and processing the visa program. The H-4B immigrant worker is also responsible for the administrative costs of the application. The H-4B visa is valid for three years and is nonrenewable. After three years in the H-4B program, the worker may enter the H-4A program and begin that process. Since introducing the bill, Rep. Jeff Flake, Sen. John McCain and I have been attacked by both pro- and anti-immigration groups. We have no doubt there will be significant hurdles in moving this bill along. But as the death toll in the desert climbs and our economy suffers from lack of workers, we are reminded that we cannot give up. This is too important.

Responses by Arizona Readers:

Traitors (Score:1) By *Dalgast* on Friday October 31, 2003 at 9:35 am MST

I hope you have the balls to read this but I doubt it. You are nothing more than a traitor to your country, as are those that side with you. You are a liar, jobs that Americans don't or won't do. You are a coward, you hide behind your politician status.

Why don't you come out and face a group of out of work U.S. citizens. You better take heed, this country is heading for a revolution. When your covered in hot tar and feathers see if your illegals come to you aid. At the very least, there are people out here that will certainly remember your actions and won't vote for you again. And since your nothing but a vote whore that ought to help change your mind, then again your relying on your illegal votes aren't you. As a retired veteran, You and your cohorts disgust me.

RLC: Calling anyone who proposes a solution, even a partial solution to the problem of illegal aliens, including a congressman and sometimes the President of the United States, a traitor is the favorite way fanatics have of attempting to win their arguments. They never have responsible suggestions to solve the problem other than to roundup arrest and deport illegals. A "vote whore?" The congressman comes from an almost all-white district, a district with fewer Hispanics than the districts of his two Arizona Democratic Hispanic colleagues, Pastor and Tejada.

What revolution? People in both parties are trying to solve the illegal alien problem in the Congress. The only revolutionaries seem to be ignorant illiterates who form vigilante groups and toss garbage in congressional offices. As for facing "out of work" Americans, Congressmen do every two years at the ballot box. Moreover, there aren't that many out-of-work Americans to begin with in the western United States, especially in Arizona. In fact, there are a record number of 134-million or more Americans working today, more than even in the booming 90s.

You need more garbage at your offices (Score: 0)

By Anonymous on Friday October 31, 2003 at 11:46 am MST think I said all that needs to be said–just as long as you go with the rubbish when they pick it up.

RLC: Since "anonymous" is too cowardly to sign his name, the only comment necessary is to report that some of the fanatics dumped garbage in the Arizona office of the

Congressman after he introduced the bill in Congress along with Senator John McCain.

Migrant Worker Bill (Score: 0)

By Anonymous on Friday October 31, 2003 at 5:03 pm MST

America has always had problems assimilating their immigrants into our society, whether legal or not. Much of the rhetoric (sic) has always bordered on that that I read by Mr. Anonymous. Through all of this our country has prospered, not in spite of immigrants, but because of them. They fill a need. But even if they didn't, the reality is that they are here, they are coming and we must do something about it. The present situation is out of hand and intolerable.

The Kolbe, McCain and Flake bill addresses an orderly process of dealing with what is now a disorderly process. The only thing that I would add to the Kolbe outline, would be to prohibit felons from remaining, renewing or becoming citizens. It has been talked about since I was President of the State Senate, but it was never addressed in such a practical manner. It is certainly a start in the right way. Thank you for daring!!

Leo Corbet

RLC: *There appears to be some sanity in Arizona. Corbet is a Republican.*

Re: Migrant Worker Bill (Score: 0)

By Anonymous on Friday October 31, 2003 at 7:24 pm MST Which "process" are you talking about Mr. Corbet? Is it the process of lowering wages and benefits for all working americans (sic)?

Is it the "process" of overpopulating the United States of America with people who refuse to learn the language or haven't been screened for infectious diseases?

Is it the "process" of lining your pockets with money from what amounts to slave labor?

Is it the big prize you are after, the "process" of destroying the greatest country the world has ever known?

I would love to witness the "process" of Kolbe being covered in hot tar and feathers and then laid atop the heap of S**T at Arizona's southern border.

RLC: What part of legal doesn't "anonymous" understand? The primary complaint of the fanatics is that illegals are illegal. Thus, one would expect that when a process for legalization is put forward for implementation, anti-illegals would be mollified. They are not. Once the issue of legal is settled, they bring up overpopulation. Then they bring up wage, benefits and living standards. Then they bring up "slave labor." Then they revert back to treason and "destroying the country." Then, they advocate violence. "Anonymous" represents the worst elements of American fanaticism, xenophobia and, of course, cowardice. There wasn't one single fact in his tirade. There rarely are.

Arrest all illegal aliens, don't hire them (Score: 0)

By Anonymous on Friday October 31, 2003 at 10:41 pm MST

RLC: *"Anonymous" posts this reprint of an article written by professional anti-immigrant FAIR, the Federation for Americans Immigration Reform. Dr. John Tanton founded this group. He is a former hot shot in Zero Population Growth. He raised the founding funds for FAIR and the Center for Immigration Studies (CIS) from the Pioneer Fund, an organization founded by American Nazi Party founder, Harry Laughlin. The Pioneer Fund funds such laudatory research as a study to correlate Black male penis size to crime rates. No accredited university in the country solicits or receives funds from this group, the very one that funded FAIR and CIS, two groups that hold themselves up as legitimate organizations with legitimate views of immigration.*

October 31, 2003

Why Amnesty Isn't the Solution

Federation for American Immigration Reform http://
www.fairus.org/news/NewsPrint.cfm?ID=1185&c=13

October, 2002

In 1986, Congress passed the Immigration Reform and Control Act (IRCA) giving amnesty – legal forgiveness – to all illegal aliens who had successfully evaded justice for four years or more or were illegally working in agriculture. *As a result, 2.8 million illegal aliens were admitted as legal immigrants to the United States. In addition, they have so far brought in an additional 142,000 dependents. _Various Amnesties of Illegal Aliens IRCA (including dependents) 2,831,351 NACARA 405,000 Haitian Act 50,000 INA Section 249 (from 1987-1997) 69,670*

Total: 3,356,021

The amnesty permanently added millions of poor to our society.

RLC: *Wrong. Most of the amnestied illegals weren't poor when they were legalized. In fact, the amnesty law required that amnestees be in the country for a minimum of five years prior to the amnesty date. Thus, assuming at least five years in the country and, presumably, working, one can estimate that few of these long time residents were in poverty. This article suggests they regressed. The loudest complaint was that the agricultural workers who were amnestied didn't stay in agriculture but rather moved on to better jobs. Perhaps most galling to FAIR and its supporters is the fact that former United States Senator Pete Wilson personally introduced the bill that amnestied the agricultural workers. Yes, the same Pete Wilson who, as Governor of California, campaigned for the infamous Proposition 187.*

An Immigration and Naturalization Service study found that after ten years in the United States, the average amnestied illegal alien had only a seventh grade education and an annual salary of less than $9,000 a year. (1)

RLC: *The study referred to is silly and the statement totally wrong. To be amnestied by the 1986 IRCA, one had to be an adult over the age of 18. Anyone under 18 had to be granted legalization under separate rules. Thus, to suggest that amnestied people after 10 years still had a 7th grade education profoundly misrepresents the fact that hard-working adults, most of who had been in the United States for years, if not decades, would not drop their jobs to attend school, or to attend school at night. Thus, the conclusion is bogus.*

Unlike immigrants with a sponsor who guarantees they will not become a burden on the public, when Congress enacts an amnesty, it makes the American public financially responsible for those amnestied. The cost of amnesties to the American taxpayer is staggering. According to a study by the Center for Immigration Studies, the total net cost of the IRCA amnesty (the direct and indirect costs of services and benefits to the ex-illegal aliens, minus their tax contributions) after ten years comes to over $78 billion. (2) . . .

RLC: *The CIS (A Tanton financed anti-immigrant front group) conclusion is false. It suggests that costs of amnestied people amounted to $78-billion. In fact, that is a lie. The State of California ran its own study and concluded that after 5-years only 5% of amnestied people were using social benefits. As California is home to many of the amnestied, the State is the best source of data on amnestied people. To suggest as the CIS does, for example, that any money spent to educate the children of amnestied is somehow a cost, is bogus and a con job. And, as usual, the antis at the CIS and other places always state that illegals and the amnestied don't pay taxes, or, if they do, don't pay enough. That, too, is a lie and a con job.*

For example, CIS refuses to believe that illegals pay school taxes, thus draining resources from legal resident children. False. If an illegal pays rent, the rent includes the property taxes that support schools. To state otherwise is a lie. To promote the idea that what taxes they pay aren't enough is also a misrepresentation of fact. No homeowner ever pays *enough to educate one child, unless the home owned is worth more than a million dollars. In California, for example, one pays one percent of the sales price (adjusted by 2% upward every year) in property taxes. Half of that goes directly to schools. Property tax on a $350,000 purchase amounts to $3500 a year. Half of that would be $1750 for the year. The current cost to educate one K-8 child in California is over $7,000, thus the $1750 paid doesn't come close to paying for one child's education. Thus, the CIS and other groups who make the claim illegals—or amnestied people—don't pay enough to educate a child, much less multiple children, are guilty of a blatant misrepresentation of the factual situation. If the study referred to had been made by the Census Bureau, or a University, one might be taken aback by the study's conclusions. But, as it was done by the Tanton-sponsored front group, the Center for Immigrations Studies with its goal to reduce legal immigration to a tiny White European base, one must discard the study as trash.*

Amnesty disguises the extent of illegal immigration. Apologists for illegal immigration have actually had the nerve to claim that, because the number of illegal immigrants living in the U.S. today (between 8.7 and 11 million) is about the same as the number living here ten years ago, illegal immigration must not be that big of a problem. In doing so, they rely on the public's forgetting that, without the amnesty, there would be closer to 12 or 14 million illegal aliens in the country. It's akin to pardoning and releasing everyone in prison, then claiming there is no crime problem because the prisons are empty.

RLC: *Wrong. The Public Policy Institute of San Francisco reports that its study of illegal's ingress and egress from the country concludes that while 70% of illegals returned to Mexico within 7-years prior to 1996, that figure no longer applies because of tighter border enforcement. Such enforcement makes it more difficult to return to Mexico even for Christmas holidays, a traditional passage over the years, and then to return to their American jobs. The entry of criminal* *alien smugglers into cross-border passage has raised the traditionally no cost border crossing, thus making it extremely costly to cross the border. The result is fewer people returning to Mexico, thus increasing the numbers of those who stay permanently every year. Of course, FAIR and the CIS rarely mention that almost half of all illegal aliens in the country come into the country legally to begin with and overstay their legal visits. American Consular officials in their home countries interview these people and issue the visas. These interviews obviously aren't very effective.*

Free market forces discount any FAIR/CIS conclusion that without the 1986 amnesty there might be millions more illegals in the country. The free market decides how many illegals come. No jobs, no illegals come. For example, if there are ten million jobs unfilled by American workers who don't want those jobs or the pay that comes with them, people will come north to take those jobs, not 15-million, not 20-million, but just enough to fill open jobs.

When there are few jobs, few Mexicans will come. Life is hard enough on those who can find work. No jobs, no one comes. An amnesty sends the message that it is okay to break the law. An amnesty says that eventually you will be forgiven, even rewarded, for breaking the law. Furthermore, it makes a mockery of the legal immigration process, wherein those who obey the rules wait years to immigrate (instead of "jumping the line" and hoping for absolution later).

RLC*: What baloney! Every day in the United States, District and U.S. Attorneys, and judges grant immunity to criminals for testimony that puts other criminals in prison. Few illegals aspire to amnesty in the future, they only hope to get through the day without being arrested and deported. As this is written (April 2004), California is implementing a tax amnesty for California taxpayers that have not filed state income tax forms, or cheated on their filings. No penalties will be assessed and no criminal charges will be filed on those taking advantage of the amnesty. The amnesty of illegal aliens* *skews the average educational and skill level of legal immigrants downward.*

As the ex-illegal aliens naturalize and become U.S. citizens, they are able to petition for their relatives to join them here as immigrants. Each one will be able to sponsor parents and brothers and sisters as immigrants. Naturally, the profile and characteristics of the relatives will be similar to their sponsoring immigrant-which, as was noted above, will detract from the high-skills, high-education, high-wage economy we are aiming for in the 21st century.

RLC*: Wrong, again! Where is the study that proves their view that anyone amnestied people petition to bring to the country legally are of the same educational and economic level as the amnestied? It maybe a good guess, but that's all it is. Notice they didn't quote even a phony study. It is just a conclusion, a stereotype and caricature, they promulgate as part of the urban myth that all Hispanics are lacking education, even those who are born and raised in the U.S.A. The statement "Naturally, the profile and characteristics of the relatives will be similar to their sponsoring immigrant..." totally exposes the basic bigotry of the writers and sponsors of this article.*

Amnesty has set a dangerous precedent. The 1986 IRCA amnesty has created the atmosphere for illegal aliens' home governments to push our government toward another amnesty or other forms of legal "forgiveness. " Mexico's President Vicente Fox began in 2001 to push the United States to "regularize" the status of the estimated three to six million illegal aliens from Mexico in this country. Those who profit from illegal immigration have jumped on the bandwagon and political pressure is building to repeat what was billed in 1986 as the first and last amnesty for illegal aliens. Amnesty threatens homeland security. Aliens who apply in the home countries to become legal immigrants to the United States are screened by U.S. consular officials to weed out any criminals or likely terrorists. Millions of illegal aliens in the U.S. have evaded this screening; amnesty would make them legal aliens without the necessary safeguards to ensure that they are not dangers to our national security. No Stealth Amnesty! [Guest Worker Programs] Since 1986, Congress has already passed 7 amnesties for illegal aliens. The 1986-amnesty program cost $78 billion to American citizens in services and benefits, about $26,000 per legalized immigrant.

RLC: *Wrong conclusion of a bogus study. In fact, it is a FAIR lie.*

Currently, at least 1.5 million legal and illegal immigrants arrive in the United States each year. Under President Bush, at least 2.5 million immigrants, legal and illegal, entered the United States and 2.7 million factory jobs vanished. One out every five Mexicans in the world now lives in the U.S.

RLC: *"2.7 million factory jobs vanished." Here is a leap in logic, what would legal immigrants have to do with jobs disappearing to technology, productivity and offshore factories in China? The statement "One out of five Mexicans in the world now lives in the U.S." is false and really pretty stupid. There are approximately 110-million people in the world who are of Mexican nationality or people descended from Mexicans who are citizens of their respective countries. In other words, if they are citizens of the United States, for example, they aren't Mexicans. Only Mexican nationals can be counted. One in five would amount to almost 25-million Mexicans living in the United States. After all, the 2000 Mexican census reported 97-million Mexicans, total. So, how could 20% of all Mexicans live in the United States? They don't and can't. FAIR lies again. This observation is another example of bigoted stereotyping. All Mexicans look alike, I guess, to the cowardly "anonymous."*

There are Nearly 800,000 illegal aliens are believed to be residing in Arizona. Estimates are that nearly 70% of Mexicans in the U.S. are illegal aliens. There are more illegal aliens in America than the entire population of Arizona. The number of illegal aliens in this country is approximately: 12 million. The number of Americans who cannot find full time jobs: 12 million.

RLC: *Best estimate of the number of illegals in Arizona is around 200,000, not 800,000 as estimated by "anonymous." That number he touts is interesting because the 2000 Census reported that there were 792,725 Hispanics in Arizona. Seems he views all Hispanics as being illegal immigrants, period. He doesn't seem to differentiate between legals and illegals. What else is new? His statement that "Estimates are that nearly 70% of Mexicans in the U.S. are illegal aliens is not only a lie, but a big lie. Mexicans make up the largest number and percentage of legal immigrants, plus amount to only about 60% of all illegal aliens, thus numbering, perhaps, 5-6-million, about a third of all Mexican origin people in the U.S. The number of illegal aliens in the country is probably far less than 12-million. No one with legitimacy estimates 12 million illegals in country or that all illegals are Mexican. There are not 12-million Americans who cannot find full-time jobs, period. There are some, of course, but if they can't find full-time jobs, how is it that illegals that can't speak English and must look over their shoulders every minute of every day for "la migra," and don't have legitimate Social Security cards, manage to find work?*

Nationally, nearly half of all people charged with federal drug offenses between 1984 and 1999 were "Hispanic," Approximately 65 percent of all the cocaine that enters this country from Mexico, and the majority of marijuana comes in from Mexico.

RLC: *"Half of all people charged with federal drug offenses between 1984 and 1999 were "Hispanic," is a ridiculous statement to make. Are all "Hispanics" illegals from anywhere? Of course not. The statements "65 percent of all cocaine that enters this country. And the majority of marijuana comes in from Mexico," are incomplete or false. No cocaine comes from Mexico; it all comes from South America. Some comes through Mexico, but as much comes in by air or ship directly from South America. As for marijuana, the joke is on* *"anonymous" for most marijuana sold in the United States is grown here in the United States. Marijuana is the largest cash crop in Hawaii and maybe also in California. Most marijuana grown in California is grown in Northern California and is grown and sold by White non-Hispanics, much less Mexicans. Recently, Canadians have begun smuggling white Canadian grown marijuana into the United States.*

Billions of dollars worth of illegal drugs come through Maricopa County each year. In Pinal County, Hispanics make up 5.4 percent of the total population, but they accounted for 46 percent of drug trafficking arrests in 2002. 90 percent of the meth (methamphetamine) manufactured in this country is manufactured by Mexican national (Mexican non-U.S. citizen) drug organizations."

RLC: *"Billions of dollars worth of illegal drugs" do not go through Maricopa County (Phoenix). "Billions" hardly even come into the entire United States, though the anti-Mexican fanatics claim that $65-70 billion dollars is sold in the USA. Retail values, however, are far more than the value actually shipped in. Methamphetamine production and distribution has always been a non-Hispanic White activity. It is noted that some Mexican drug gangs have entered the meth market, but certainly not 90%.*

Call write and fax your members of Congress and DEMAND that they stop the invasion of illegal aliens, arrest and deport all illegals in the country and tell them NOT to support any "guest worker" (stealth amnesty) programs for illegal aliens. The last thing this country and Arizona needs is more immigrants, legal or not. Congress toll free: 1-888-355-3588 White House toll free: 1-800-321-8268

Arrest & Deport All Illegal Aliens Now!

RLC: *This person and the people who believe like him hate all immigration and lump legal in with illegal, as they do legal Hispanics and illegals from Mexico. The shock of it all is that Anonymous may be your next-door neighbor.*

Hey Rep. Kolbe ! (Score:1)

By opinionated on Saturday November 1, 2003 at 9:28 am MST

I'm a legal immigrant and now a U.S. citizen. It took me seven hard years to fight my way legally through all the INS Catch-22's to get into the USA, so I understand why people come here illegally.

I hope you read the foregoing posts in this thread (ignoring Mr. Corbet) because they contain the facts and logic that seem to have escaped the political class.

Only two minorities support your position and you continue to be timid to confront either of them:

Leftist who will sell out our American sovereignty (sic) for the illegal vote;

Conservatives who will sell out our American sovereignty to avoid paying living wages to Americans.

Two solutions:

Enforce *existing* immigration laws passed after the *last* amnesty you granted – *no more phoney amnesty solutions; jail time for illegal employers; deportation for aliens who illegally cut in line.* If you can't find the political capital for that, then at least *Demand Reciprocity* from foreign governments as a condition for relaxing U.S. immigration restrictions against their citizens coming here. For example: *On November 4th, I dare you to ask Vicente Fox why his Mexican Government doesn't extend the same rights to Americans who want to live and work in Mexico as he demands that we extend to his citizens who want to live and work here?* Why not quit fawning to the powerful (but still minority) interests a. and b. above? Otherwise please *resign* your office to make room in Congress for people who represent the *majority* of U.S. citizens who care more about Us Sovereignty, political and economic *security*.

Otherwise you don't represent us – you are just selling us out.

RLC: *This is a typical whine from someone who says he is a legal immigrant, but offers no proof. As for asking President Fox of Mexico for reciprocal rights for Americans in Mexico, just what kind of an idiot are we dealing with here? Any American who is requested to work in Mexico by a Mexican business or company applies for a work permit and pays an annual fee for the permit that allows him to work and live in Mexico. Such a program is what Congressman Kolbe has proposed for this country to implement. The problem with these critics is that they are uniformed and, if they are informed, just plain whiny liars.*

Million Illegals Entered Through Arizona in 2003

Posted by PHX – Todd Hartley on Wednesday October 29, 2003 at 10:10 am MST, PHXnews Editorial

In March of 2003, I spent a few days in Nogales (Mexico & U.S.) investigating Arabs who were paying $60,000 per person to be smuggled into the U.S. While at the border, I met up with a buddy who is a high-ranking member of the border patrol. As he has done in the past, he was very candid with me and shared the latest developments in America's homeland security.

RLC: *A quick check with inside Homeland Security officials reveals that the information about smuggling fees $60,000 being charged Arabs is false. In fact, most Arabs crossing the border are Iraqi Christians (Chaldeans) who left Iraq before the American invasion. They aren't Muslims, nor are there any recorded terrorist incidents among Iraqi Christians who have ever entered the United States. There may be 100,000 or more of them in the Detroit and San Diego areas.*

At one point during our conversation, I asked my friend, "How many illegals get successfully over the border? He said the official Border Patrol line is that 25% of those trying to gain illegal entrance into the U.S. get apprehended. But after some blunt discussion he admitted that figure was way too high. He then said softly, "We aren't allowed to talk about the real percentage we catch, but…the flow is so heavy, we're only nabbing 10%." WOW! That means 90% of attempting illegals are getting into the U.S. safely.

RLC: *Ridiculous. The Tucson Sector has the highest number of agents on the Border than any other part of the 2,000 mile border. It is not real difficult to find and arrest illegals in the desert. There are hi-technological tools like body heat sensors, night vision goggles and helicopters to aid in locating unsophisticated people in the desert. The alleged high-up Border Patrolman either doesn't exist, or was putting on the writer.*

Hold on to Your Hats! The U.S. Border Patrol in the Tucson sector recently announced 347,256 illegals were apprehended during their fiscal year '03 that ended in September. 347,000 is a pretty high number, but thatv's (sic) the number of people caught. Some 3,472,650 (the other 90%) are not getting caught each year. Does that sound like a lot to you? Well, it's not! Three-million illegal aliens are coming in successfully through the Tucsonv (sic) sector alone each year, but what about the other 21 secures protecting our borders? Sounds to me like the real number of illegal aliens we get each year is closer to 10 million, and that's being conservative.

RLC: *There are two types of logic, inductive and deductive. What we have here is neither. We have guess work based on false information. There is no way many more illegals get through than those officially apprehended. As mentioned, locating mobs of illegals is not hard in the desert. Night vision equipment, alone, makes location easy, as do thousands of body heat sensors scattered in and around known routes illegals take. There are not scores of Border Agents in the Tucson Sector; there are hundreds of them. It is the most patrolled sector on either the Mexican or Canadian borders. There are not 3.5 million illegals flowing through the Tucson Sector of the border. Nor are there 10-million illegals coming through every year. If there were, there would certainly be far more illegals in the country than even the most fanatical and rabid anti-illegal immigrant people speculate. Remember,* *"anonymous" claimed 12-million and that is the highest estimate I have ever seen.*

My friend with the Border Patrol also mentioned, that Americans would freak out if they knew how many Arabs are coming over this border each month. This was all said to me off the record because under the new Office of Homeland Security, the Border Patrol is not allowed to talk about Arab "migration".

Todd Hartley

RLC: *No high-ranking agent or Homeland Security officer would make such a statement, especially to a media person. Any such statement would be illegal and grounds for firing. Better yet, if such were actually true, the government would find and arrest the so-called Arabs and trot them out for all to see as a victory in the War on Terror. In reporting year-end apprehension figures in October, Homeland security officials reported that not a single suspected terrorist was captured on the Southern border. Of the three hundred thousand plus apprehensions, not a single one was suspected of being a terrorist.*

Oh well (Score:0)

By Anonymous on Wednesday October 29, 2003 at 11:24 am MST

Todd, Janet would ingore (sic) your post because it proves her term in office is a total waste. She has done everything in her power to increase the flow of these criminals. We have stopped building the machine and given up trying to do anything at all. The blood is on her hands, but few seem to care anymore. It only takes 2 or 3 terrorists to make it here to do their thing. I will hate to say I told you so on that account. Janet might as well be one of them. KMH

RLC: *Exactly how many terrorist suspects have been caught sneaking into the USA from Mexico? How many of the September 11th terrorists were from Mexico? How many*

of the September 11th terrorists entered the country illegally through Mexico? NONE!!!!!

Hire Americans (Score:0)

By Anonymous on Wednesday October 29, 2003 at 11:27 am MST, Just hire Americans Letter to the Editor

We will never stop the flow of illegal aliens until it becomes too costly for the people who hire them. Our manufacturing businesses moved factories overseas for the cheap labor, and now the service industry (which can't move overseas) has learned that it can increase profits by hiring uneducated, poor Mexicans.

The big lie is that the illegal aliens are doing jobs Americans won't do. The truth is that Americans can't do the jobs for the pay Mexicans will work for. I recently spent a year in Ohio. To my surprise most of the hotels, restaurants, and carwashes were staffed by American citizens. How nice it was to be able to have a decent conversation in English with the person serving me. The landscaping crews I saw were American citizens also. I didn't see hundreds of people standing on the sidewalks hoping for a job. Most people I saw in the service industry were high school and college students, or those lacking much education. Interestingly the food and services did not cost any more than they do out West, even though the companies were paying their employees better wages. American companies could hire Americans, but that would mean their profit margins wouldn't be as great. With unemployment at a 20-year high it's time American businesses do the right thing by paying decent wages and by hiring Americans. It is also time for immigration officials to start inspecting companies and heavily fining those who hire illegal aliens. Americans also should boycott companies that hire illegal aliens. The United States would do just fine without the millions of illegal aliens already here, and the million coming every year.

Tim Johnson Tempe

RLC: *Unemployment is at a 20-year high? Who says so? In fact, it is relatively normal and slightly lower than in the boom 1990s, this after a mini-recession from which we are coming out. As for Americans doing the work of illegals, tell that to the poultry industry in the South that cannot hire any Americans at any price, or the farmers of Arizona and California who can't hire Americans to work crops no matter the pay. As for Americans doing all the low-pay jobs in Ohio, please. Ohio is in the heart of the Rust Belt and suffers from a heavy loss of jobs to overseas companies and countries. San Diego, Phoenix and Orange County have thousands of Help Wanted signs and newspaper help wanted advertisements. Where are all those Americans who need work when you need them?*

Re: Hire Americans (Score:0)

By Anonymous on Wednesday October 29, 2003 at 11:39 am MST

Sonoran   News   http://www.sonorannews.com/ front_page.html July 16, - July 22, 2003

INA Section 237: Any alien who is present in the United States in violation of this Act or any other law of the United States is deportable.

Washington, D.C. Immigration issues seem to be at the top of every politician's agenda these days. Regardless of how individuals feel about immigration or illegal immigration, there appears to be consensus in one area ... the system is in shambles and cannot continue on the same path.

On June 26, 2003, The Center for Immigration Studies (CIS) held a panel discussion on Capitol Hill to present a report by James R. Edwards, Jr. The report had recently been published on the subject of state and local law enforcement cooperation with the immigration authorities. CIS Executive Director Mark Krikorian, who moderated the event, stated, "... this is an issue that's politically become important and ...

one that's likely to see legislation that's gained saliency and importance since 9/11, with increased concern and awareness of the importance of immigration enforcement." Krikorian introduced Sen. Jeff Sessions, R-AL, who served as assistant United States Attorney for 15 years followed by 12 years as United States Attorney, and served as attorney general of Alabama for two years, prior to being elected to the senate. "Basically, we are not allowing state and local law enforcement to be participants in any meaningful way in the enforcement of federal laws dealing with immigration. They have been shut out of it." Sessions noted that there are only 2,000 INS agents in the heartland of America, while there are 600,000 state and local law enforcement officers on the streets every day, enforcing all the laws that apply in America, except immigration laws. Sessions attended a conference with a group of police chiefs. They told him, when illegal aliens are apprehended, in most cases they are released. Phoenix Police told Sessions that they don't even bother to call the INS in most cases, and that the INS people told them not to call unless there were at least 15 of them. Then, they might be able to send someone out. There is no way the limited number of INS officers that are out there can do the job. "The only way we can enforce immigration laws in America, if we desire to do so, is to engage and employ and utilize our state and local law officers," Sessions said, adding, "That's so basic as to be without dispute, it seems to me."

Sessions continued, "I cannot tell you how deeply I believe that America's strength is based on its commitment to law," and recited the words" equal justice under law," that are chiseled on the wall of the Supreme Court. "The fact that we enforce laws effectively in America is our strength. And to me, to have a major part of our legal system eviscerated by a systematic approach to things that guarantees it wont work, guarantees that those who violate the law can continue to violate the law, is just not good for a whole lot of reasons, not the least of which is a lot of the terrorism that we threats that we have to this country today involve people who are here illegally ..." Sessions says he supports immigration but believes there is a need for a system that is enforceable and is enforced. He said, "I do salute Judge Al Gonzáles in the White House. He's written an opinion that says there is an inherent right of state and local law enforcement to arrest for felony offenses. That's the clear statement that we've needed for some time." "We don't need, in most cases, tougher immigration laws as much as we need to enforce the ones we have."

Sessions also saluted James R. Edwards, Jr., who authored the paper, citing Edwards report was "right on" and very consistent with what he'd learned, "anecdotally," by talking to state and local law enforcement officers. In conclusion, Sessions stated, "The role of state and local police in immigration law enforcement is a matter of tremendous importance. We've got to keep working on it. You know, if you raise these questions, some people automatically think that you're hostile to immigrants or you don't like people to come here; you don't want them to succeed; we're trying to be Big Brother. That's not it. We believe in the rule of law. We believe that people can come here and be citizens of this country and reach their fullest and highest potential. But, we believe that any nation has the right to set the standards by which it accepts people, and then if it sets those standards it ought to create a legal system that would enforce those standards. Otherwise, it undermines respect for law and undermines the whole scheme of immigration that we've worked to create

RLC: *Senator Sessions is wrong and that discussion is elsewhere in this book. Suffice it to say if 600,000 local cops are busy querying me or the other 38-or more-million Hispanics about our legality, they won't have much time for protecting and serving the community. Crime will rise because not enough police will be available to prevent crime from happening, or for investigating crimes after they occur.*

Re: Oh well (Score:0)

By Anonymous on Wednesday October 29, 2003 at 9:58 pm MST (

Maybe the solution is "Revolution".... Liberals and conservative Politicians hate American Citizens, selling out to get votes from third world countries, with support from newspapers like the Arizona (Republic) Liberal Democrat. Check the "Opinion Page" of the *Daily News-Sun* today, October 29, 2003, "How do we solve illegal-immigration dilemma?" And see how many people are disgusted with the whole situation, Prop 414, CPS, etc. The *Daily News-Sun* posted a "Questionnaire" June 10th, 2002, in regards to "concerns" to submit to politicians before election time. The results July 15th, 2002, the Number One concern happen to be "ILLEGAL IMMIGRATION." It seems people like Saturday Night Live McCain, Jeff the Flake, Cowboy Kolbe who disguise Senate Bill 1461 and House Bill 2899 as a "Guest-Worker" Program, when it is really a Two-Stage Amnesty Program, throw in Rep. Ed Pastor and Governor NapoReno and all the other Liberals, to many to list. Why is it so hard for these politicians to understand crossing the Borders of the United States is *illegal*, without a legal and proper invitation! Wake up America, you have lost your country...

RLC: *Anonymous strikes again. Revolution? One in 29 people in the entire country may be in the country illegally. Very few of the remaining 28 people in the U.S.A. are for "Revolution." Most would prefer for the situation to be resolved. They know we can't arrest and deport 10-million people; that is impossible. They know we can't line them up and shoot them. We must, then, legalize them.*

Re: Oh well (Score:1)

By Dalgast on Thursday October 30, 2003 at 12:19 am MST

I agree maybe it is time for a revolution. When the government becomes so bad I think it is not only our right, its our duty as Americans to over throw the government and replace it with one that works. At the rate they are going the southwest will fall into the hands of enemies is a very short order (grammar sic). They say what I sugjest (sic) is treason, I say what they are doing is. Its time for American to decied (sic) who the trators (sic) really are.

RLC: And they say illegals can't read and write English.

Re: Hire Americans (Score:1)

By opinionated on Friday October 31, 2003 at 5:48 am MST

"The big lie is that the illegal aliens are doing jobs Americans won't do. The truth is that Americans can't do the jobs for the pay Mexicans will work for."

Absolutely agree. If American employers weren't illegally undercutting their competitors by exploiting cheap labor, perhaps currently undesirable wages for these jobs would increase sufficiently for Americans to do them. Paying higher wages for the jobs illegals do would be unlikely hurt the rest of us either. After all, we are currently getting stuck with higher taxes from all the indirect social costs the illegal employers pass on to us (Prop: 414, anyone?) Bottom line? You can either pay more for your hotel or restaurant meal to hire an American hospitality worker, or you can pay higher taxes for free social services for illegal aliens. At least with hotels and meals you get a choice!

RLC: *There we go again. Pay more and Americans will get on their knees ten hours a day to pick strawberries. The truth is very few Americans have ever done that work; it has always been Mexicans willing to work, or Blacks in the South who could not work at any jobs not dictated by Jim Crow laws and attitudes. This subject is covered extensively in other sections of this book.*

CHAPTER 47

LAWS AND LAW BREAKERS

The problem of illegals is more than one problem. It is really several problems. They—the illegals—are here, but we don't know how many are here. That, then, turns into more problems: (1) If they are working, they are working illegally; (2) there may or may not be a displaced American worker sidelined by the illegal worker. (3) If they are working, their employer is breaking the law if he knows the illegal is illegal. (4) If the illegal crossed the border without being interviewed and documented, the illegal has violated civil immigration law. (5) If the illegal entered the country legally and overstayed his or her visa, civil immigration law was also violated. These crimes, however, are not crimes of violence, nor are they as serious as violating speed laws or drunk driving laws that result in the deaths of thousands of Americans every year.

What laws are they violating? First, the Constitution is clear, the "Congress" is charged with making a "uniform rule of naturalization." The word "Naturalization" means incoming immigration and has since the country was founded. The Constitution and myriad Supreme Court decisions are clear: Immigration and naturalization are federal responsibilities. The states may not attempt or enter into schemes to regulate, or control immigration, or even legally describe legal residency and, of course, can in no way grant legality or legal residency to anyone not a natural born United States citizen.

Attempts, like 1994's California's Proposition 187 (that would have set state standards for defining and searching for legal residency and denied certain public benefits to "suspected" illegals and the children of illegals, even if the children were U.S. citizens by birth), are illegal on their face. Such attempts have not survived even minimal legal challenges. Proposition 187, for example, was declared an unconstitutional state "scheme" to regulate immigration by setting up rules to identify and punish "suspected" illegal aliens. Proposition 187 was so declared in a summary judgment by a single judge, no trial was necessary. That point must be highlighted—in the proposition, there was no mechanism for due process hearings or investigation to determine federally defined legal residency. The use of the word "suspected" at least a half-a-dozen times in the poorly written law and expulsion of children from school based on "suspicion" and the denial of medical care in every California hospital, public or private, to citizen children made the original proposition illegal. Every city or county law enforcer, including meter maids and building inspectors, was mandated to check legal residency of anyone "arrested" and that documents necessary to prove "legal residency" were to be determined by individual sheriffs and police chiefs. These "rules" significantly influenced a federal judge declaring Proposition 187 unconstitutional.

It was so declared in a Federal district court summary judgment. It never went to trial; despite its proponents claiming their court test was torpedoed. It never had a trial because it wasn't legal on its face. The Proposition simply didn't meet the test of constitutionality. The consistent use of the word "suspected illegal status," for example, could be spotted as unconstitutional by a kindergartner in Norway. The actual decision was made in a federal district court summary judgment and any appeal was destined to be fruitless, according to most legal experts. Nonetheless, many of the anti-immigrants continue to complain to this day that the people of California were cheated out of their court test of the unconstitutional law they approved at the ballot box. How soon they forget that we live under a constitution, not majority rule that denies rights and law to those not in the majority.

Remember school segregation, which was totally legal and approved by a majority of citizens.

The fact of the matter is the United States Supreme Court refused –let me *repeat*—*refused*, to intervene in the court tests of Proposition 187. The court torpedoed the desire of the Proposition's supporters for Supreme Court review of the schooling question. They fervently and hysterically wished the Court might overturn prior decisions on the subject of illegal immigrant children in public schools. As those decisions stood, certainly no district court judge can overrule a Supreme Court decision, nor can any appeals court even if the Supreme Court decision was a 5-4 one. At the risk of redundancy, the United States Supreme Court, led by conservatives Scalia, Thomas, Renhquist, O'Conner and Kennedy refused to take up the question. They could have (with five votes) by simply agreeing to look at Proposition 187 and to review the 1982 Plyler v. Doe Supreme Court decision that allowed illegal resident children to enroll in public schools, K-12.

After hypothetically agreeing to look into Proposition 187, five justices could have simply sent a one-line fax to district judge Marianna Pfaelzer stating: Certify the Proposition 187 case to this court for review. The court did not so order Judge Marianna Pfaelzer. One does not have to be a mind-reader to see that the United States Supreme Court did not want to legitimize Proposition 187's flagrant abuse of the United States Constitution, a Constitution in which one cannot find the word "suspected," as one can several times in reading Proposition 187. By omission, the Supreme Court of the United States ruled that Proposition 187 was illegal and unconstitutional. Period, the argument ends here. Critics might call this a flight of fantasy, but legal experts agree that this thesis is legally correct.

Whose Problem Are Illegal Immigrants?

Only Congress can make immigration law, just as it generally regulates employers through the "commerce clause" of the Constitution. That clause allows Congress to regulate interstate commerce and, thus, wages and working hours. The combination of its exclusivity with immigration law and its ability to regulate interstate commerce allows the federal government to wield great power and authority in the solving the problem of illegal aliens. Back to the problem of illegal immigrants in the United States—We see that many problems result from their crossing the border illegally or overstaying their legal entry. We see that some of them involve themselves in some crime or another, in gangs, in drug commerce and some in violent crimes. California prisons report that slightly over 10 percent of its inmates are illegal aliens (approximately, 18,000 inmates of which, the state reports, less than half committed violent felonies).

In fact, as of March 31 2004, the California Department of Corrections reports that of the 162,120 inmates in state prisons, 18,212 had Immigration holds on them (11.2 percent). Of the 18, 212 Immigration holds, 15,495 were Mexican nationals (9.55 percent). So much for Heather McDonald's dumb statements about an illegal alien Mexican crime wave. The federal prison system reports that 25% of its 160,000 prisoners are Mexican nationals. Some are in for smuggling of illicit drugs and other contraband, including people, most for convictions of felony border crossing, a recent (1996) development in border crossing law (getting caught twice is a felony)—but not violent crimes such as murder, etc.

Nationally, these U.S. Department of Justice statistics (2002) are noteworthy. There are 3,437 sentenced Blacks per 100,000 Black males; 1,176 sentenced Hispanic men per 100,000 Hispanic males and 450 White males per 100,000 White males in the justice system, either in prison, on probation or parole. On the surface, one must be shocked so many Blacks are in prison. The Hispanic figure would be shocking also if the 1,176 Hispanic males per 100,000 were illegal aliens, but they are not. Consider first that the total Hispanic prison inmates number a third of Blacks. Then, one must consider that there is a distinct segmentation of the Hispanic prison numbers into three segments. One, the legal resident Hispanic (including citizen); Two, the illegal resident; plus, of course, the Puerto Rican who is not an immigrant and is a native born citizen no matter where born. Illegals are certainly not half the Hispanic prison population. They are, perhaps, a third, or a fourth, a fifth or sixth of the Hispanic prison population, debunking, therefore, emotional cries that all illegals are violent criminals, or, other than breaking border crossing laws, criminals at all. We also know that the illegal immigrant problem is not a zero-sum problem, despite emotional claims to the contrary.

Justice William Brennan wrote in the landmark 1982 Plyler v. Doe case, that all children, including illegal resident ones, be educated in the public schools. He also wrote that children should not be "punished for the sins of their fathers." With many Supreme Court cases to rely on, he wrote that "today's illegal immigrant" may be tomorrow's legal resident. Certainly, president George W. Bush and most Republicans and Democrats in the Congress of the United States know that to be true and can make it happen.

CHAPTER 48

IMMIGRANTS FIGHT FOR AMERICA, WHILE ANTI-IMMIGRANTS RUN AND HIDE

Take, for example, the recent Iraq War experience in which immigrant soldiers and Marines played a huge part. One immigrant Marine came from Guatemala to the United States illegally as a teenager and was able to get legalized. He left college to enlist in the U.S. Marines and was one of the first combat casualties in the war. Being an illegal border crosser does not mean one will never be a legal resident and contributing member of American society. According to the Department of Defense, as many as 37,000 soldiers, sailors and Marines were green card carrying immigrants when they joined. As a matter of fact, the Army has discovered that there are some illegals serving who joined the army with less-than-perfect paperwork. The first case that became public, however, was of an Iraq War combat veteran. The Army wanted to keep him because he was a good soldier; he was also Mexican.

Thanks to the war, President George W. Bush and Congressmen like Darrel Issa, the grandson of Lebanese immigrants and, himself, a former U.S. Army officer, Congress passed laws cutting the citizenship application time for active duty immigrant servicemen and women to practically nothing. In less than 6-months, 10,000 immigrant military men and women applied for citizenship under President Bush's expedited system. Interestingly and predictably, anti-immigrant elements are against immigrants serving in the Armed Forces of the United States, despite a noble history of such service dating back to the American Revolution. Mark Krikorian, of the Center for Immigration Studies (CIS), the fanatical anti-immigrant nonprofit founded and funded by notoriously anti-immigrant Dr. John Tanton of Michigan, wrote a published op-ed piece in which he called these immigrant fighters "mercenaries" serving only so they could short circuit the normal naturalization process. Of course, the falseness of this emotional charge is laid bare by the fact that the President sponsored quick-legalization for the military's immigrants long after they joined and only as a result of the Iraq war.

As if someone pushed a button, anti-immigrant letter writers flooded the nation's newspapers promoting the same point of view. The question that raised is: Is there a centrally directed conspiracy against immigrants, legal and illegal, working throughout the United States? Is that why Dr. John Tanton has organized front groups all over the country, so they can rise in protest to the "darkening" of America by people who look like me?

CHAPTER 49

POSITIVE ILLEGAL IMMIGRANT CONTRIBUTIONS

For every problem caused by illegal immigrants, however, there are many countervailing positive aspects to their being and working here, no matter how emotional and irrational the anti-immigrants rant and rave. For example, the United States Government published a report four years ago that over 50% of all farm workers in California were illegal aliens. Thus, if they weren't here, who would plant crops, pick them and send them to our tables? Snap shots of the farm workers population have from time to time shown high rates of unemployment among farm workers, but those studies are only valid between crop harvests. It should be remembered that California, with these illegals, produces most of the fruits and vegetables eaten in the USA. The problem is to have enough workers on hand for crop harvests, not 365 days a year. If the workers were allowed to go back to their Mexican homes between peak employment periods, the problem of unemployed farm workers would go away, the problem would take a holiday.

Clearly stated, that means legal farm workers who can come for a few months to work harvests could come and go as the demand for their labor increases or decreases. Some workers would come just to plant crops, for example, work for two or three months and return to their families in Mexico without fear of apprehension, as they fear now. Thus, the current problem of illegals staying permanently or semipermanently because they fear crossing the border and/or paying much money to smugglers for passage, would simply go home when their jobs end. California farmers constantly complain that there aren't enough workers at the proper time –at the proper time—to harvest crops. For example, for several years there haven't been enough workers in California's Central Valley at grape harvest time to pick table grapes in available quantities. The farmers have brought in machines to shake grapes off of vines that are then dried and prepared for the less profitable raisin market. Harvests of table and wine grapes have in recent years fallen by as much as 40% according to Fresno's Nisei Farmers League. These farmers should know, in contrast to the expounded views of immigration critics, few of whom know anything about farming in California or anywhere else.

These Fresno-area farmers know our good farmer-professor Victor Davis Hanson and are quick to suggest he simply doesn't know what he is talking about, despite his being a part-time farmer and neighbor of theirs. Asparagus fields in the San Francisco Bay area have gone unharvested for lack of Mexicans and the price of asparagus has hardly ever reflected the amount of asparagus actually planted. The price reflects the amount harvested. Thus, if there aren't enough workers to dig up asparagus, less asparagus reaches supermarket produce sections at prices higher than they should be. Less supply means higher prices. On top of it all, as asparagus is usually in short supply because of labor problems, many American processors have turned to China for asparagus that is cheaper, even after being flown across the Pacific Ocean, all 10,000 miles of it.

As labor shortages cut harvests and developers come waving cash, less and less land is devoted to farming and more and more farm land is permanently retired from production. When that happens in Kansas or Nebraska, little is lost because slightly higher per acre production can keep wheat and other cereal product supply at current or higher levels. In fact, of course, cereal farmers in the Plains states who might be affected simply ask for more money from the Federal government for them to stop producing, or to lower production. In California, however, the crops usually aren't subsidized and once land is developed into houses, that production cannot be grown elsewhere. Thus, less produce, higher prices and less over-all food supply. Ask the people of New York what they pay for fruit and vegetables, now while there are thousands of Mexicans in the fields.

Labor Supply

Belying the fact that up to 95% of California's farm work force is from Mexico and most are probably illegally present, many immigration critics maintain that there are plenty of Americans who will do this work. For example, an anti-immigrant web site, the Citizen Lobby.com, declared that "illegal alien workers displace over 659,000 American workers every year (What happened to 1,880,000 Americans FAIR claims lose their jobs *every year*) and cost (taxpayers) $3.5 billion." At the bottom of its page, it lists sources for its myriad anti-immigrant and anti-Mexican statements including, among others, the U.S. Department of Justice, Department of Labor, the anti-Immigrant Federation for American Immigration Reform, and, the best of all, *The Spotlight*, a publication considered less credible than the *National Enquirer*. These statements are made in the face of studies that conclude that 95% of all farm workers in California were born in Mexico. There is no proof that American worker displacement is actually the case. In the cities, everyone knows where illegals congregate to offer their labor to Americans who drive by looking for casual labor. Rarely does one ever see places where native-born Americans congregate to look for casual labor jobs.

One can hire casual labor White males from places like San Diego's St. Vincent De Paul Center, but once hired, they rarely show up or return for a second day's work. In Los

Angeles, one used to see unemployed South-Central Blacks standing on corners offering their services as painters, etc. However, they always wanted more money than immigrant day laborers on other corners, so the market system manifested itself and no one hires the higher priced native-born Americans. Not understanding free market principles, they priced themselves out of the market. One can say that economic profiling is manifested by skin color because American Blacks have simply abdicated the labor demand to those willing to work for the money offered. Moreover, if one uses South-Central Los Angeles, what used to be called Watts, as an example, one sees illegals everywhere looking for work, or doing menial tasks like selling ice cream bars from hand carts, etc., and making themselves available by the hundreds at congregation points where contractors, builders, private citizens, or warehouse operators can hire ones, twos, or dozens of casual laborers for reasonable rates. Over and above casual labor jobs, illegals are found working in thousands of jobs in factories, warehouses, canneries, auto body shops, car dealerships, restaurants and fast food businesses throughout California and the country.

The question is: When Boeing fired 30,000 workers at its various factories, did illegal aliens take their place? When General Dynamics sold its San Diego operations employing thousands upon thousands of workers, did illegal immigrants take those jobs? Or, where the jobs abandoned in California simply resurrected in Arizona and other low-cost labor states with Americans working just like they have since industries started moving out of the Old Rust Belt?

CHAPTER 50

ILLEGAL IMMIGRANTS, TAXES AND SOCIAL SECURITY

Based on a number of government sponsored studies, the Government reports that most illegals are paid by check and have taxes and Social Security "contributions" withheld and sent to the Social Security Administration. It should also be noted that many illegals have taxes withheld from their paychecks but don't file tax returns on April 15th because they are either using false Social Security numbers or, they simply want to stay invisible and hard to locate by "la migra," immigration. As this tax season ends, newspaper stories abound about illegals filing tax returns using Tax Identification Numbers issued by the IRS to people without Social Security numbers. Their reason: They hear that filing taxes may be a prerequisite for some sort of legalization in the future. So much for illegals not paying taxes.

Even more apparent is the hypocrisy of the anti-immigrant, anti-Mexican lunatic-fringers represented by FAIR. In a recent earthshaking release of another phony study, FAIR claims that the Mexican immigrant doesn't pay as much in taxes as the native-born American. What happened to the declaration that illegal immigrants don't pay taxes at all? What happened to the middle position that illegals don't pay enough in taxes, as immigrants, in general, don't pay enough in taxes? The FAIR "study" whines that the average American pays slightly over

$3000.00 in federal income taxes while the Mexican immigrant pays slightly over $2000.00 in federal income taxes. The "study" claims it draws its numbers from the Census Bureau, though it makes its own conclusions. What can we conclude from this phony study allegedly done by "researchers" at FAIR (The John Tanton front group founded with Pioneer Fund money, money usually spent on determining if Black male penis size is related to Black male crime rates)?

We can conclude that illegal and legal Mexican immigrants pay federal income taxes. That Mexican immigrants pay taxes at all, much less federal taxes is finally admitted by the fanatics at FAIR. We can conclude that Mexican immigrants contribute to the public benefit treasury based on their income levels. We know that Mexican immigrant income levels are lower than the general population, but we also know (see other parts of this book) that those income levels rise the longer the immigrants are in the United States. Moreover, we also know from myriad studies quoted in this book, that the children of these immigrants are better schooled and make more money than their parents, thus increasing tax contributions as they join the labor market.

Of course, even before the FAIR "study," critics came out of the woodwork claiming that illegals don't make enough money to pay taxes so they are filing just to recover refunds of subsidy payments. There might be elements of truth to that in some cases, but the reality is that these people are risking exposure and endangering their working status. What they are doing is dangerous and courageous concurrently, but may count someday in some legalization plan we have yet to see. The United States government, then, includes that illegally contributed money into the Social Security checks sent out every month to 96% of Social Security recipients who happen to be non-Hispanics. The illegals cannot collect Social Security benefits. It is said by experts that illegals may have paid $40-billion into Social Security in recent years. '

That is a direct subsidy paid to America's senior citizens by illegals, the price illegals pay so they can work here.

It should be mentioned, in passing, that many anti-immigrant critics are the very senior citizens who complain loudest about illegals, though they don't send their Social Security checks back because they include money paid by illegals. Their checks consist of far more money paid by illegals in recent years than those FICA taxes the recipients paid in the 50s when the Social Security system collected pennies to today's dollars. At the local and state level, illegals pay the same taxes as natural-born citizens. For example, local property/school taxes are usually built into the property tax on houses and apartments. When rent is paid, the property taxes are part of the rent. Thus, illegals that rent, have property taxes—school taxes—in their rent. All renters do. Property owners, landlords, collect the property taxes in rents and pay them to the county or the state. Few landlords have the community spirit to pay taxes on their rental properties without accounting for those taxes in the rent they collect, even when they get checks from the Federal government subsidizing the rents of their Section 8-qualified renters.

When the illegal buys merchandise, he, or she, pays the same sales tax native-born Americans pay. When an illegal buys a lottery ticket, the state keeps the same amount as from a native-born American citizen. When an illegal buys gas, he or she pays the same .36 cents a gallon in taxes that native-born Americans pay in California, plus sales taxes that are percentage based, thus reaching very high amounts in this age of higher priced gasoline. Most pay the same payroll taxes native-born Americans pay for Medicare yet can't receive the medical care paid for by those taxes. That is theft on a grand scale. When they use telephones, they pay the same taxes native-born Americans pay. When they buy tires, they pay the same federal excise taxes legals do. When they gamble at U.S. approved Indian casinos, they don't get credits because they are here illegally despite complaints by "Native

American" activists that White Europeans are the real illegal immigrants. Ergo, illegals pay taxes. When they are paid by check, the full 7.5% (seven dollars and fifty cents per hundred) of their checks is paid directly to the Social Security Trust Fund, and, matched by the employer. Currently, illegals can never collect Social Security benefits, at least under current laws they can't.

The George W. Bush Administration is talking about negotiating an agreement with Mexico that would allow Americans to collect Mexican Social Security benefits they paid for while working in Mexico (Like me between 1967 and 1971). Conversely, Mexicans who worked a certain number of quarters in the United States and paid into the Social Security system would be able to collect Social Security benefits they paid for while working in the United States. It goes without saying that the antis are in a rage about those negotiations.

A study by the Rand Corporation once concluded that we make money off of illegals when one adds taxes, productivity and lower prices for the goods and services they produce in the economy. Studies done by anti-immigration experts claim otherwise, but those studies are easily debunked by the Rand study because they are never done by respectable organizations using respectable, scientific methods. How, for example, does the Colorado Alliance for Immigration Reform stack up intellectually to Rand Corporation of Santa Monica? It doesn't. Another example: A decade ago, a study was done in Los Angeles that claimed illegals cost the county of Los Angeles and the State of California billions of dollars in education, health and welfare costs. That study, however, was quickly debunked. (a) It didn't acknowledge that illegals paid property taxes. (b) It included all children who might have been born to one or two parents who might be immigrants in estimating school costs, even if the child was an American citizen. (c) It didn't quantify any taxes or fees paid to the Federal government. (d) It didn't deduct from all funds spent

on illegals in California those funds actually supplied—offset—
by the Federal government.

PART 8

CHAPTER 51

STANDING ON THE CORNER...

Thus, in general, the situation of illegal immigration is fluid because the problem is fluid. For every negative, there is a positive. The fact they are here is a positive. There are those who believe otherwise. The question is, are there more positives than negatives, or, conversely, more negatives than positives? Fact: There are millions of illegal residents in the United States of America. Most of these millions have regular jobs. There are far more illegals working than there are unemployed Americans, for the number of unemployed Americans who will do the work illegals do is limited. That is not an urban myth. Facts contradict those who say that Americans will do the work illegals are do throughout the economy. Farmers have offered up to $20.00 an hour to American citizens to pick peaches in Central California groves and no one shows up to work (Even Dr. Victor Davis Hanson states that fact in his book, *Mexifornia*).

California's Alameda County once ran an experiment to help take American citizen welfare recipients off welfare by having farmers offer jobs picking peaches. The money they earned would not have replaced welfare checks; it would have supplemented the checks for no loss in dollar intake. No one took advantage of the program. Just 30 miles south of South Central Los Angeles, there are vegetable fields as far as the eye can see in between industrial buildings. All the workers working the crops are Mexican. One will not find a single unemployed South Central native-born American in the fields, not one. One does see hundreds, thousands of unemployed native-born complaining Americans just 30-minutes north of the Orange County fields. A simple bus ride will take all these unemployed complaining Americans to jobs paying $60-70 for a-ten-hour day.

There are world famous flower and strawberry fields in Carlsbad, California, five minutes south of 160,000 person Oceanside, California. One finds hundreds of unemployed American citizens in Oceanside, but none who ever present themselves to Carlsbad field foremen at dawn seven days a week looking for work that can pay up to $20.00 an hour picking tomatoes, strawberries or flowers. There is no proof whatsoever that legal resident Americans will ever seek work currently done by illegals. This is especially true of work in the fields that used to be done by interstate immigrants from the old Dust Bowl states back in the Thirties.

World War Two created hundreds of thousands of aircraft construction and defense jobs in old orange groves that pulled the "Okies" and "Arkies" out of the fields forever. Their replacements were and still are Mexicans. One must notice that some critics point out that when they travel to Rust Belt states, they see Americans making hotel beds, working as dishwashers, working in construction and doing other jobs done by illegals in the West. They can't have it both ways, however, because those Rust Belts are not growing job havens. They are, in fact, areas that don't feed themselves or others to any great extent; nor do they produce economic products for the future. Moreover, these are the very areas losing jobs to places like China, South Carolina, Mississippi, India, Mexico, et al.

Every study of immigrant domicile patterns has concluded that immigrants go to where there are other immigrants and that they do better there than in places where there aren't many immigrants. That is true of illegals also, they zero in on available jobs. The Ohio 40ish former steelworker does not sell everything to pile into an SUV to head for California, Nevada or Arizona, places where the jobs are. Empty words from critics don't prove Americans will crawl on their hands and knees to pick strawberries for any amount of money.

Sovereignty. On sovereignty, the illegal immigrant's phantom violation of American sovereignty is a major complaint of the antis. They see a Mexican or Central American who crosses the border not as a misdemeanant, but as a sovereignty-violating criminal intent on taking over America. They look at employers of those who make it as traitors to the USA. They look at the President as a "traitor;" they look at this writer, the President and others who support regularization of immigration as part of the *Treason Lobby*. One wonders, however, if a fifteen year-old Indian from the two Mexican states that send the most illegals to the United States, Oaxaca, or Michoacan, even knows what sovereignty is. One must also wonder if many of the critics even know what sovereignty is.

Sovereignty is defined in my Webster's Collegiate Dictionary as, "Supreme power over the body politic, and, freedom from external control, and, autonomy." Now, exactly how does the Indian man or woman looking for a job threaten our freedom, our autonomy or control over our body politic? They know they are breaking some law or another, but can they be compared with German spies who came to sabotage, maim and kill, during WWII, or to Mohammed Atta and his 17 hijacking murderers on September 11, 2001? No. They want to work. It is not a crime to want work. It is not a violation of our "sovereignty." Setting aside complaints that these people are violating America's sovereignty, the overwhelming number of them don't break criminal laws. They stay out of the way of law enforcement as much as possible. They only want to work.

They want to earn money to send home if they have family, to save if they don't.

During the 1990s, during the huge influx of illegals from Mexico, the national and California crime rates have plunged to levels not experienced since 1967. Is that an accident? Crime is still falling in California, even as the number of illegals increases. In April 2004, the Attorney General of California announced that 1775 people were murdered in California in 2003, 64 fewer than in 2002, a percentage decrease of 3.4%. He also announced that murders in Los Angeles dropped by 21.6 percent and in Long Beach, 26.9 percent. Where is Ms Heather MacDonald when real facts are released? The Los Angeles-Long Beach metropolitan area is, perhaps, the highest impacted area of the country by illegal aliens. Nonetheless, the murder rates there are falling dramatically.

Legal Residency, a Wild-eyed Congressman & Farmers

Illegals would prefer to be legal. Congressman Tom Tancredo, on the other hand, would institute a police state to root them out and deport them, even as he hires them to remodel his own residence. There is one aspect of the illegal problem that troubles some. They, led by Republican Congressman Tom Tancredo of Colorado, point to what they claim are facts about farm economics. They say that if the illegal alien labor market is curbed by stringent law enforcement at the Border with Mexico, that farmers will simply develop more farm mechanization to take up the labor deficit and that prices will not rise much. Recent mechanization of orange groves in Florida shows that Florida orange growers can still not compete with Brazilian frozen orange juice concentrate, even after they shift production from Mexican farm workers to machines that shake oranges off trees. Mechanization, thus, cannot necessarily better the production interests of the American farmer.

Tancredo uses the tomato example. He relates that tomato farmers were hooked on legal Mexican labor from 1943 through 1965. In 1965, the Kennedy-Johnson Administration arbitrarily ended the twenty-year-old joint-labor agreement with Mexico.

Tancredo: The farmers complained they would be ruined. Tancredo relates that farmers developed machines to pick tomatoes—a false statement—and that they are now doing just fine (another false statement). His actual words were, "We (farmers) cannot possibly grow tomatoes, we cannot harvest tomatoes, without the help of this kind of labor. So we ended up in a situation where we went ahead and eliminated this bracero program. And what happened? Did tomato growers go out of business as they said they would? No. They were forced to actually invest in technology, to invest in different kinds of technology and actually develop some sort of mechanized approach to doing the labor that had been done heretofore by individuals. So today tomato growers in the United States are far more productive than they ever were before when they relied solely on individuals picking tomatoes. Now they can do it with machines, now they can do it more cost effectively, and they are more productive in the process." (House of Representatives – June 09, 2003, Page: H5075)

2004 reality escapes Tancredo. The machines developed to pick tomatoes and the tomatoes created to be picked by machines were created by university scientists. Apparently Congressman Tancredo has not tasted these scientifically engineered tomatoes that taste like cardboard. Moreover, American tomato farmers are abandoning tomato farming because they can't compete with Mexican farmers who use human labor to pick tomatoes that are tastier, riper and better-colored tomato red than tomatoes bred to be picked by machine. Machine picked tomatoes are not very lush red in color, are almost always unripe and truly taste like cardboard.

In the Florida orange juice case recently reported in "Rural Migration News," farmers had to plant orange trees farther apart and to keep them precisely pruned by human labor. After all this effort and expense, they managed to lower their prices to 90-cents per pound of frozen juice concentrate, still 15-cents above the American-delivered Brazilian product. Brazil defeats the machines. Arguments like Tancredo's simply don't hold up under examination.

Another argument is that if all illegal resident farm workers were deported, the cost of farm produce would only rise slightly. That is false, according to farmers. They suggest the two ultraconservative anti-immigrant University of California, Davis professors, who came up with a projected result of massive deportation, simply don't know what they are talking about. The professors suggest that produce prices would only rise by pennies. At the University of Iowa, a professor has calculated the farm-product prices would rise by 3-5 percent. That figure has already been discussed and shown to be billions of dollars in regressive increases in food prices. The models they apparently used suggest that the amount of produce raised would stay the same because native-born farm workers would suddenly materialize if farmers would simply pay more than the $7.00 an hour they currently average paying farm workers. Would $10.00 an hour produce more native-born strawberry pickers, $20.00, or $25.00? The answer is, no amount of wage increases will produce the same number of farm workers that presently exist in the illegal alien- dominated farm worker labor market. Even if wages rose, the number of farm workers would be less than today. Farmers would have to cut back on plantings because they need to keep labor costs as low as possible. Of course, plantings would shrink because x-number of farm workers can only pick x-quantities of produce.

Then, of course, the Chinese farmer is looming with similar farm products that are cheaper than farm products grown in the United States. Check the price of garlic now that Chinese garlic is coming into the country, or asparagus. Another Example: Strawberry farmers state that they spend at least $10,000 an acre before they pick a single strawberry. Culling back on plantings will decrease supply; decreased supply means higher prices. How much higher, no one knows. Tom Tancredo doesn't know. Two anti-immigrant UC Davis professors don't know, either, nor does the Iowa professor. Market prices are dependent on market supply. No computer model in the world can predict what acreage farmers will plant or not plant.

Higher food prices and less food are two projected negatives if the anti-immigrant group gets its way insofar as rounding up and deporting all illegal aliens. A supply and demand instigated inflation would set in across the board in the American economy. Who wants that? Who loses in that scenario? The poor uneducated unskilled high school dropout laborer, the whiners like to declare so injured by the presence of illegal aliens, is who.

A lower standard of living is in store for middle class American families who would face sticker shock if they had to pay retail for scarce formal child-care after having their nanny deported. Moreover, the supply of retail child-care might increase after years of high demand, but the costs would negate any outside income generated by a mother choosing to work. Many of these women would be forced to quit their jobs, plunging many families into less than ideal financial situations they may currently enjoy with illegal alien nannies taking care of their children. The economy could shrink and the Gross Domestic Product could decrease into a disastrous depression. The great American middle-class of the West, the best in the world, would shrink and disappear in many cases. The general standard of living in the entire United States of America would go down, not up.

Legalization of the economy

Arrest and deportation is one proposed solution. Legalization, of some sort, is the other. Both methods carry heavy economic consequences. Can anyone objectively state that the American hospitality industry—hotels and restaurants—would not suffer shock if the bulk of behind the scene workers were deported? Has anyone ever studied that consequence of massive deportation? Yes, one study suggests that total deportation would cause a $220-billion, loss, a fifth of a trillion dollars loss in the Gross Domestic Product of the United States.

Can anyone objectively predict what would happen to agriculture in the West if all illegals were deported? Can anyone predict what would happen to the illegal-alien-heavy beef packing industry in Iowa, Kansas and Nebraska if all illegals were deported? What would happen to the pork processing industry in those same three states if all illegals were deported? Can anyone project any positive consequences to the chicken and turkey processing industries in Oklahoma, Arkansas, North Carolina and throughout the South if illegals were massively deported?

Can anyone project what might happen to beef; chicken and turkey prices if half or more of the work force in those industries were deported? Could enough American citizens fill those critical vacant jobs, at any wage? Are there enough American citizens willing to move to those states for stressful, boring jobs, no matter the wages? Iowa is losing population now and has for years, would that improve if all its illegal resident Mexican workers were deported?

Let's look at an actual case: The California Restaurant Association reports that today (January, 2004) there are 150,000 job openings in the 34-million person state of California—150,000 job openings presently unfilled by anyone, much less Americans. If the illegals weren't here, that shortfall might by 250,000 or 350,000, or 550,000. In other words, restaurants would have to go out business for lack of workers. Less competition would mean higher prices and less choice to the public. Legal residency totally depends on Congress.

Congress can grant or not grant legal residency to anyone it wants, when it wants. Congress has granted mass citizenship and legal residency three times in the past. In 1917, Congress granted Puerto Ricans citizenship because it wanted to draft Puerto Rican men into the World War I Army. In 1924, Congress granted American Indians citizenship. In 1986, Congress granted over three million illegals amnesty, some of whom applied for Permanent Residence and have gone on to become citizens. Of course, one must also count the estimated 75,000 people who inhabited the Southwest when it was taken from Mexico in the Mexican and American War. Those people were legalized when the U.S. Senate ratified the Treaty of Guadalupe Hidalgo. The Treaty validated the real estate seizure and allowed the contemporaneous inhabitants two choices, become citizens, or move to what was left of Mexico. Within the citizenship option the people could formally apply, or just wait and automatically become citizens one year after ratification of the Treaty by both countries. The Treaty also guaranteed the right to worship as they pleased and due process to their land claims.

It should be noted that the United States Supreme Court has prohibited Congress from making laws removing American citizenship (Afroyem v. Rusk, 1967). The Court's rational in that case was simple; Congress can change its mind and take back what it can grant. Thus, leaving some citizens fearful that Congress might wake up one day and decide it doesn't like Polish-origin naturalized citizens, or Russians, Mexicans or Canadians who have become American citizens through the naturalization process. Citizenship, like statehood, the Court ruled, is forever.

The precedent was the Court's decision after the Civil War when Texas claimed that it and the other secessionist states of the Old Confederacy had the right to secede from the United States (in an effort to force payment of bonds issued by Confederate Texas). The Court said no, the Constitution carefully outlines how a territory becomes a state but makes no mention of withdrawing statehood, or dissolution of the

United States of America, or secession by a state from the Union. Thus, once a citizen, always a citizen except in very tightly defined situations.

Texas also challenged the citizenship of the former Mexicans who were automatically enabled by the Treaty to become citizens. The challenge was as interesting as it was bogus. Texas maintained that because the existing federal immigration law of 1848, the year the Treaty was negotiated and ratified, was very specific in that only "free White persons" could become citizens in that year and previously, these Mexicans could not be considered citizens because they weren't white. The Supreme Court rejected that Texas challenge because, it ruled, treaties have the weight of the Constitution and override acts of Congress for the simple reason that the Constitution itself explicitly states that a treaty must be ratified by a super-majority of 2/3rds of voting Senators.

A Happy-face Police State

Currently, there are efforts (led by Rep. Charlie Norwood R-GA) in Congress to allow local police to be deputy immigration law enforcers, as well as attempts to assign military troops to the Mexican border, just as there are countervailing moves to legalize those people who are here illegally today. The proposed law is titled the Clear Law Enforcement for Criminal Alien Removal (Clear) Act. While many immigration critics insist that it is necessary to use local law enforcement agencies to hunt down illegals for deportation, scores of sheriff's offices, national police associations, chiefs of police and state and local government associations in 37 states have asked Congress to defeat the bill.

The school of massive enforcement of immigration law maintains that all illegal immigrants must be rounded up and deported; secondly, they want the border tightly wrapped with more enforcement of entry laws and law enforcement backup by our military. It is this force behind the various moves in Congress to limit all immigration, to forcefully roundup and deport illegals and to seal the border with Mexico. Moreover, they always seem to be in the forefront demanding the closure of the border with Mexico to trade, as well, despite the fact that trade with Mexico is the largest the United States has, second only that with Canada.

Trade means jobs; better paid jobs for hundreds of thousands of Americans who would otherwise be making 20 or 30 percent less money than they make now. The critics, however, disagree and insist, like Pat Buchanan, that we do not trade at all so that 60 year old American furniture makers can hold on to jobs that are better performed by 20-year old Chinese furniture makers for half the price. There are significant problems with both these positions. To roundup and deport millions, maybe 10,000,000 people, is a monumental task that would require the emergence of a giant police state like the world has never seen. Federal agencies would need the assistance of thousands upon thousands of local police who are already overburdened at the local level. Those supporting Rep. Norwood's bill state that there are 600,000 local law enforcement people in the United States. Those numbers alone depict exactly the scenario I have outlined about checkpoints and street confrontations.

To implement a roundup of illegals would require hundreds of thousands of badge-wearing, gun-toting cops and deputies and soldiers manning highway and street checkpoints, official national identification cards, warrantless door-to-door searches, seizures and confrontations, and the worst "racial profiling" in the history of the country. Is this realistic? Yes and would be necessary to round up 10,000,000 or more people. Each and every Hispanic/Latino looking person in the country would have their rights violated by virtue of most illegals being Hispanic and most cops/deputies being lazy.

Studies of police stops in San Diego, California, for example, prove conclusively that Hispanics are stopped more often and arrested less than other groups. Why are they singled out for more stops, because they appear Hispanic? Cars are searched without probable cause other than alleged nonworking taillights. The number of actual tickets or arrest percentage of these stopped people is less than among Whites or Blacks. For those who don't think clearly, the studies prove that Hispanics are pulled over more often because they are Hispanic looking, not for suspected violations. Otherwise, their violation rate would equal or be in proportion to white and black drivers also pulled over for traffic violations. There is no getting around such a scenario, for how would anyone visually pinpoint an illegal without this massive violation of several rights carefully defined in the Constitution?

Now, if all these hundreds of thousands of people were dedicated to sniffing out illegals and arresting them for deportation, how could they protect us from other crime and criminals? They couldn't. Drugs, robberies, burglaries, car thefts and all other crimes, especially violent crimes, would flagrantly be committed against society for the simple reason that police officers would be busy hassling any Hispanic they see to determine legal residency. A "Blade Runner" society would emerge with Hispanics –not "replicants"—on the short end of law enforcement. If the reader doesn't understand, rent the movie "Blade Runner" and they can experience—with shudders—what might be in the Republic of Tom Tancredo."

This 2003 proposed form of law enforcement would not be new to the country. Twice before it has done exactly what this would require today. In the Depression years after 1930, police, federal Marshals and Immigration officers swept the streets of Los Angeles and other cities in California and Texas and rounded up anyone they "suspected" of being in the country illegally. They transported them to the border in trucks, buses and trains—without hearings or trials of any sort—for ad hoc deportation. In fact, to save money, they would arrest people and warehouse them in local jails until a 1000 or more were accumulated, no matter how long it took. Then, a train would be chartered for special pricing, it would be packed just like the German cattle cars a few years later without water or sanitation facilities and sent rolling south 150 miles to Mexico.

The Feds and local police picked up American citizen children and deported them with their suspected illegally present parents. They picked up many adult citizens and deported them, also. Who could fight back? Who could fight back with *writs*? Where was the ACLU? It was in New York protecting Communists. There were no civil rights lawyers practicing at the time. Looking Mexican was enough reason to deport someone. Segregated schools in San Diego and Orange County, separating Mexican children from Anglos, were the norm, so why should we think that those with badges bothered to observe the law rather than skin color? There were no "due process" hearings before immigration judges, there were no immigration judges; there were no consent forms agreeing to voluntary deportation. It was just, you look Mexican, thus, you look illegal—you are out of here.

The Border Patrol had been organized under law in 1924 only to keep Mexicans out. It was unleashed in Los Angeles to confront and deport anyone an individual Border Patrolman decided on the street was illegally in the United States. Each patrol agent was prosecutor, judge and jury. Twenty years later, Operation Wetback deported over a million people from California and Texas. As defined by federal officers and local cops helping them, anybody looking Mexican was ipso facto an illegal unless they could produce proper documentation, not at home or at work, but on the street—were they were stopped.

They refined and defined for all time racial profiling, as we now know it, to a high degree. Civil rights lawyers were busy fighting the battles of Blacks in the South. The ACLU was busy defending people from the House Un-American Activities Committee of Congress then busy searching for traitors and Communists in Hollywood. It overlooked the greatest un-American activities in young America's history by federal officers on the streets of Los Angeles. Driving while "Black" pales in comparison to being arrested on the street and slammed into a cattle car to be taken to another country for the crime of not being able to produce a birth certificate on the street.

There is no other violation of civil rights by United States federal officers on such a grand scale. Charlie Norwood's law would dwarf the 1950s experience of "Operation Wetback." It will unleash 600,000 untrained cops to harass the Hispanic population of 38-million, to hound American citizens, to disrupt the entire society and economy by street stops and arrests for nothing more than not being able to prove one is a citizen on the street. No one else would be so harassed; certainly not the Anglo-Protestants that are so favored at Harvard. Hispanics, who would look like illegals to the locals, would be doomed for life to harassment. One can only imagine how many millions of laws suits would be filed by American citizens who would be detained by these local cops who, in their wildest imaginations could never conceive of the training and expertise necessary to determine the intricacies of legal residency.

One case comes to mind about expertise on legal residency. A legally resident Mexican couple took their newborn American citizen baby to visit relatives in Mexico. They carried the baby's birth certificate with them, along with their legal residency papers to present to U.S. Immigration officers at the border upon their return. They were not allowed to bring the baby back. The birth certificate, complete with baby footprints, wasn't enough. The baby was placed in foster care while the investigation was organized and implemented.

It took the Immigration and Naturalization Service nine months to decide the baby was an American citizen...Nine months.

These were immigration professionals dallying for nine months. How, then, can we expect local cops to know the difference between an illegal and a legal resident? We can't, they hardly know the Vehicle Code. Most can barely read and write (Please, I come from a law enforcement family of a father, two brothers being retired police officers and having some experience in the field my self four and a half decades ago). Then, there is the argument that illegals don't have the same rights as citizens. That is not true, of course. More importantly, to find the one in 29 people who are in the country illegally, the rights of the other 28 people (280-million) would be violated by massive violations of the Constitution. Search and seizure provisions of the Constitution (4th Amendment) would evaporate. Our right not to incriminate ourselves (5th Amendment), our right to a fair trial (6th Amendment), to due process and equal protection (5th and 14th Amendments) to name but a few rights that would have to be cast aside by people with badges. These are the very people sworn to "protect and defend" the Constitution of the United States, the document in which all these rights are enumerated and enshrined.

As for the military option, there are almost 2,000 miles of Mexican border. A soldier would need to guard a 50 or 100 yard strip of the border 24-hours a day. Thus, at any given moment, we would have to have at least 35 soldiers per mile times 2000 miles times three eight hour shits totaling the need for 210,000 soldiers on the line. Then, these troops would need to be quartered, fed, serviced and replaced during leave. A quarter-million troopers might be necessary to militarily patrol the Mexican border. Illegals would still get through. One must remember that almost half of all illegals come into the country legally, then overstay. Only half or so cross the Mexican border.

How many support troopers per field soldier would be necessary for border duty? One to one, two to one, three to one, or more? It looks like three or four times the number of people we have in Iraq today would be necessary to patrol the border. Can we do that with today's military force? No. We would need to institute a draft to raise another 500,000 soldiers, just to patrol the border. What would be the cost, billions of dollars? Illegals still would get through. The military would be compromised and turned into a frontier patrol, not the world's finest military force that can dash across hundreds of desert miles to take Baghdad in a matter of days. Can anyone see United States Marines yelling "Alto!" To a 15-year old kid who wants to work? Or can Marines see themselves shooting at unarmed 15-year olds looking to be busboys so their families can eat?

Who would be searching for international terrorists if the American military was stationed on the border with Mexico? Who would have found Saddam Hussein, Tom Tancredo, Charlie Norwood? The military option is impractical. It is also illegal. The military cannot be used to enforce civil laws, which is what immigration law is—civil, not criminal, except in very special and narrow incidents.

The problem must have a solution because it is growing so large. Furthermore, ever since the Clinton Administration decided to throw a bone at the anti-immigration people by flooding the San Diego Border with Mexico with thousands of Border Patrol agents to smother the border crossings used by illegals with enforcement, people have died by the hundreds. When the Clinton Administration started "Operation Gatekeeper " Mexicans moved east of San Diego into high mountains and the great Sonoran Desert of California and Arizona. In less than a decade, over a thousand people died in the desert or mountains trying to cross in the heat of summer or cold of winter. That is, a thousand or more that we know about. How many bleached bones lie in the desert and mountains that we haven't yet found? How many families in Mexico wonder where the man in the family is—at work, or dead?

CHAPTER 53

THE PRESIDENT SPEAKS AND THE NATION AWAKENS, JANUARY 7TH, 2004.

On that day, President George W. Bush set the tone for the current debate by departing from the status quo of the illegal alien problem. President Bush stepped out by stating that the current situation is unacceptable. A new plan to handle the problem must come from Congress and must come soon. The current situation cannot continue, he said. As President George W. Bush courageously set out his policy path on January 7th, the critics swarmed out from their nooks and crannies to shriek political epithets at the President including calling him a "Traitor."

On the Left, the complaints were that the President didn't go far enough. Needless to point out, Plantation Chicanos objected, prodded by their patrons of the Democratic left that demands loyalty from the Chicanos, but, never delivers for them. After all, it was the Democratic Party's President Bill Clinton who lowered an Iron Curtain on the San Diego-Tijuana border, forcing illegals into the California mountains and deserts, places they froze in during winter, or died of thirst on desert trails in summer.

As we have seen, this 1994 operation was nothing but a sop to help Clinton's reelection in 1996. More illegals came to America than before; they came at breakneck speed in record numbers, drawn by the booming job market of the 1990s. That job boom, incidentally, was fed by the North American Free Trade Agreement (NAFTA), which simultaneously helped Mexico become more productive and chased subsistence farmers off poorly farmed land in rural Mexico. Not enough new jobs were created in Mexico to accommodate the peasant farmers that cheap American corn and wheat drove off unprofitable patches of land cultivated for too long in the old Indian way, however, so they came north.

President Bush knows that 10-million illegals among us are real problems that need real solutions. Machine-gunning them at the border, or to issue "shoot on sight permits" as advocated by the Emigration Party of Nevada are not solutions, they are nothing but hate symbols by haters. Moreover, the solutions do not include plunging the country into a "police state" where millions of people will be lined up and harassed in the streets, in their homes, or in their work places for the crime of looking Hispanic, thus looking illegal. To solve the problem of illegal immigration, the country cannot violate the Constitution. The country can use the Constitution to solve the problem. Congress can simply change the laws so that people can come and work, come and go, carry work permits with pictures and pay more in taxes than in the current world of shadows in which they live.

Despite being accused of "pandering" to the Hispanic vote by ideologues, professional plantationeers and Mexican haters, the President spoke out courageously like no President in history, with the possible exception of Abraham Lincoln. With his words, President Bush set out a path to make it possible for hard working people to quit looking over their shoulders, to quit dying in the desert, or in the mountains, while seeking a job picking lettuce or busing tables. This policy suggestion was that of a "compassionate conservative." This policy will regularize the ten million-person segment of the population that is real and here.

With this new Bush Policy embedded in law, we, the people of the greatest nation on earth, can turn our attention to and focus on protecting the country from foreign enemies, none of whom are busboys. The Border Patrol should be chasing terrorists, not busboys.

On that day, January 7th, the country was treated to a cacophony of shrieks, hysterical shrieks of pain on the airwaves and in newspapers by a coterie of critics and Mexican haters the likes of which few had ever experienced before. Some of us, of course, are quite used to such hate and bigotry as descended on the President that day and in its aftermath, but the American public is not used to experiencing their President being called a traitor. The shrieks came from tiny minorities of people led by Tom Tancredo and Pat Buchanan who at once detest immigrants of all sorts, Mexicans in particular, and more specifically, Mexicans who have braved the dangers of the desert, of smugglers and bandits, of vigilantes in Arizona and Texas.

One must recognize that two elements are at work here. One, is pure racial white supremacy as promoted by Vdare.com writers Peter Brimelow and columnist Sam Francis, Georgie Ann Geyer and, of course, Pat Buchanan, who has a lifetime of racial prejudice and hate crimes committed in his youth. Pat Buchanan, he with a lifetime of racial bigotry and "hate crimes," ran for President in 1996 against "JOSE." He reran in 2000 after hijacking Ross Perot's Reform Party and its 12-million federal dollars against "JOSE." Pat Buchanan received less than one half a percent of the vote for President. The other element at work in this hatred of Mexicans and illegals from Mexico is jealousy. Reasonable people look at men, women and children who risk their lives to bus tables, pick strawberries or work in sweat shops so American women can wear $1000 dresses and surreptitiously, I submit, admire such courage. Men and women who have never accomplished anything with physical courage are rife in the anti-immigrant, anti-Mexican cabal.

They even stepped forward to criticize a Guatemalan illegal that came to Los Angeles as a lone teenager, became legal, joined the Marines and died in Iraq in the first hours of the Iraq War in 2003. He died fighting for this country, something none of these critics—Tom Tancredo, Pat Buchanan, Sam Francis, Michele Malkin, Georgie Ann Geyer, Peter Brimelow, Rush Limbaugh, Glenn Spencer, Chris Simcox, Samuel Huntington, Victor Davis Hanson, Jon E. Dougherty and legions of others—have ever done. With the deftness of a word surgeon, President Bush carefully explained why and what he wants in immigration reform and destroyed arguments by the "patriot" writers like Pat Buchanan and the others that criticize but never offer realistic solutions.

To those who denigrate contributions by any immigrants to America, President said: "America is a stronger and better nation because of the hard work and the faith and entrepreneurial spirit of immigration." To those who claim that immigrants don't fit in, President Bush said: "…14 percent of our nation's civilian workforce is foreign born." To those who demand we enforce current immigration laws and massively round up millions and deport them, President Bush says: "As a nation that values immigration, and depends on immigration, we should have immigration laws that work and make us proud. Yet today we don't." To those who claim there are plenty of unemployed Americans to do available work, President Bush says: "Reform must begin by confronting a basic fact of life and economics: some of the jobs being generated in America's growing economy are jobs American citizens are not filling."

President Bush probably didn't even know that as he spoke 150,000 California restaurant job openings couldn't be filled by anyone, much less Americans. To those who say that illegals are degenerate thieves of the American way of life, President Bush said: " Many undocumented workers have walked mile after mile, through the heat of day and cold of night. Some have risked their lives in dangerous desert crossings, or entrusted their lives to the brutal rings of heartless human smugglers. Workers who seek only to earn a living end up in the shadows of American life—fearful, often abused and exploited."

To those who say arrest and deport, President Bush said: "If an American employer is offering a job that American citizens are not willing to take, we ought to welcome into our country a person who will fill that job." To those who say that temporary and guest workers never go home, President Bush said: "...new laws should provide incentives for these temporary, foreign workers to return permanently to their home countries." Specifically, he stated: I also support making it easier for temporary workers to contribute a portion of their earnings to tax-preferred savings accounts, money they can collect as they return to their native countries."

Temporary legalized foreign workers will never leave their jobs or the country, some say, to them President Bush says: "...participants (of the new Bush program) will be issued a temporary worker card that will allow them to travel back and forth between their home and the United States without fear of being denied reentry into our country." If they can travel back and forth, why would they stay, why, in fact, would they bring their families, though the Bush program allows that in limited circumstances?

To those who say that the country will be flooded with new illegal job seekers and immigrants, President Bush says: "All who participate in the temporary worker program must have a job, or, if not living in the United States, a job offer." If there are ten million jobs offered to present or new employees from Mexico under this Bush program. There will be some additional job growth as there always is in a growing immigrant community, but would the number of illegal border crossings increase? Why and how would or could that happen?

Border crossings are directly related to the job market. There is no one who can prove that people come here regardless of whether they can work or not work. When jobs are plentiful and the American job seekers gravitate upward, illegals come to fill the jobs left behind by upwardly mobile American job seekers and holders. That is an economic fact of life. That one for one job filling by Mexican illegals is the quintessential free market at work. What the critics don't understand is that the free market must and will prevail. It is the very free market that has drawn 10-million or so illegals here, to work. It is the free market that separates us from the socialist countries of Old Europe. It is the free market that is the very foundation of our economic system and it is our free economic system that makes us politically free.

Real freedom is not possible without the free market and the free market is not possible in this day and age without political freedom. Note how the socialist countries of Europe have destroyed themselves by interfering with the free market. Unemployment is as high today in Germany as it was the day Adolf Hitler took control of the German nation. None of the European countries have recently shown economic growth like we take for granted. China and India are steam rolling themselves into modernity with more free market philosophy than Europe; thus, those countries make the future look brighter in these traditionally socialist and communist countries.

Under the Bush plan, and the proposals of several Congressmen currently in the legislative hopper in Washington, employers would have to advertise the job on the Internet. If no American wants the job, the employer can offer the job to a Mexican on the prospective employee rolls of the same Internet site. So, one job, one job offer; job filled— simple. Multiply that by the millions of jobs that are open every day and there will be a limited number of jobs open and being filled as the economy grows. There will be, however, no huge jump in jobs at anytime, thus any huge increase in new Mexican employees. With jobs properly advertised and filled with legal workers how can there be an increase in illegal border crossers?

If there were no jobs available, why would anyone come to work when there is no work? To collect welfare they can't collect? To collect unemployment they can't collect; to attend college for in-state tuition? Sure. Everyone should understand one factor, that factor is the network most illegals or potential illegals have in this country about job openings. They do not come here and find jobs in a vacuum. They can usually locate someone they know, a relative or someone from their village, town or city when they arrive and those contacts can let them know who is hiring. Thus, in the future, those same contacts will let people know in Mexico even before a job opens up officially that a job is coming online. Is that bad? No, it is good. Such an informal job notification network will set up an unofficial but very accurate system that will cut down on people planning illegal entry. It won't take long for the telephone wires to buzz with job information and when to apply and when a job is filled. The network will probably work faster and more accurately than the official system.

To those who demand better Border protection, President Bush said: "…when temporary workers can travel legally and freely, there will be more efficient management of our borders and more effective enforcement against those who pose a danger to our country." To those who say that lawbreakers should not be rewarded, President Bush said: "This new system will be more compassionate. Decent, hard-working people will now be protected by labor laws, with the right to change jobs, earn fair wages, and enjoy the same working conditions that the law requires for American workers. Temporary workers will be able to establish their identities by obtaining legal documents we all take for granted. And they will be able to talk openly with authorities, to report crimes when they are harmed, without the fear of being deported."

To those of the anti-immigrant minority and to the ultra-liberal activist minority, President Bush has outlined a policy that will benefit our society to the highest degree possible. Concurrently it will lift those who have risked life and limb to pick our lettuce, set our tables, dig our ditches, and care for our children to legality and dignity. It will protect a basic foundation of millions of hard working people of our free enterprise system and bring them out of the shadows into sunlight. To those on the left fringe of America who complain the Bush proposal isn't enough, I ask, what did you do when you were in power?

Democratic Party Chairman Terry McCauliffe states: "President Bush could have shown his commitment to immigrants by supporting a meaningful earned legalization proposal and by consulting Democrats in Congress, who for many years have worked on immigration issues." His President Clinton, the man who personally tossed aside the normal Party procedures and forced the Party to take McCauliffe as Chairman, instituted a policy of herding illegals into the desert to die, where over a thousand have died. That's what Democrats did, Chairman McCauliffe. Certainly, the Bush proposal does not encompass every wish and desire critics and supporters demand, but, it is a start and for those who do not understand politics, a half loaf gained is better than a whole one unattained. In other words, our current situation is not acceptable and the policy proposed by President Bush is a giant step forward in confronting and slowing the problem of illegal aliens.

The Bush plan is miles down the road to reform and it can be accomplished by marrying it to several proposals already in Congress and already supported by key Democrats and Republicans. What will the complainers complain about then?

President George W. Bush has once again manifested his superior ability to control the country's agenda. He offers a substantive policy change recommendation for the ineffective immigration policy that confuses, befuddles us and plain encourages law breaking by otherwise honest people. He offers a plan that will eliminate a death count exceeding a thousand people and growing. In the process he exposes critics of his plan for what they are, hypocrites, uninformed partisans, partisan slashers, bigots and clueless people who prove beyond all doubt that they have no ability to recognize reality, or to recognize real problems and solutions that might work.

The President has proposed a total revamp of our immigration policy as it affects millions of people who are currently in the country illegally and the millions of Americans for whom they work, Americans who themselves are breaking laws. Estimates of the number of illegals range between 8-12-million such people, with about 50 or 60% being Mexican. How many are actually working is unknown just as the number of those not working or under working age and in schools is unknown. As described, the President's proposals include a work permit system for those here already and for those in the future that can document a legitimate work offer from an American employer. Those already here would pay a "fee" for the privilege of legalizing. Those coming in the future will not be charged. There are suggested time limits in the proposal of three years per permit, plus an additional extension of three years. Congress can change these year parameters after debate and consideration. Some would be able to apply for permanent status and some would be required to return to their native country at the end of the extensions.

As mentioned, critics break into two camps. The candidates for the Democratic presidential nomination all jumped on the President because his proposal didn't "go far enough." The Democratic National Chairman, Terry McCauliffe, joined in on the criticism with the aforementioned quote. The question to these people is a simple one:

When confronted by exploding illegal immigrant numbers what did these democrats do to solve the problem, despite that they controlled the congress and the presidency in 1993 and 1994 and the presidency from 1993 until January 2001?

There are three candidates for President who shot off their mouths minutes after the President finished his speech on immigration reform. Did Senator John Kerry introduce work permit and legalization legislation? Did then Speaker of the House Dick Gephardt introduce a legalization program? Did Senator Carol Mosley Braun introduce legalization legislation? Did Governor Howard Dean of Vermont even know there were illegal immigrants in the country? The answers to these questions are one word, NO.

What did their President Bill Clinton do in those years about the illegal immigrant problem? He flooded the border at El Paso and San Diego with Border Patrol Agents in moves that cut down the illegal entries at those two popular crossing points, but simply moved the illegals into the mountains and deserts. That move also permitted at least two of the September 11th Arab murderers to slip into the country through the little guarded Canadian border. Like streams and rivers, the illegals simply moved away from Border Patrol agents lined up at the easy crossing points. The Clinton results: More illegals than ever and well over a thousand bodies in the mountains and deserts. At least one was shot in the back and killed by a Border Patrol Agent in a charged murder. At least one American citizen was shot and killed by a Clinton-assigned Marine sharpshooter at the border who was watching a flock of goats.

Two illegals were crossing the border from Mexico into Arizona on foot. Two Border Patrol agents were patrolling in the area and hiding among rocks. They were armed with M-16 rifles. At dusk, the two illegals walked by the two hidden agents. Neither agent cried out "Freeze" or "Alto" (stop). One of the agents fired his M-16 hitting one of the illegals in the back. The unwounded illegal ran away chased by agent bullets. The agent who wounded the Mexican dragged the wounded man into an arroyo (gully). He then aimed his rifle at his agent partner and threatened him with death if he told anyone about the shooting. They left the area and drove to a roadside beer bar to drink at the end of their shift. The wounded Mexican bled to death over the next 8-hours.

The following day, the partner agent disclosed the shooting to his superiors. A rescue team rushed to the arroyo and found the Mexican dead, he had bled to death. The county coroner later testified that had the man received medical attention within six hours of the shooting he would have survived. The shooter was charged with murder under Arizona law. The partner who disclosed the shooting was fired by the Border Patrol for not revealing the shooting immediately. The shooter was tried in state court. The shooter claimed he feared for his life when he shot the young Mexican in the back and dragged the unarmed wounded man into the arroyo to bleed to death. The shooter was acquitted of murder. He was allowed to resign from the Border Patrol.

The Clinton Administration did not prosecute the shooter for any charge, much less murder or denial of civil rights, both federal charges that could have been brought. The Clinton Administration did nothing to punish the shooter, in fact, it allowed him to leave the Patrol, and it did not fire him with prejudice because it didn't want a fight with the Border Patrol agent union. This is the same union that used to run the Border Patrol. Now that that agency has been absorbed by the Department of Homeland Security, the union is out. Interestingly, it was to protect this very union that the Democratic Senators blocked the formation of the Homeland Security Department for weeks and months. They did not want the President to have the same authority he has to hire and fire in departments of the federal government concerning safety and security. They wanted their precious union member agents to continue their membership in their union. They eventually failed.

This case alone testifies to the lack of Clinton effort on the border and his disdain for Mexicans. His administration allowed a murderer to walk. The murderer is walking the streets today, a free man, thanks to Janet Reno, Clinton's Attorney General, who refused to charge the man with federal charges. She is the same Attorney General that personally ordered a military-style snatch of a little Cuban boy in a predawn raid in Miami. She is the same Attorney General that ordered an attack in Waco that killed 20 or so innocent children. No one should ever forget the face of Democratic policy towards Hispanics that we all saw when armed federal agents smashed their way into a blue-collar home in Miami to kidnap at gunpoint a little boy. He had survived days at sea while he and his family were escaping from Communist Cuba. He survived the death of his mother.

Nonetheless, President Clinton and Janet Reno personally ordered that this helpless little boy be returned to Communist Cuba. Would that have happened if the scene had been the border between Communist East Germany and the West under any President? Of course not. Elián González was sacrificed to Fidel Castro because President Clinton simply didn't have a clue about how Hispanics should be treated. President Clinton never offered any plan to legalize illegals or to handle them in any humane way. He only ordered more guns to the border and there are over a thousand corpses to memorialize his shortsightedness.

A brief summary of the Clinton immigration policy regarding illegals is punctuated by a quantum leap from the numbers on January 20th, 1993, when Bill Clinton raised his right hand and swore to "defend" the country, and dead men, women and children strewn across the Southwest. In other words, the Clinton policy was disastrous; it was a total failure, a failure of Democrats. Other critics, foundation funded left wing groups like The National Council of La Raza and the Mexican American Legal Defense Fund complain that the President's policy doesn't go far enough. They want total amnesty and potential citizenship in the manner of the Reagan-signed 1986 amnesty. Columnists like James Goldsbrough of the San Diego Union/Tribune join the non-representative groups in criticizing President Bush's proposal. He criticizes the plan by calling it a farce.

Of course, Goldsbrough wouldn't know a Mexican if he tripped on one. He is more sympathetic to the French than to Mexicans, as any reader could see during the build-up to the

War in Iraq. This twice-weekly columnist in the largest American city on the Mexican border has never written any reports, glowing or otherwise of the Mexican citizens who died in the war in Iraq. Nor has he taken notice of the Guatemalan young man who walked across the entire country of Mexico as a teenager to enter the USA illegally to eventually die in the Iraq desert as a United States Marine. Nonetheless, he calls the Bush plan a "farce." Joining the leftist critics are those from the right like columnists Pat Buchanan, Michelle Malkin, Georgie Anne Geyer and talk show hosts like Michael Savage, Mike Gallagher, Bill O'Reilly and others.

Unlike the leftist critics who have no credibility on the subject because they didn't offer any policy other than the deadly and ineffective Clinton immigration policy and enforcement, the rightists work overtime at creating Red Herrings as the basis of their opposition. For example, Buchanan continues to lament that Mexicans will come here to work for a "dollar an hour" thus cheating Americans out of work. That is, of course, false. Malkin calls the proposal an "abomination" because it absolves millions who have used phony Social security cards or phony driver's licenses in the pursuit of their goal of working in the USA. She does not object to convicted reckless drivers and speeders and drunk drivers getting driver's licenses. She does not object to rich white Americans getting amnesty from criminal charges and penalties for tax fraud.

Gallagher quotes Pat Buchanan on the loss of manufacturing jobs to China as a reason to oppose the President. Bill O'Reilly objects because the proposal doesn't call for putting the Army on the Border (an illegal act under current law, a law passed a hundred and 30 years ago, by the way). That proposal has been discussed in depth elsewhere in this work. O'Reilly has never served in the military, as far as we know, thus his comments about putting military troops on the border don't hold up well under examination by anyone who has ever served in the military. Buchanan, Gallagher, Goldsbrough and their allies and like thinking congressmen like Tom Tancredo (R-CO), Dana Rohrabacher (R-CA), Elton Gallegly (R-CA) and former Ku Klux Klansman Senator Robert Byrd (D-WV) also object to the proposal because it will draw "millions" more Mexicans and doesn't shut down the border. Both are false assumptions.

They overlook the President's statement that the border enforcement will improve with his plan because most of the Mexicans crossing the border will overwhelmingly be legal. The President is right. Predictions that millions more illegals will cross the border is unfounded, for two reasons: (1) those already here are filling jobs and will continue to do so legally. (2) Those future workers will come with job offers only. Thus, millions of new illegals won't come except to replace existing workers who return home when their visas expire, or when new jobs are created by economic growth. That's not difficult to understand, but these people don't want to understand that what we have here is not a zero sum situation. As for Malkin's phony Social Security cards and driver's license problems, they will mostly disappear because real ones will be available for the very first time. She should concentrate her ire on all those millions of white crooks that steal identity and cause billions of dollars of credit card fraud.

For those that think that these workers will simply stay when their work permits expire in six or more years, the President's proposal has the foundation of a monetary reward for returning to Mexico. Two financial rewards are part of the plan. One, a Social Security credit applicable to the Mexican Social Security system's benefits upon retirement. Secondly, the proceeds from Tax-free savings accounts that can only be redeemed when the worker returns to Mexico after his legal work time in the USA expires. Now, that's a plan.

My suggestion would be that Congress expand the President's three year permits to seven year permits with one seven year renewal and the ability to apply for a Permanent

Resident (Green Card) after ten years of honest work, taxpaying, noncriminal time in the U.S. The President proposed an outline of what he thinks Congress should pass into law. Details will be debated in a public fishbowl, in public view and will certainly result in compromises that will go miles towards solving the problems. These things are for sure; fewer people will die in the desert heat or mountain cold. Fewer people will come into the USA illegally. Legal workers will pay more in taxes and collect fewer benefits because fewer of them will bring families due to being able to cross the border legally at will.

Lastly, this proposal gets us several more years towards 2015 when demographers predict that there won't be surplus Mexican labor in Mexico to feed the job machine in the United States. Reason: Birth rates have plunged in Mexico in the past two decades thanks to Herculean efforts by the Mexican government to make planned parenthood available in the tiniest villages of rural Mexico. Every village in Mexico has a paid government representative that educates women and girls on birth control and this has been in effect for twenty years with some serious positive effects on the birth rate in rural Mexico.

The birth rate in Mexico City is reported by the Mexican government to have plunged in recent years to levels approaching that of the United States, much closer to two children per family than to the 4 or higher of past decades. In 2015 and later, there simply won't be enough surplus Mexican men and women of working age to make the trek north for jobs. There will be plenty of jobs in Mexico at much higher wages than currently for them to fill. The free market works in Mexico, as well as the United States of America. What will the critics complain about then?

Time, along with the Bush plan will solve the problem of illegal working immigrants coming to the United States. The solution may be in the various congressional proposals that have been introduced recently by Republican Senators John

Cronyn of Texas and John McCain of Arizona. Similar guest worker bills have been introduced by Arizona Representatives Flake and Kolbe. Additionally, a bipartisan bill to legalize 500,000 agricultural workers has been negotiated among Senators Crappo and Craig, Republicans of Idaho and Ted Kennedy, Democrat of Massachusetts. Details aside, these proposals call for legalizing those illegals that are in the United States today with employer requested temporary work permits. For those coming in the future, they would respond to offers of work by American employers who can prove that no Americans wanted the advertised jobs. They would be required to advertise any job openings for a period of time before they could hire a vetted worker from Mexico (or wherever). The workers would be work permitted for a fixed period of time and could after several years apply for permanent residence (a green card) and after several more years apply for citizenship. What's wrong with such a program? Nothing...

The Tom Tancredo led-anti-Mexicans are shrieking about rewarding criminals for illegal behavior, yet are mum when thousands of criminals are granted immunity from prosecution by prosecutors and judges every day in the country's criminal courts. Isn't such immunity rewarding criminal activity?

How about tax amnesties that are granted by states all the time for criminals who have violated tax laws over the years. More visible to the naked eye are the millions of American drivers who flagrantly violate speed laws and drunk driving laws every minute of the day. People are killed every day, every hour, by speeders and reckless drivers, yet Tancredo and gang are obsessed with Mexicans looking for honest work.

Some opposition for such programs comes from left-wing immigrant advocates who claim that the 1940s-era Bracero program mistreated Mexican workers and allowed American employers to exploit Mexicans with low pay and bad housing, but, those complaints cannot be projected for the future, for no one can predict the future. Moreover, most of those complaints are imaginary. One complaint is being fought out in the courts currently. There is a claim that money that was supposed to be set aside from the Braceros pay checks in a trust fund guaranteed by the American and Mexican governments has disappeared. What else is new?

Isn't the United States government under court order to produce hundreds of millions of dollars of American Indian trust fund money that has disappeared in the last 100 years into the ether? Yes...We have no idea what will occur in the future on the subject of illegal aliens, but we do know that this country will not tolerate a police state that squashes our rights because one in 29 people are here illegally. In spite of the emotion and passion of the Tancredo people, the courts will never permit wholesale violations of the Constitution and the Bill of Rights in order to root out people who can be legalized with an act of Congress. Courts, in most cases, thankfully, are reluctant to make law when that is the function of the legislature.

The President has now proposed a good way to solve the problems of illegal aliens; it is now up to Congress to dispose of the problem of illegal aliens with a comprehensive restructuring of an immigration policy that makes no sense, nor is enforced, nor is effective even when enforced. The President is offering a real solution, a compassionate solution; he is offering a solution that is good for the economy and all individuals involved. It is bad, of course, for Mexican haters. That offer is contrary, of course, to Congressman Tom Tancredo's one-sided and blind view of Mexicans and any immigrants from Mexico. It is contrary to the view that the President is a traitor and a member, like this writer is alleged to be, of the Treason Lobby; and, finally, contrary to the view of the Mexican haters of the country.

President George W. Bush deserves support for his plan to solve the problem that vexes many, the problem of illegal aliens. Why, for the illegals are not daggers into the heart of America, they are but the latest contributors to the great American nation, its economy, its standard of living and its history.

San Diego, California

The 5th of May, 2004

PART 10

CHAPTER 54

DEMOCRATS PLAY CATCHUP, THEY HOPE!

NATIONAL IMMIGRATION FORUM

Press Release

FOR IMMEDIATE RELEASE Contact: Douglas Rivlin (rivlin@immigrationforum.org) May 4, 2004 (202) 383-5989 or (202) 441-0680 (mobile)

Advocates Praise Comprehensive Immigration Reform Legislation Call for Enactment of "Down Payments" This Year

Washington, DC – The National Immigration Forum joined advocates, labor leaders, and community groups across the country in praising new comprehensive immigration reform legislation unveiled today in Washington. The new bill, the Safe, Orderly, Legal Visas and Enforcement Act of 2004 or SOLVE Act, introduced at a Capitol Hill press conference by Senator Edward Kennedy (D-MA) and Representatives Bob Menéndez (D-NJ) and Luis Gutiérrez (D-IL), would go a long way toward fixing our broken immigration system. "Everyone in the country, be they native born or immigrant, knows that our immigration system is in desperate need of repair," said Frank Sharry, Executive Director of the National Immigration Forum. "This bill promises to rewrite the rules so that they can be fairly and evenly enforced across the board."

Sharry said the bill will reunite families by reducing the years of family separation caused by a backlogged bureaucracy and unduly restrictive laws. It will reward the hard work of immigrants who are in the U.S., raising families, paying taxes, and learning English, eager for a chance to earn legal residency over time and get on the path to citizenship. It respects workers by reducing exploitation and downward wage pressures by creating a "break-the-mold" worker visa program that protects the wages and working conditions of U.S. workers, and provides equal rights to immigrant workers admitted in the future. Finally, Sharry said the bill will reduce illegal immigration by devising fair and reasonable rules that are realistic and enforceable. "This bill will, over time, replace a chaotic, deadly, and illegal flow of exploitable workers and desperate family members with a safe, orderly, and legal flow of workers with full labor rights and family members with legal immigrant visas," Sharry said.

The new legislation marks a new chapter in immigration reform. From the President's speech in January through the introduction of this legislation, it is clear that both parties are now ready to get serious about reform. Sharry noted that the strong support for this legislation from the American labor movement is a sign of major progress. Add to that the support that American businesses and trade associations have demonstrated for earned legalization, and the necessary ingredients for bipartisan reform seem to be taking shape. He cautioned, however, that comprehensive immigration reform legislation is unlikely to pass before Election Day. "The shape of the immigration reform debate has been defined," Sharry said. "We've moved beyond tired notions of building a big wall around the country or deporting 10 million workers and their families. Immigration is an overwhelmingly positive feature of America's history and will remain so in the future. This bill recognizes that managing immigration fairly and effectively makes more sense than our current policy of trying to overly suppress immigration and drive it underground."

Sharry said that while the President and Congress were unlikely to negotiate and agree on a comprehensive reform package this year, they each could demonstrate their sincerity by enacting the AgJobs and Dream Act bills already under consideration and with wide bipartisan support. AgJobs, which would legalize some farmworkers and streamline existing temporary worker programs, has the support of business and labor and, with 60 Senate co-sponsors, seems poised for passage. The Dream Act puts undocumented students who came here as children on a path to legal residency, so they can work legally and without fear of deportation. It also enjoys support on both sides of the political aisle, and could be passed this year if leaders in each party made it a priority.

"Agjobs and Dream Act would serve as a good down payment on comprehensive immigration reform," Sharry said. "It would show the country that Congress and the President are serious about reform and willing to roll up their sleeves and work out their differences to get good policies passed." Sharry said passage of these measures this year would "set the table" for comprehensive reform, along the lines of the new bill introduced today, to happen next year. "The fact that there are rallies and press conferences supporting this bill in about 30 cities shows the groundswell of support across the country for fixing our broken immigration system," Sharry said. "Labor, religious, ethnic, and community leaders have been waiting for a serious, comprehensive piece of legislation to mobilize their constituencies and who will make their voices heard. The SOLVE Act fits the bill."

Part 11

About the Author